■■ Microsoft

Microsoft
Visio 2016
Step by Step

Scott A. Helmers

198159

006
- 6
VIS

PUBLISHED BY
Microsoft Press
A division of Microsoft Corporation
One Microsoft Way
Redmond, Washington 98052-6399

Library of Congress Control Number: 2015936021
ISBN: 978-0-7356-9780-5

Printed and bound in the United States of America.

2   17

Microsoft Press books are available through booksellers and distributors worldwide. If you need support related to this book, email Microsoft Press Support at mspinput@microsoft.com. Please tell us what you think of this book at http://aka.ms/tellpress.

This book is provided "as-is" and expresses the author's views and opinions. The views, opinions, and information expressed in this book, including URL and other Internet website references, may change without notice.

Some examples depicted herein are provided for illustration only and are fictitious. No real association or connection is intended or should be inferred.

Microsoft and the trademarks listed at www.microsoft.com on the "Trademarks" webpage are trademarks of the Microsoft group of companies. All other marks are property of their respective owners.

Acquisitions and Developmental Editor: Rosemary Caperton
Editorial Production: Online Training Solutions, Inc. (OTSI)
Technical Reviewer: John Marshall
Copyeditor: Jaime Odell (OTSI)
Indexer: Susie Carr (OTSI)
Cover: Twist Creative • Seattle

Contents

Part 1: Create Visio diagrams

Give us feedback
Tell us what you think of this book and help Microsoft improve our products for you. Thank you!
http://aka.ms/tellpress

3 Manage text, shapes, and pages...............................95

Part 2: Add data to your diagrams

Part 3: Enhance and share diagrams

Give us feedback

Tell us what you think of this book and help Microsoft improve our products for you. Thank you!

http://aka.ms/tellpress

Introduction

Welcome! This *Step by Step* book has been designed so you can read it from the beginning to learn about Microsoft Visio 2016 and then build your skills as you learn to perform increasingly specialized procedures. Or, if you prefer, you can jump in wherever you need ready guidance for performing tasks. The how-to steps are delivered crisply and concisely—just the facts. You'll also find informative, full-color graphics that support the instructional content.

Who this book is for

Microsoft Visio 2016 Step by Step is designed for use as a learning and reference resource by home and business users of Microsoft Office programs who want to use Visio to create a variety of diagrams for business and personal use. The content of the book is designed to be useful for people who have previously used earlier versions of Visio and for people who are discovering Visio for the first time.

The *Step by Step* approach

The book's coverage is divided into parts representing general Visio skill sets. Each part is divided into chapters representing skill set areas, and each chapter is divided into topics that group related skills. Each topic includes expository information followed by generic procedures. At the end of the chapter, you'll find a series of practice tasks you can complete on your own by using the skills taught in the chapter. You can use the practice files that are available from this book's website to work through the practice tasks, or you can use your own files.

Adapt procedure steps

This book contains many images of user interface elements (such as the ribbon and the app windows) that you'll work with while performing tasks in Visio on a Windows computer. Depending on your screen resolution or app window width, the Visio ribbon on your screen might look different from that shown in this book. (If you turn on Touch mode, the ribbon displays significantly fewer commands than in Mouse mode.) As a result, procedural instructions that involve the ribbon might require a little adaptation.

Simple procedural instructions use this format:

1. On the **Insert** tab, in the **Illustrations** group, click the **Pictures** button.

If the command is in a list, our instructions use this format:

1. On the **Home** tab, in the **Editing** group, click the **Layers** arrow and then, in the **Layers** list, click **Layer Properties**.

If differences between your display settings and ours cause a button to appear differently on your screen than it does in this book, you can easily adapt the steps to locate the command. First click the specified tab, and then locate the specified group. If a group has been collapsed into a group list or under a group button, click the list or button to display the group's commands. If you can't immediately identify the button you want, point to likely candidates to display their names in ScreenTips.

Multistep procedural instructions use this format:

1. Display the Backstage view.

2. In the left pane of the Backstage view, click **New**.

3. On the **New** page, click **Categories**, click the **Business** thumbnail, and then double-click the **Organization Chart** template.

On subsequent instances of instructions that require you to follow the same process, the instructions might be simplified in this format because the working location has already been established:

1. On the **New** page of the Backstage view, click **Categories**, click the **Business** thumbnail, and then double-click the **Organization Chart** template.

The instructions in this book assume that you're interacting with on-screen elements on your computer by clicking (with a mouse, touchpad, or other hardware device). If you're using a different method—for example, if your computer has a touchscreen interface and you're tapping the screen (with your finger or a stylus)—substitute the applicable tapping action when you interact with a user interface element.

Instructions in this book refer to Visio user interface elements that you click or tap on the screen as *buttons*, and to physical buttons that you press on a keyboard as *keys*, to conform to the standard terminology used in documentation for these products.

When the instructions tell you to enter information, you can do so by typing on an external keyboard, tapping an on-screen keyboard, or even speaking aloud, depending on your computer setup and your personal preferences.

Download the practice files

Before you can complete the practice tasks in this book, you need to download the book's practice files to your computer from *http://aka.ms/Visio2016sbs/downloads*. Follow the instructions on the webpage.

 IMPORTANT Visio 2016 is not available from the book's website. You should install that app before working through the procedures and practice tasks in this book.

You can open the files that are supplied for the practice tasks and save the finished versions of each file. If you later want to repeat practice tasks, you can download the original practice files again.

The following table lists the practice files for this book.

Chapter	Folder	File
1: Get started with Visio 2016	Visio2016SBS\Ch01	ExploreDrawing.vsdx
		GetStarted.vsdx
		ManageShapesWindow.vsdx
		PanAndZoom.vsdx
2: Create diagrams	Visio2016SBS\Ch02	PositionShapes.vsdx
		ResizeShapes.vsdx
		SelectShapes.vsdx
		UseAutoAddAutoDelete.vsdx
		UseAutoConnect.vsdx
		UseDynamicConnectors.vsdx
		UseLines.vsdx
3: Manage text, shapes, and pages	None	None
4: Create business process diagrams	Visio2016SBS\Ch04	CreateSubprocesses.vsdx
5: Create organization charts	Visio2016SBS\Ch05	AlterLayout.vsdx
		OrgChartData.xlsx
		Photos folder with 27 images of people

Chapter	Folder	File
6: Add style, color, and themes	Visio2016SBS\Ch06	AlignSpaceShapes.vsdx
7: Create network and datacenter diagrams	Visio2016SBS\Ch07	ChangeDrawingScale.vsdx
		CreateRacks.vsdx
8: Work with shape data	Visio2016SBS\Ch08	CreateModifyReports.vsdx
		EditShapeData.vsdx
		InsertFields.vsdx
		ModifyDataAttributes.vsdx
		RunReports.vsdx
		Vegetation Report.vrd
9: Visualize your data	Visio2016SBS\Ch09	CreateDataGraphics.vsdx
		RiskManagementTaskMap.pdf
10: Link to external data	Visio2016SBS\Ch10	Photos\Oleg Anashkin.jpg
		OrgChartData.xlsx
		OrgChartData_Supplement1.xlsx
		UseQuickImport.vsdx
		UseCustomImport.vsdx
11: Add and use hyperlinks	Visio2016SBS\Ch11	EnhanceDiagrams.vsdx
		FollowHyperlinks.vsdx
		Human Resources Policy Manual.docx
12: Print, reuse, and share diagrams	Visio2016SBS\Ch12	CreateGraphics.vsdx
		CreateTemplates.vsdx
		PreviewDrawings.vsdx
		PublishToWeb.vsdx
		SaveInFormats.vsdx
13: Add structure to your diagrams	Visio2016SBS\Ch13	AnnotateShapes.vsdx
		OrganizeByContainers.vsdx
		OrganizeByLists.vsdx

Chapter	Folder	File
14: Validate diagrams	Visio2016SBS\Ch14	ReuseRules.vsd
		RuleSets--BPMN 2.0.html
		RuleSets--Cross-Functional Flowchart.html
		RuleSets--Flowchart.html
		RuleSets--SharePoint 2010 Workflow.html
		RuleSets--SharePoint 2016 Workflow.html
		ValidateBPMN.vsdx
		ValidateFlowcharts.vsdx
		ValidateSwimlanes.vsdx
15: Collaborate and publish diagrams	None	None
Appendix A: Look behind the curtain	Visio2016SBS\AppA	ViewShapeSheet.vsdx
Appendix B: Keyboard shortcuts for Visio	None	None

Ebook edition

If you're reading the ebook edition of this book, you can do the following:

- Search the full text

- Print

- Copy and paste

You can purchase and download the ebook edition from the Microsoft Press Store at *http://aka.ms/Visio2016sbs/details*.

Get support and give feedback

This topic provides information about getting help with this book and contacting us to provide feedback or report errors.

Errata and support

We've made every effort to ensure the accuracy of this book and its companion content. If you discover an error, please submit it to us at *http://aka.ms/Visio2016sbs /errata*.

If you need to contact the Microsoft Press Support team, please send an email message to *mspinput@microsoft.com*.

For help with Microsoft software and hardware, go to *http://support.microsoft.com*.

We want to hear from you

At Microsoft Press, your satisfaction is our top priority, and your feedback our most valuable asset. Please tell us what you think of this book at *http://aka.ms/tellpress*.

The survey is short, and we read every one of your comments and ideas. Thanks in advance for your input!

Stay in touch

Let's keep the conversation going! We're on Twitter at *http://twitter.com /MicrosoftPress*.

Part 1

Create Visio diagrams

Get started with Visio 2016

Microsoft Visio is the premiere application for creating business diagrams of all types, ranging from flowcharts, process maps and organization charts, to datacenter layouts, floor plans, and brainstorming diagrams.

Much more than just a diagramming app, Visio makes it easy to connect diagrams to live data sources, and then publish the results to Microsoft SharePoint to create near-real-time dashboards. On top of all that, you can use Visio to create a pattern for a quilt or to design a new kitchen for your house!

Visio 2016 includes many new features, including one that eliminates the curse of the blank page when you're starting a new diagram. Between that feature and the techniques you will discover in this chapter, you'll be off to a running start with Visio.

This chapter guides you through procedures related to getting started in Visio 2016, exploring the Backstage view, beginning quickly by using starter diagrams, exploring the drawing window, managing the Shapes window, and panning and zooming in the drawing window.

In this chapter

- Identify the editions of Visio 2016

- Discover new features in Visio 2016

- Get started in Visio 2016

- Explore the Backstage view

- Understand tool tabs and add-in tabs

- Begin quickly by using starter diagrams

- Explore the drawing window

- Manage the Shapes window

- Pan and zoom in the drawing window

Practice files

For this chapter, use the practice files from the Visio2016SBS\Ch01 folder. For practice file download instructions, see the introduction.

Identify the editions of Visio 2016

Visio 2016 is available in three editions. The first two editions use the traditional desktop purchase and installation model and mirror the two editions that were offered in most prior Visio releases. The third edition is part of the Microsoft Office 365 suite of subscription-based applications.

- **Visio Standard 2016** This is the starter edition of Visio. It provides significant capability for creating business diagrams and includes 26 templates that are divided into six categories.

- **Visio Professional 2016** This edition expands on the Standard edition by offering more than four dozen additional templates, for a total of 76 across eight categories. In addition, Visio Pro offers the ability to link diagrams to a wide variety of data sources, and includes a diagram validation capability that is especially well suited for the expanded set of business process diagrams it supports.

- **Visio Pro for Office 365** This edition of Visio provides the identical features and templates as Visio Professional 2016. The key differences in this edition are in packaging and delivery. As part of Office 365, there is no up-front license fee. Instead, you pay a monthly subscription fee and can install the software on up to five computers.

Discover new features in Visio 2016

Visio 2016 is sleek-looking, colorful, connected, portable, collaborative, and helps protect your document content.

The following list describes key new capabilities of Visio 2016:

- **Starter diagrams** Creating a diagram from a blank page can be daunting, especially if you're working with a new diagram type. Visio 2016 helps you get started more quickly by providing dozens of starter diagrams.

> **SEE ALSO** For more information about starter diagrams, see "Begin quickly by using starter diagrams" later in this chapter.

- **Modernized shapes** Dozens of Visio shapes received makeovers for Visio 2016. The updated shapes look modern, as shown in the comparison of Visio 2013 furniture shapes, on the left in Figure 1-1, with the equivalent shapes from Visio 2016 on the right. In addition to changes in appearance, some new shapes exhibit smart behavior. For example, if you increase the length or width of the Visio 2016 table in Figure 1-1, additional chairs appear!

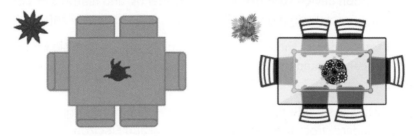

Figure 1-1 *Many Visio 2016 shapes have a fresh, new look*

You will find updated masters in stencils associated with templates for office layouts, site plans, floor plans, home plans, and electrical diagrams.

- **Tell Me** The Microsoft Office Tell Me feature makes finding any one of the 800 commands in Visio as easy as entering a word or phrase. Tell Visio what you want to do, and it responds with a list of executable commands.

Some commands in the response list might be dimmed (unavailable) because the Tell Me feature is context-aware. For example, if you start entering the word *container* when a container is not selected, most commands are unavailable, as shown on the left in Figure 1-2. However, if a container is selected, additional commands are available, as shown on the right.

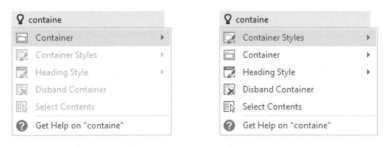

Figure 1-2 *Tell Me provides instant access to relevant commands*

- **Information Rights Management (IRM)** In Visio 2016, you can assign access rights so only authorized people can read or modify your diagram.

   SEE ALSO For more information about IRM, see the sidebar "What is Information Rights Management?" in Chapter 12, "Print, reuse, and share diagrams."

- **High-resolution device support** All buttons, menus, and features of Visio 2016 now operate properly on high-resolution displays like the Microsoft Surface.

- **Support for standards** Three types of diagrams included with Visio Professional 2016 have been updated to comply with the latest versions of the relevant international standards.

  - The Basic Electrical template in the Engineering template group complies with standards from the Institute for Electrical and Electronic Engineers (IEEE).

  - The BPMN Diagram template (available only in Visio Professional) in the Flowchart template group conforms to Business Process Model and Notation (BPMN) 2.0.

     SEE ALSO For more information about BPMN, see Chapter 4, "Create business process diagrams."

  - The six UML templates in the Software and Database template group comply with Unified Modeling Language (UML) 2.4.

- **Quick Import** The new Quick Import wizard (available only in Visio Professional) links a diagram to external data, links data to individual shapes, and then applies a data graphic to each shape—all in a single, seamless operation.

   SEE ALSO For more information about Quick Import, see Chapter 10, "Link to external data."

Get started in Visio 2016

The Visio Start screen is shown in Figure 1-3. In addition to a list of recently opened diagrams, the Start screen displays thumbnails of available templates.

> ✓ **TIP** The New page of the Backstage view, which is shown in Figure 1-12 in the following topic, presents the same template options as the Start screen. When you first start Visio, you can create a diagram from the Start screen. If Visio is already running, you can create one from the New page.

Featured templates   Template categories

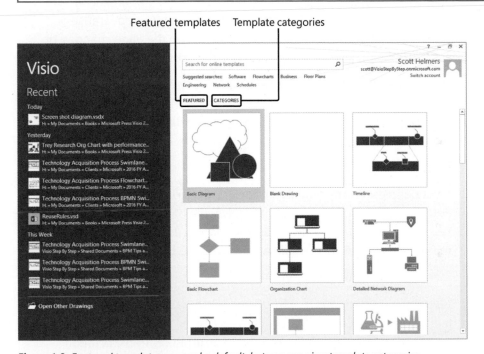

Figure 1-3 *Featured templates appear by default, but you can view template categories*

> ⚠ **IMPORTANT** The Start screen always displays featured templates first. It's easy to overlook the Categories button that presents a more traditional view of templates organized into logical groups.

Understand shapes, masters, stencils, and templates

Before you explore the rest of Visio, it's helpful to understand a number of commonly used terms:

- **Shape** An object on a Visio drawing page.

  A shape can be very simple, such as a line, a polygon, or an image. A shape can also be a sophisticated object that changes appearance or behavior as data values change, as its position on the page changes, or as properties of another shape change—the possibilities are endless.

  Usually, you create shapes by dragging a master from a stencil to the drawing page; however, you can create shapes in other ways. You will learn more about shapes in Chapter 2, "Create diagrams," and throughout this book.

- **Master** An object in a Visio stencil.

  Most people who create diagrams by using Visio use either the masters that ship with Visio or masters that they download from the Internet. You can also create your own masters, and you'll find enough information to get started in Appendix A, "Look behind the curtain."

- **Stencil** A collection of masters.

  Visio includes both metric and US unit versions of more than two hundred stencils. Each stencil contains several, or several dozen, related masters. Examples include stencils named Furniture, Transportation Shapes, Workflow Shapes, Network Locations, and Timeline Shapes. Appendix A, "Look behind the curtain," describes how to create a custom stencil.

- **Template** A Visio document that includes one or more drawing pages with preset dimensions and measurement units.

  A template generally contains one or more stencils, and it might include background pages, themes, shapes, or text. A template can include special software that only operates in that template.

- **Workspace** A collection of Visio windows and window settings.

  At minimum, the workspace consists of the drawing window and the zoom settings for the pages in the drawing. Frequently, it includes a Shapes window containing one or more stencils. The workspace can also include the Shape Data, Size & Position, and Pan & Zoom windows, in addition to template-specific windows.

  Unless you change the default action, Visio saves the on-screen workspace whenever you save a document. Consequently, the next time you open the document, Visio restores the workspace.

TIP Despite the distinction made in this list between a master and a shape, many people refer to an object in a stencil as a *shape*. Indeed, when you think about it, the window that displays stencils is called the Shapes window! Consequently, unless the distinction is important in a specific context, the text in this book will usually refer to objects in stencils and on the drawing page the same way—as shapes.

To begin a diagram based on an existing template, you can do any of the following:

- Search online for templates by entering keywords or by clicking any word in the Suggested Searches list.

  > ⚠ **IMPORTANT** Searching with a keyword will not produce the same result as selecting a template category that matches the keyword. For example, clicking the Flowchart search term yields some of the same templates that you find in the template category named Flowchart. However, it also returns a list of several—or several hundred—templates that is likely to include both Visio templates and templates for other apps in the Office suite.

- Use a template in the Featured section. The presentation of thumbnails in this section is dynamic: the templates you use most frequently rise to the top.

  > **TIP** The Blank Drawing template shown in Figure 1-3 opens the drawing page but does not open any stencils.

■ Use the Categories view to locate templates that are organized into groups. Visio Standard displays six categories: Business, Flowchart, General, Maps and Floor Plans, Network, and Schedule. Visio Professional adds two categories: Engineering, and Software and Database.

At the end of the template categories list is an additional entry called New From Existing, as shown in Figure 1-4. When you click this thumbnail, you can select any existing Visio diagram. Visio then opens a copy of the diagram as a new document and leaves the original untouched.

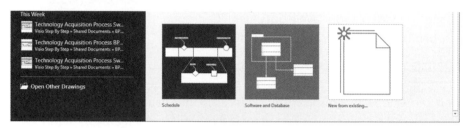

Figure 1-4 *The New From Existing button helps protect your diagram*

Clicking any template category displays thumbnails for the templates in that category. Figure 1-5 shows several of the templates in the Maps And Floor Plans category.

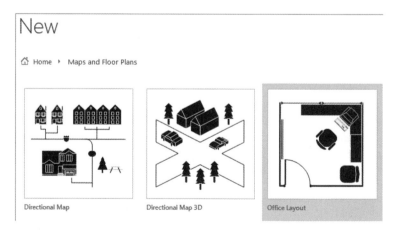

Figure 1-5 *Sample template thumbnails*

If you click once on a diagram thumbnail, Visio displays information about that template, as shown in Figure 1-6. If you double-click a diagram thumbnail, Visio launches a new diagram.

> ⚠️ **IMPORTANT** Many Visio templates include starter diagrams that provide additional options for creating diagrams. See "Begin quickly by using starter diagrams" later in this chapter for more information.

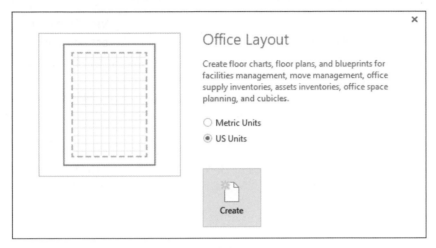

Figure 1-6 *The template information panel includes a description of the template*

> ✓ **TIP** When you create a new diagram, Visio names it Drawing*n*, where *n* is a sequence number that is incremented for each new drawing created within one Visio session. Closing and restarting Visio always resets the sequence number to 1.

Visio templates are provided in two sets of measurement units:

- **Metric** Metric drawings are based on paper sizes specified by the International Organization for Standardization (ISO); the default size is usually A4. Metric templates also include other ISO drawing and paper sizes. All measurements are in millimeters or other metric measurement units.

- **US Units** Diagrams created with US Units use the 8.5-by-11-inch, letter-sized paper that is common in the United States and parts of Canada and Mexico. Templates created for US Units also include additional drawing and paper sizes that are common in those countries/regions. The default measurement units are inches and feet.

Depending on your system configuration, you might be offered a choice between the two, as shown in Figure 1-6.

> **SEE ALSO** Microsoft provides a Quick Start guide for Visio 2013 (and other Office 2013 apps) at *office.microsoft.com/en-us/support/office-2013-quick-start-guides-HA103673669.aspx*. As of this writing, there is no Visio 2016 guide; however, the majority of the Visio 2013 guide is correct for Visio 2016.

To open a recently used diagram

1. In the **Recent** column on the **Start** screen of the Backstage view, click the name of the diagram you want to open.

To open a diagram that is not on the Recent list

1. In the **Recent** column, click **Open Other Diagrams**.

2. On the **Open** page of the Backstage view, click the location, and then open the diagram you want.

To use a Featured template

1. If the Featured tab is not already active, click the **Featured** button above the thumbnails on the **Start** screen.

2. Do either of the following:

   - Double-click a template thumbnail.

   - Click the thumbnail for the template you want, and then click the **Create** button.

To use template categories

1. If the Categories tab is not already active, click the **Categories** button above the thumbnails on the **Start** screen.

2. Click the thumbnail for the category you want.

3. Do either of the following:

   - Double-click a template thumbnail.

   - Click the thumbnail for the template you want, and then click the **Create** button.

To search for a template

1. On the **Start** screen, do either of the following:

   - Enter keywords in the **Search for online templates** box, and then press the **Enter** key.

   - Click one of the keywords in the **Suggested searches** list.

To use an existing diagram as a template

1. If the Categories tab is not already active, click the **Categories** button above the thumbnails on the **Start** screen.

2. Do either of the following:

   - Double-click the **New from existing** thumbnail.

   - Click the **New from existing** thumbnail, and then click the **Create** button.

3. In the **New From Existing Drawing** dialog box, navigate to, and then open the diagram you want.

Explore the Backstage view

The Backstage view is the central location for managing files and setting the options that control how Visio 2016 operates. You access the Backstage view by clicking the File tab on the left end of the ribbon in the Visio window.

Of the 11 commands in the left pane of the Backstage view, only four—New, Open, Account, and Options—are available if you do not have a diagram open. The remaining seven appear when you open a diagram.

> **TIP** If you are in the Backstage view and have a diagram open, you can return to the diagram by clicking the left-pointing arrow in the upper-left corner of the Visio window. If you don't have a diagram open, clicking the arrow will return you to the Start screen.

Most of the commands and accompanying pages in the Backstage view will be familiar if you have used other apps in the Office suite. In this topic, you will explore the Backstage view, with an emphasis on features that are unique to Visio.

The Info page

When you have a diagram open and click the File tab, Visio presents the Info page shown in Figure 1-7.

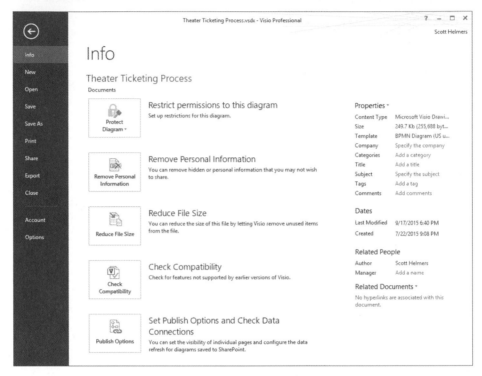

Figure 1-7 *You use the Info page to view and change document attributes*

The center section of the page includes five buttons:

- **Protect Diagram** You will explore this button in the sidebar "What is Information Rights Management?" in Chapter 12, "Print, reuse, and share diagrams."

- **Remove Personal Information** You will learn about this button in Chapter 12, "Print, reuse, and share diagrams."

- **Reduce File Size** You can click this button if document size is a major consideration and you want to create a smaller file.

- **Check Compatibility** This button identifies features in the current diagram that are not compatible with previous versions of Visio.

- **Publish Options** You will learn about the SharePoint publishing settings behind this button in Chapter 15, "Collaborate and publish diagrams."

The right side of the page provides information about the open document, along with a Properties list that you can use to view and set document attributes. You will work with the Properties list in several places in this book, including Chapter 11, "Add and use hyperlinks," and Chapter 12, "Print, reuse, and share diagrams."

The Info page can contain additional buttons, such as the following:

- If you open a document in read-only mode, the Save As button, shown in Figure 1-8, will appear at the top of the Info page.

Read-Only Document

This document has been opened in read-only mode. Changes cannot be made to the original document. To save changes, create a new copy of the document.

Figure 1-8 *Altered read-only documents must be saved as new documents*

- If you open a file created in Visio 2010 or earlier, it will open in compatibility mode, and the Convert button, shown in Figure 1-9, will appear at the top of the Info page.

Compatibility Mode

Some new features are disabled for improved compatibility with previous versions of Visio. Upgrading to the current file format will enable these new features. Affected objects include themes and shape formatting.

Figure 1-9 *You can upgrade older diagrams to the Visio 2016 format*

SEE ALSO For more information about current and former Visio file formats, see "Understand the Visio 2016 file formats" in Appendix A, "Look behind the curtain."

- When a document is stored in SharePoint or OneDrive, the Check Out and View Version History buttons, shown in Figure 1-10 and Figure 1-11, will appear.

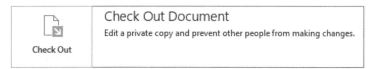

Check Out Document

Edit a private copy and prevent other people from making changes.

Figure 1-10 *You can protect documents from simultaneous edits by other authors*

As the description next to the button shown in Figure 1-10 suggests, you use the Check Out button to prevent others from making changes to a document you are editing. When you click the Check Out button, it is replaced by a Check In button that you use to mark the document as available.

You use the View Version History button to view and manage the current and previous versions of a document.

Figure 1-11 *SharePoint can track each time a document is saved*

The New page

The New page, the upper part of which appears in Figure 1-12, is very similar to the Start screen shown in Figure 1-3 in the preceding topic. On the New page, you have access to the same featured templates, template categories, and online template search options that were described for the Start screen.

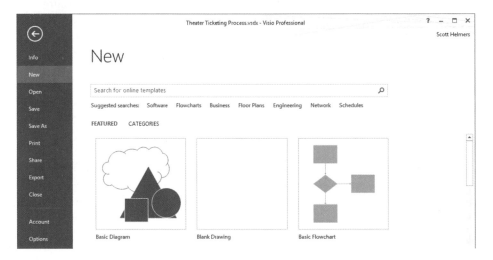

Figure 1-12 *The New page shows both featured and categorized templates*

> ⚠ **IMPORTANT** The New page always displays featured templates first. It's easy to overlook the Categories button that presents a more traditional view of templates organized into logical groups.

1

The Open page

As it does throughout the Microsoft Office suite, the Open page, shown in Figure 1-13, displays a list of both online and local locations where documents can be stored. You can click any location in the left column to see recently used diagrams stored in that location. You can also add more online locations to the list, or browse to locate the diagram you want.

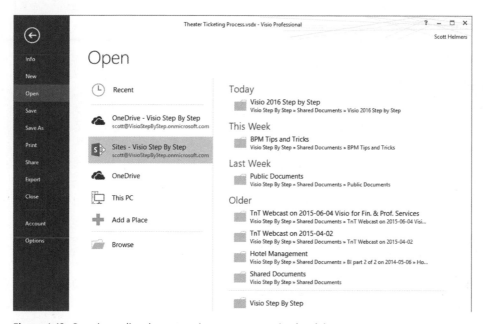

Figure 1-13 *Opening online documents is as easy as opening local documents*

The Save command

Clicking Save for an unsaved diagram displays the Save As page that is described in the following topic. Clicking Save for a previously saved diagram saves the changes.

The Save As page

On the Save As page, shown in Figure 1-14, you can choose a local or online location and then select a recent folder or click the Browse button to navigate to the location you want.

> **SEE ALSO** For information about storing Visio diagrams in other formats, see Chapter 12, "Print, reuse, and share diagrams" and Chapter 15, "Collaborate and publish diagrams."

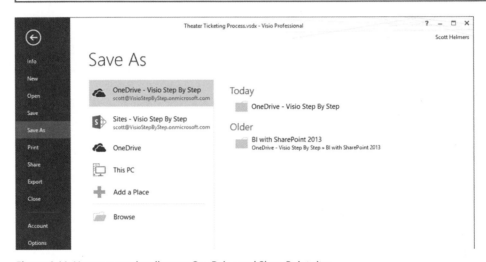

Figure 1-14 *You can save locally or to OneDrive and SharePoint sites*

The Print page

The Print page provides a print preview and printing options. You will explore print options in Chapter 12, "Print, reuse, and share diagrams."

The Share page

You can share your diagram two ways by using the Share page.

You can click Share With People to send people a link to your diagram via email. Your diagram must be stored in SharePoint or OneDrive to use the share function. If it is not, you will be asked to save it in one of those locations first, as shown in Figure 1-15.

1

Figure 1-15 *Sharing diagrams with other people requires two steps*

After the diagram is available online, you can use the form shown in Figure 1-16 to send links to one or more people.

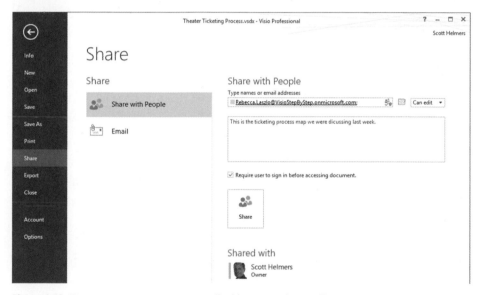

Figure 1-16 *You can enter one or more email addresses to share a diagram*

You can click the Email button to share your diagram using any of the options listed on the right side of the page shown in Figure 1-17.

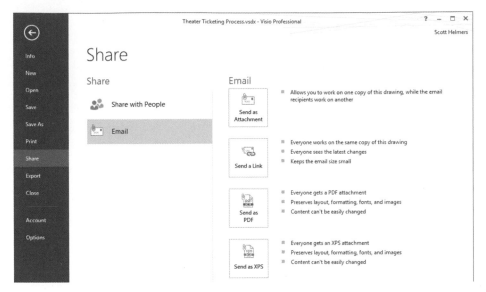

Figure 1-17 *One option for sharing by email automatically creates a PDF of your diagram*

 TIP Send A Link is available only if your diagram is stored online or in a shared folder.

The Export page

You can use the Export page to create a PDF or XPS document and to save in a variety of other file formats. You will explore other file formats in Chapter 12, "Print, reuse, and share diagrams" and Chapter 15, "Collaborate and publish diagrams."

The Close command

Clicking Close closes the active diagram but does not exit Visio.

The Account page

The Account page, shown in Figure 1-18, summarizes information about the Microsoft Account that you have linked to Visio. You can click the links in the User Information area to change your Microsoft Account details and to switch to another Microsoft Account if you have more than one.

The same area provides lists you can use to alter the Office Background and Office Theme used for Visio and all other Office applications.

1

In the Connected Services area is a list of OneDrive and SharePoint sites to which you are currently connected. You can click the Add A Service button to link to additional OneDrive and SharePoint sites.

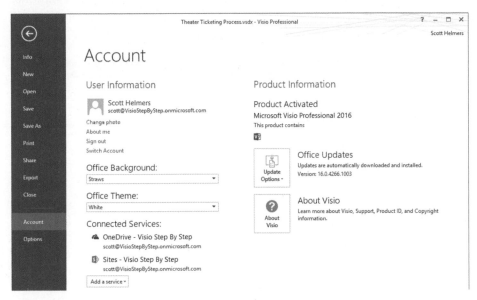

Figure 1-18 *Both user profile and application-level settings are on the Account page*

Clicking the About Visio button in the Product Information area opens the About Microsoft Visio dialog box (see Figure 1-19), which displays version information and your product ID.

> **TIP** The About Microsoft Visio dialog box does not indicate whether you are running Visio Standard or Visio Professional; that information is located below the Product Activated heading in the Product Information area.

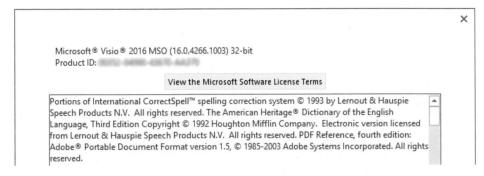

Figure 1-19 *The About Microsoft Visio dialog box displays important information*

The Visio Options dialog box

The Options button opens the Visio Options dialog box, which contains dozens of settings you can use to customize the operation of Visio. Many people use Visio without ever needing to change any of these options, but it's a good idea to examine the option categories shown in Figure 1-20 for potential future use.

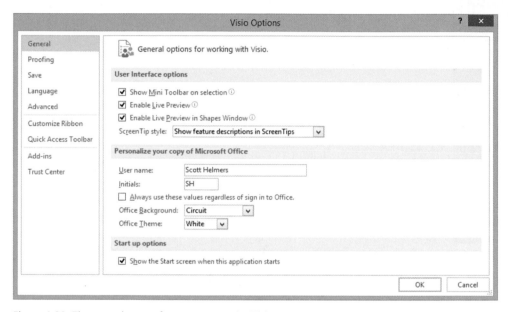

Figure 1-20 *There are dozens of ways to customize Visio*

You can use the options in the Visio Options dialog box to perform many actions, a few of which are mentioned in the following list:

- **General** Enter your user name and initials, and set various global options, including Live Preview and color choices for all Office apps.

- **Proofing** Set autocorrect, spelling, and grammar options.

- **Save** Enable AutoRecover, set the default Visio save format from among three choices (Visio Document, Visio Macro-Enabled Document, and Visio 2003-2010 Document), and set a personal templates location.

- **Language** Set editing, display, help, and ScreenTip language parameters.

- **Advanced** Set dozens of options in five categories: Editing, Display, Save/Open, Shape Search, and General.

1

- **Customize Ribbon** Add and rearrange commands on built-in ribbon tabs; create new tabs and commands.

- **Quick Access Toolbar** Add and remove command buttons for the Quick Access Toolbar.

 SEE ALSO For more information about customizing the Quick Access Toolbar, see Appendix A, "Look behind the curtain."

- **Add-ins** View, add, and delete Visio add-ins.

- **Trust Center** View and edit macro settings and other trust-related options.

To display the Backstage view

1. Click the **File** tab.

Understand tool tabs and add-in tabs

Most tabs on the Visio ribbon are visible 100 percent of the time. However, two types of tabs appear only when necessary.

 SEE ALSO For information about the Developer tab, which might not be visible in your copy of Visio, see Appendix A, "Look behind the curtain."

Use tool tabs

A tool tab group appears only in a particular drawing context, usually when a specific type of shape is selected on the drawing page. Tool tab groups usually appear to the right of the View tab and are not always activated automatically when they appear; that is, you might need to click the tab to view its contents. A tool tab group includes a colored header and might contain one or more tool tabs under the header.

For example, the Picture Tools tab group, shown in Figure 1-21, appears whenever you insert or select a graphic on a Visio drawing page. The green Picture Tools tab contains a Format tool tab that includes buttons to crop, rotate, and otherwise modify a picture.

Figure 1-21 *You can use the Format tool tab in the Picture Tools tab group to edit images*

Another example, the Container Tools tab group, shown in Figure 1-22, appears whenever you insert or select a Visio container. The orange Container Tools tab group contains a Format tool tab, which includes buttons to size and style containers, and to control container membership.

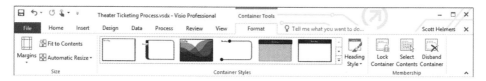

Figure 1-22 *You can use the Format tool tab in the Container Tools tab group to customize containers*

 SEE ALSO For more information about containers, see Chapter 13, "Add structure to your diagrams."

Use add-in tabs

Add-in tabs are associated with software that adds capabilities to Visio. Some add-ins are packaged with Visio by Microsoft, and others are sold by third-party software vendors.

Unlike tool tabs, add-in tabs look and behave exactly like permanent Visio tabs, with one exception: they appear when an add-in application is active and disappear when it is not.

For example, the Org Chart add-in is included with Visio and is activated whenever you create or edit a drawing that uses either of the Visio organization chart templates. The Org Chart add-in tab is shown in Figure 1-23.

Figure 1-23 *You can change the look and layout of an organization chart by using the options on the Org Chart tab*

> **SEE ALSO** For more information about organization charts, see Chapter 5, "Create organization charts."

An example of a third-party add-in is TaskMap, which provides easy-to-use process mapping, analysis, and improvement functions. TaskMap can be used with either Visio Standard or Visio Professional. The TaskMap add-in tab is shown in Figure 1-24.

Figure 1-24 *The TaskMap add-in tab includes functions that integrate Visio with Microsoft Excel, Project, and PowerPoint*

> **SEE ALSO** For more information about the TaskMap add-in, go to *www.taskmap.com*.

Begin quickly by using starter diagrams

Visio templates have always included stencils full of shapes that you can use to build a new diagram. However, even when you use a template to create a diagram, the new drawing page is blank and it can be difficult to know how to begin.

Visio 2016 significantly reduces the challenge by providing several dozen starter diagrams, each of which includes a properly arranged and formatted set of shapes along with a set of tips.

Figure 1-25 shows an example of the starter diagrams that are provided with the Timeline template in the Schedule template group. You can click any of the starter diagram thumbnails to read a description of that sample diagram and the circumstances in which it might be useful.

In all cases, the blank page option is still available by selecting the thumbnail in the upper-left corner.

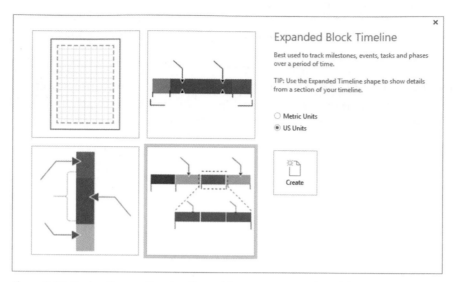

Figure 1-25 *Starter diagram thumbnails provide an accurate preview of diagram content*

Selecting one of the thumbnails opens a one-page document that includes the starter diagram. Figure 1-26 shows the Expanded Block Timeline diagram.

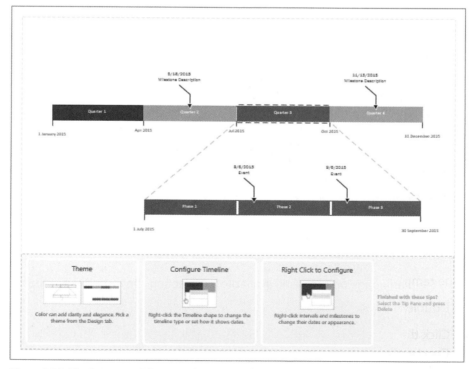

Figure 1-26 *The first page of the Expanded Block Timeline starter diagram*

1

In addition to the diagram itself, every starter diagram includes a tip pane that contains both general and domain-specific tips. When you are finished using the tips pane, you can delete it from the page.

Starter diagrams are available for these Visio Standard templates:

- Audit diagram

- Basic Flowchart

- Basic Network Diagram

- Cross-Functional Flowchart

- Gantt Chart

- Organization Chart Wizard

- Timeline

- Work Flow Diagram

In addition to those templates, the Professional edition of Visio includes starter drawings in these templates:

- BPMN Diagram

- Detailed Network Diagram

- Microsoft SharePoint 2016 Workflow

- UML Class

- UML Sequence

- UML Use Case

- Value Stream Map

To use a starter diagram

1. Click the thumbnail for any template.

2. In the template information panel, do either of the following:

   - Double-click the thumbnail of the starter diagram you want.

   - Click the thumbnail for the starter diagram you want, and then click the **Create** button.

To remove the tips pane from a starter diagram

1. Do either of the following:

    *   Click anywhere inside the tips pane, and then press the **Delete** key.

    *   Right-click the tips pane, and then click **Cut**.

Explore the drawing window

When you open a document in Visio, two windows normally appear below the ribbon, as shown in Figure 1-27.

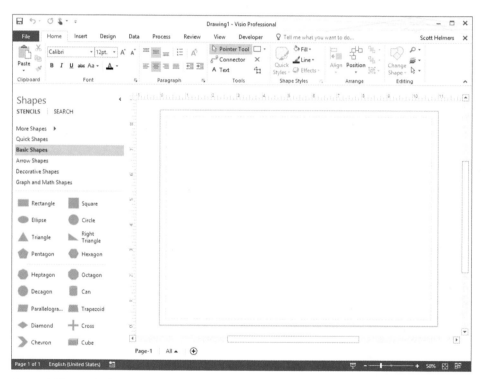

Figure 1-27 *A typical view of Visio includes the ribbon, the Shapes window, and the drawing window*

The Shapes window contains one or more stencils, each represented by a header bar containing the name of the stencil. Depending on the number of open stencils in the Shapes window, a scroll bar might appear at the right of the headers when you move the pointer into the Shapes window. You will investigate the Shapes window in the next topic.

TIP The width of the Shapes window is adjustable. Consequently, the Shapes windows on your computer might be narrower or wider than those that appear in this book.

The larger window on the right is called the *drawing window* because it contains the drawing page. The drawing window is bounded on the top and left by rulers that display inches, millimeters, or whatever units you've selected (or your template has selected) for measuring page dimensions. The gray area between the drawing page and the rulers is referred to as the *canvas*; shapes on the canvas are visible in the drawing window but do not print.

 TIP All versions of Visio prior to Visio 2013 displayed an alignment grid on the drawing page by default. In Visio 2016, the opposite is true. To make the grid visible, select the Grid check box in the Show group on the View tab.

At the lower left of the drawing window is a set of page controls, as shown in Figure 1-28.

Figure 1-28 *Page controls are located at the bottom of the drawing window*

These controls provide the following functions:

- **Page Name tabs** These display the name of each page; the name of the active page is displayed in a different color. Click any tab to switch to that page. Right-click any page name tab to access page management functions, including the Duplicate Page function.

- **All Pages button** Click this button to display a list of all pages in the diagram. The name of the active page is highlighted in the list.

- **Insert Page (+) button** Click this button to add a new page.

Below the Shapes and drawing windows is a status bar that contains a variety of indicators, buttons, and controls. The buttons and indicators on the left end of the status bar are context sensitive, so they show different information depending on the state of the drawing.

If nothing is selected on the drawing page, the left end of the status bar looks like the image shown in Figure 1-29.

Figure 1-29 *The left end of the Visio status bar when no shape is selected*

These areas of the status bar provide the following functions:

- **Page Number** This shows which page is active and displays the total number of pages in the current drawing. Click this button to open the Page dialog box.

- **Language** This area displays the language of the current drawing. The drawing language is normally derived from Windows or Visio language settings.

- **Macros** Click this button to start the macro recorder.

If you have selected a shape on the drawing page, the left end of the status bar appears as shown in Figure 1-30.

PAGE 3 OF 3   WIDTH: 1.5 IN.   HEIGHT: 1.5 IN.   ANGLE: 0°   ENGLISH (UNITED STATES)

Figure 1-30 *The left end of the Visio status bar when a shape is selected*

The Width and Height buttons display the dimensions of the selected shape. The Angle button displays its angle of rotation. Clicking any of these three buttons opens the Size & Position window.

 SEE ALSO For information about using the Size & Position window, see Chapter 3, "Manage text, shapes, and pages."

The right end of the status bar, shown in Figure 1-31, contains buttons and controls that affect the view of your diagram.

Figure 1-31 *Zoom and window control functions are located on the status bar*

- **Presentation Mode button** Click this to view the active diagram in full-screen presentation mode.

- **Zoom slider** Move this to zoom in or out.

- **Zoom Level button** This displays the current zoom percentage. Click it to open the Zoom dialog box.

- **Fit Page To Current Window button** Click this to resize the drawing page so the entire page is visible in the drawing window.

- **Switch Windows button** Click this to switch to another Visio window.

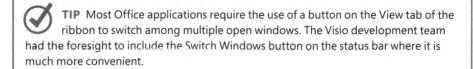

> **TIP** Most Office applications require the use of a button on the View tab of the ribbon to switch among multiple open windows. The Visio development team had the foresight to include the Switch Windows button on the status bar where it is much more convenient.

If you right-click anywhere in the status bar, the Customize Status Bar menu appears. You can use this menu to turn on or off the display of any of the buttons and controls on the status bar.

To view a list of all pages in a diagram

1. Do either of the following:

   - To the right of the last visible page name tab, click the **All Pages** button.

   - At the left end of the status bar, click the **Page Number** button.

To view a different page

1. Do either of the following:

   - Click the page name tab for the page you want.

   - Open the list of all pages, and then select the name of the page you want.

To switch windows

1. Do either of the following:

   - On the right end of the status bar, click the **Switch Windows** button.

   - On the **View** tab, in the **Window** group, click the **Switch Windows** button, and then click the name of the window you want.

How do I scroll through page name tabs?

Versions of Visio prior to Visio 2013 included four page navigation buttons in the lower-left corner of the drawing window that you could use to scroll through the pages in your diagram. Two of the buttons scrolled page name tabs left and right, and two jumped to the first or last page. The navigation buttons were especially helpful when the number of pages or the length of the page names meant that some page names were not visible.

Although those controls are not present in Visio 2016, there is an invisible button that you can use to scroll pages from left to right—to use it, click in the space immediately to the left of the first visible page name tab. You can scroll pages in the opposite direction by clicking the right-most visible page name tab.

Unfortunately, there are no buttons you can use to jump to the first or last page with a single click. However, you can jump to any specific page, whether or not its name tab is visible, by using the techniques described in the procedures at the end of the preceding topic. As an example, clicking the All Pages button results in a clickable list of page names, as shown in Figure 1-32.

Figure 1-32 *The color of the current page name is different from all other page names*

Two keyboard shortcuts are very helpful for moving from page to page:

- **Ctrl+Page Down** Move one page to the right.
- **Ctrl+Page Up** Move one page to the left.

Manage the Shapes window

The upper part of the Shapes window contains the title bars of all open stencils, and the lower part displays the shapes from the currently selected stencil, as shown in Figure 1-27 in the preceding topic. You can switch to any open stencil by clicking its title bar. When you click the title bar of any stencil, the title bars remain stationary, and the stencil always opens in the same place, below all title bars. This is a significant improvement in behavior over versions of Visio prior to Visio 2010.

By default, the Shapes window is docked to the left of the drawing window, and it usually displays one or two columns of masters. However, you might find that you want to adjust or reposition the Shapes window, depending on the diagram you are creating or editing.

You can minimize or expand the Shapes window by using arrow buttons. The minimize button is shown on the left in Figure 1-33, and the expand button is shown in the image on the right. The minimized view of the Shapes window is most useful when the icons depicting the masters in the stencil are easily recognizable.

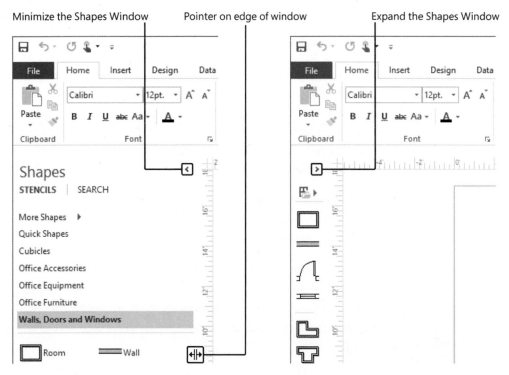

Figure 1-33 *You can view as little or as much of the Shapes window as you want*

You can undock and float the Shapes window at any time if you would like it to be in a different position within the main Visio window. You can also close the Shapes window entirely, as shown in Figure 1-34.

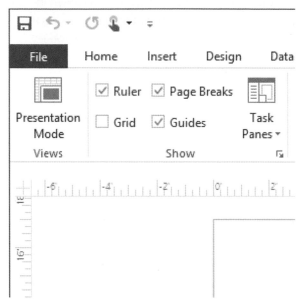

Figure 1-34 *The Shapes window has been hidden*

You can adjust the width of the Shapes window one column at a time by dragging the right edge of the window. However, it's not as easy to locate the right edge as it used to be. A user interface change introduced in Visio 2013 causes window edges to fade into the background so they don't interfere visually with the content of the drawing. Consequently, when the Shapes window is docked on the left, the right edge is not visible unless the pointer is positioned directly above it.

Making the boundary visible typically requires moving the pointer slowly across the right side of the window until the pointer changes to a window resize tool. The resize tool is visible in the image on the left in Figure 1-33.

This same user interface change means that scroll bars in smaller windows only appear when the pointer is inside the window. This creates a challenge in the Shapes window because you can't determine whether additional masters are below the bottom edge of the window without pointing to the window. In the image on the left in Figure 1-35, for example, you can't tell that there are additional furniture shapes available. The scroll bar makes their presence known when the pointer is inside the window, as shown in the image on the right.

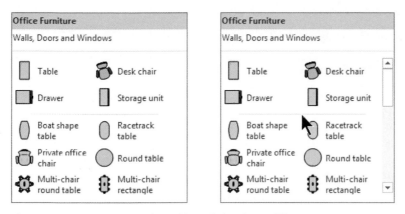

Figure 1-35 *The pointer must be inside a window for scroll bars to appear*

You are not restricted to working with the default set of stencils that opens in any particular template. You can open one or more additional stencils at any time, as shown in Figure 1-36.

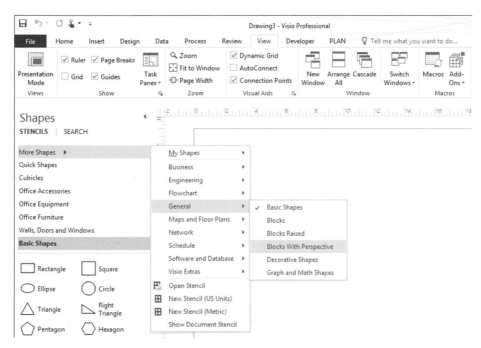

Figure 1-36 *Cascading menus offer access to all Visio stencils*

To minimize the Shapes window

1. Click the **Minimize the Shapes Window** button.

To expand the Shapes window

1. Click the **Expand the Shapes Window** button.

To adjust the width of the Shapes window

1. Move the pointer in the right side of the **Shapes** window until it changes to a window resize tool.

2. Drag the window edge to the left or right.

To undock the Shapes window

1. Drag the header of the window onto the drawing page.

To dock the Shapes window

1. Drag the header of the window to one of the four edges of the main Visio window.

To open or close the Shapes window

1. On the **View** tab, in the **Show** group, click the **Task Panes** button, and then click **Shapes**.

 TIP The various subwindows that can be opened or closed within the main Visio window are sometimes referred to as *task panes*.

To open additional stencils

1. In the **Shapes** window, click **More Shapes**.

2. In the list of template category names, point to the name of the template you want.

3. In the list of stencil names, click the name of the stencil you want.

 TIP The stencil opens in the Shape window as soon as you click its name.

1

4. (*Optional*) Click additional stencil names, within either the same template category or a different one.

5. Click anywhere outside the template and stencil lists to close the cascading menus.

Pan and zoom in the drawing window

As you work with Visio diagrams, you frequently need to zoom in and out and pan—move left-right and up-down—within the drawing window. Both can be accomplished by using a variety of techniques, some that rely on your mouse, some that use a special Pan & Zoom window, and others that entail keyboard shortcuts.

The pan and zoom examples in this topic all use the furniture diagram shown in Figure 1-37.

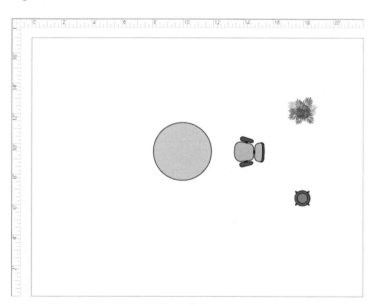

Figure 1-37 *Four furniture shapes in a full-page view*

One of the fastest techniques to view exactly the part of the page you want involves drawing a bounding box while holding down the Ctrl and Shift keys. While you draw the bounding box, Visio displays what's shown in Figure 1-38.

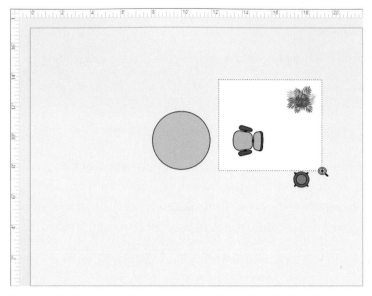

Figure 1-38 *The magnifying glass pointer indicates that this bounding box will zoom the diagram*

The result of the zoom operation is shown in Figure 1-39. The selected shapes are centered in the drawing window.

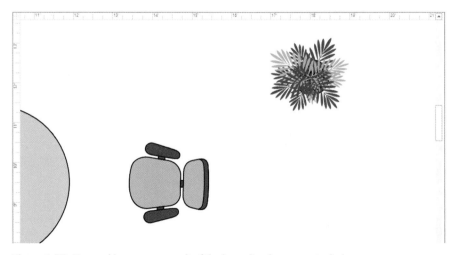

Figure 1-39 *Zoomed image as a result of the bounding box zoom technique*

As an alternative, you can draw a rectangle in the Pan & Zoom window that is shown in Figure 1-40. By dragging or resizing the rectangle in the Pan & Zoom window, you can pan or zoom, respectively.

> **TIP** For many drawings, the Pan & Zoom window isn't necessary and might even be in the way. However, it is extremely helpful when your drawing page is very large, which might be the case when you are working on engineering drawings, floor plans, or office layouts.

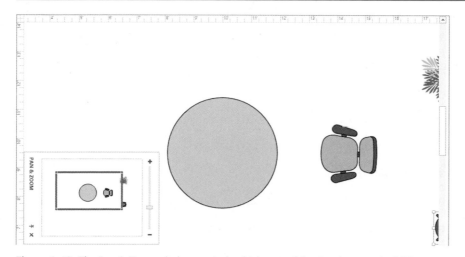

Figure 1-40 *The Pan & Zoom window controls which part of the drawing page is visible*

> **TIP** The need to zoom in and out while working with a diagram is so frequent that there are probably more techniques and keyboard and mouse shortcuts for this operation than for any other action in Visio.

To open or close the Pan & Zoom window

1. On the **View** tab, in the **Show** group, click the **Task Panes** button, and then click **Pan & Zoom**.

To zoom in

1. Do any of the following:

   - While holding down the **Shift** and **Ctrl** keys, click the left mouse button.

   - While holding down the **Shift** and **Ctrl** keys, roll the mouse wheel forward.

   - Press **Alt+F6**.

   - On the status bar, drag the handle of the **Zoom** slider.

   - On the status bar, click the **Zoom level** button, and then set a specific zoom level.

- On the **View** tab, in the **Zoom** group, click the **Zoom** button, and then set a specific zoom level.

- In the **Pan & Zoom** window, drag to draw a rectangle that is smaller than the current rectangle (if any).

- In the **Pan & Zoom** window, drag the edges or corners of the selection rectangle to make it smaller.

To zoom out

1. Do any of the following:

   - While holding down the **Shift** and **Ctrl** keys, click the right mouse button.

   - While holding down the **Shift** and **Ctrl** keys, roll the mouse wheel backward.

   - Press **Shift+Alt+F6**.

   - On the status bar, drag the handle of the **Zoom** slider.

   - On the status bar, click the **Zoom level** button, and then set a specific zoom level.

   - On the **View** tab, in the **Zoom** group, click the **Zoom** button, and then set a specific zoom level.

   - In the **Pan & Zoom** window, drag to draw a rectangle that is larger than the current rectangle (if any).

   - In the **Pan & Zoom** window, drag the edges or corners of the selection rectangle to make it larger.

To fit the drawing page to the current window

1. Do either of the following:

   - On the status bar, click the **Fit page to current window** button.

   - On the **View** tab, in the **Zoom** group, click the **Fit to Window** button.

1

To pan the diagram

1. Do any of the following:

   - Roll the mouse wheel (pans up and down).

   - While holding down the **Shift** key, roll the mouse wheel (pans left and right).

   - While holding down the **Shift** and **Ctrl** keys, click the right mouse button, and drag.

   - In the **Pan & Zoom** window, drag the selection rectangle.

Skills review

In this chapter, you learned how to:

- Identify the editions of Visio 2016

- Discover new features in Visio 2016

- Get started in Visio 2016

- Explore the Backstage view

- Understand tool tabs and add-in tabs

- Begin quickly by using starter diagrams

- Explore the drawing window

- Manage the Shapes window

- Pan and zoom in the drawing window

Practice tasks

The practice files for these tasks are located in the Visio2016SBS\Ch01 folder. You can save the results of the tasks in the same folder.

Identify the editions of Visio 2016

There are no practice tasks for this topic.

Discover new features in Visio 2016

There are no practice tasks for this topic.

Get started in Visio 2016

Start Visio, and then perform the following tasks. At the conclusion of each task, return to the Start page.

1. Open the **GetStarted** diagram in the Visio2016SBS\Ch01 folder.

2. Close the **GetStarted** diagram without exiting Visio.

3. In the **Featured** section, click the thumbnail for any template you want.

4. In the category section, click the Business category thumbnail, and then create a diagram from the **Brainstorming Diagram** template.

5. Enter a keyword to search online for templates.

6. Click a **Suggested searches** keyword to search online for templates.

7. Create a diagram by using the **GetStarted** diagram as a template.

Explore the Backstage view

Start Visio, and then perform the following tasks:

1. Open any diagram.

2. Display the Backstage view and explore the various pages.

Understand tool tabs and add-in tabs

There are no practice tasks for this topic.

Begin quickly by using starter diagrams

Start Visio, and then perform the following tasks:

1. Open the template information panel for the **Basic Flowchart** template.

2. Create a diagram from the **Decision Branches Flowchart** template.

3. After reviewing the tips pane, delete it from the diagram.

Explore the drawing window

Open the ExploreDrawing diagram in Visio, and then perform the following tasks:

1. View several pages in the diagram.

2. Display the list of all diagram pages.

3. In the same instance of Visio, open the **GetStarted** diagram located in the Visio2016SBS\Ch01 folder.

4. Switch between the two open diagrams.

Manage the Shapes window

Open the ManageShapesWindow diagram in Visio, and then perform the following tasks:

1. Minimize and then expand the **Shapes** window.

2. Make the **Shapes** window wider or narrower.

3. Dock the **Shapes** window at the top of the drawing page, and then float it over the drawing page.

4. Dock the **Shapes** window in its original location.

5. Hide the **Shapes** window, and then make it visible again.

6. Open several additional stencils.

Pan and zoom in the drawing window

Open the PanAndZoom diagram in Visio, and then perform the following tasks:

1. Open the **Pan & Zoom** window.

2. Zoom in and out on several parts of the diagram.

3. Zoom to **200%**, and then pan to the right side of the page.

4. Pan to the lower-left corner of the page.

5. Use the **Pan & Zoom** window to zoom out and view the center of the page.

6. Fit the diagram to the window.

Create diagrams

2

Creating a diagram from scratch can be daunting. Consequently, Visio 2016 provides dozens of templates for a variety of diagram types. Two dozen templates are grouped into six template categories in the Standard edition and more than 70 templates in eight categories in the Professional edition.

Each template includes one or more stencils, and each stencil contains a collection of shapes that are suitable for the specific diagram type. Some of the shapes are very simple, whereas others contain formulas that give them surprisingly sophisticated behavior. You will examine examples of both simple shapes and smart shapes as you explore various templates in this and subsequent chapters. Regardless of which template you use, you should understand how to position and manipulate shapes.

This chapter guides you through procedures related to aligning, positioning, and resizing shapes by using the Dynamic Grid; selecting, copying, pasting, and duplicating shapes; positioning shapes by using rulers and guides; resizing, repositioning, and reorienting shapes; connecting shapes by using lines and dynamic connectors; using AutoConnect and Quick Shapes; and using AutoAdd and AutoDelete.

In this chapter

- Place shapes by using the Dynamic Grid

- Select, copy, paste, and duplicate shapes

- Position shapes by using rulers and guides

- Resize, reposition, and reorient shapes

- Connect shapes by using lines

- Connect shapes by using dynamic connectors

- Use AutoConnect and Quick Shapes

- Use AutoAdd and AutoDelete

Practice files

For this chapter, use the practice files from the Visio2016SBS\Ch02 folder. For practice file download instructions, see the introduction.

Place shapes by using the Dynamic Grid

The purpose of the Dynamic Grid is to help you position or size a shape with greater accuracy as you drop it on the page or when you relocate it, thereby eliminating much of the need to drag and nudge the shape after you've placed it. Visio 2016 and Visio 2013 both feature an enhanced Dynamic Grid that provides even more visual feedback than earlier versions of the software.

> ✓ **TIP** Unless otherwise indicated, the shapes shown in the figures in this chapter are from the Basic Shapes stencil that opens when you use the Basic Diagram template that is located in the General template group.

The Dynamic Grid displays horizontal or vertical dashed lines to assist with shape alignment. In the three parts of Figure 2-1, the Dynamic Grid indicates when the circle is aligned with the top, middle, and bottom of the rectangle.

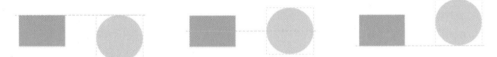

Figure 2-1 *Dynamic Grid guidelines appear while aligning shapes*

The Dynamic Grid also displays double-headed arrows of different lengths to assist with shape spacing and sizing. Double-headed arrows appear when:

- The interval between shapes matches the default spacing interval for the page. Refer to the vertical arrow to the right of the space between the rectangle and octagon in Figure 2-2.

- The space between your new shape and an existing shape matches the space between the existing shape and another shape on the page, as shown by the horizontal arrows below the spaces between the rectangle, circle, and square in Figure 2-2.

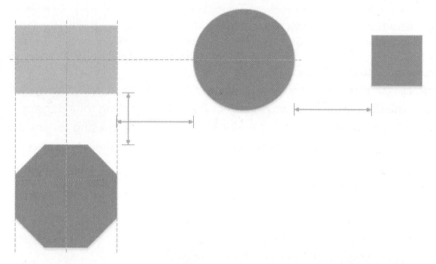

Figure 2-2 *Dynamic Grid guidelines appear while spacing and aligning shapes*

■ You are resizing a shape and its dimensions match those of one or more existing shapes on the page, as shown in Figure 2-3. (The ellipse is being resized in this figure.)

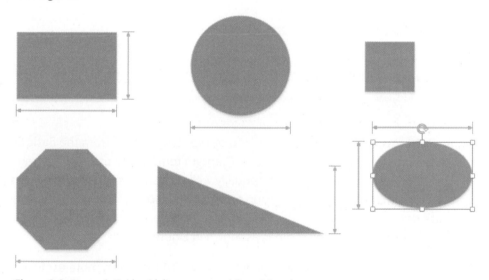

Figure 2-3 *Dynamic Grid guidelines appear while resizing shapes*

> **TIP** When two shapes that you are positioning are the same width or height, Visio displays three Dynamic Grid lines for the pair of shapes: at the left, center, and right, or at the top, middle, and bottom. See the dashed grid lines between and along the sides of the rectangle and octagon in Figure 2-2 for an example.

Because some double-headed arrows reflect the default spacing for a page, it is useful to know that you can change the default inter-shape spacing for any page. You can do so in the Spacing Options dialog box shown in Figure 2-4.

The default options in this dialog box set the vertical interval to match the horizontal interval. You can change the vertical interval separately by clearing the Use Same Spacing For Both check box.

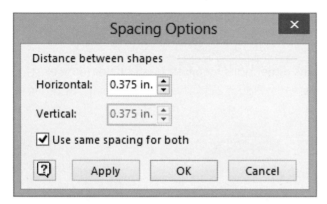

Figure 2-4 *The Spacing Options dialog box, in which you can change the vertical and horizontal spacing intervals for a page*

Figure 2-1 through Figure 2-3 were created by dragging shapes from the Basic Shapes stencil that opens when you use the Basic Diagram template to create a diagram. However, the Dynamic Grid functions equally well with shapes you create by using the drawing tools that are in the Tools group on the Home tab. To make it more convenient to create new shapes in Visio 2016, the drawing tools were added to a button in the upper-left corner of the mini toolbar, as shown in Figure 2-5.

Though the Dynamic Grid was helpful before Visio 2013, it's even more useful now because it reacts more quickly to pointer movement and shape locations, and because it provides a greater variety of visual feedback. In addition, the Dynamic Grid is more vital for aligning shapes in Visio 2016 and Visio 2013 because the background page grid is turned off by default in these versions.

> **TIP** If the Dynamic Grid lines don't appear as you move shapes near others already on the page, it is probably because the feature is turned off for this drawing. To activate the Dynamic Grid, select the Dynamic Grid check box in the Visual Aids group on the View tab.

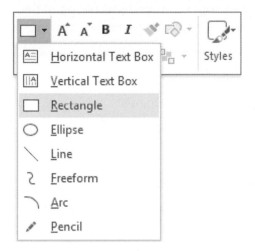

Figure 2-5 *The drawing tools button has been added to the Visio 2016 mini toolbar*

To place shapes on a page

1. Drag a shape from a stencil and drop it on the drawing page.

To align shapes by using the Dynamic Grid

1. Drag a shape to either side of, above, or below an existing shape, and then pause until Dynamic Grid lines appear.

To align shapes on both axes by using the Dynamic Grid

1. Drag a shape so it is above or below at least one shape, and at the same time is also left or right of a different shape. Note that both horizontal and vertical Dynamic Grid lines appear.

To space shapes by using the Dynamic Grid

1. Do either of the following:

   - Drag a shape to the right or left of another shape and slowly move it left and right until a double-headed arrow appears.

   - Drag a shape above or below another shape and slowly move it up and down until a double-headed arrow appears.

To change the default inter-shape spacing for a page

1. On the **Home** tab, in the **Arrange** group, click **Position**, and then click **Spacing Options** to open the **Spacing Options** dialog box.

2. If you want to set different intervals for **Horizontal** and **Vertical** spacing, in the **Spacing Options** dialog box, clear the **Use same spacing for both** check box.

3. Set either the **Horizontal** interval, or both the **Horizontal** and **Vertical** intervals, to the spacing you want, and then click **OK**.

To resize a shape to match the width or height of existing shapes

1. Drag any resize handle on one shape and note the appearance of the double-headed arrows.

To create shapes by using the drawing tools

1. Right-click anywhere on the drawing page, click the **Drawing Tools** button on the mini toolbar, and then click one of the tools.

    Or

    On the **Home** tab, in the **Tools** group, click the drawing tools button, and then click one of the tools.

2. Drag to create a shape.

To create a square by using the drawing tools

1. Select the **Rectangle** tool.

2. Hold down the **Shift** key while dragging.

To create a circle by using the drawing tools

1. Select the **Ellipse** tool.

2. Hold down the **Shift** key while dragging.

 TIP You can constrain the Rectangle and Ellipse tools so they draw only squares or circles by holding down the Shift key while dragging.

To align and size shapes created by using the drawing tools

1. Reposition and resize shapes in the same way you would for shapes created from a stencil.

Select shapes

You can use several techniques for selecting shapes in Visio, including clicking one or more shapes, using Area Select, and using Lasso Select. You can also select all shapes on a page at once, and you can remove shapes from an existing selection.

Area selection is the default behavior in Visio when you click the drawing page and drag. Only shapes that are fully surrounded by the gray bounding box are selected, unless you change the Visio selection default. For example, in the left half of Figure 2-6, the rectangle and octagon will be selected when you release the mouse button. In the right half of the figure, no shapes will be selected.

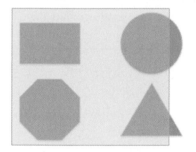 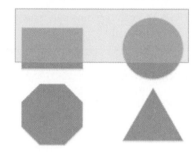

Figure 2-6 *A bounding box used to select shapes*

Lasso Select is a less common technique but provides greater flexibility by allowing you to surround the shapes you want with a freeform line. As with a bounding box, the default behavior in Visio is to select only fully enclosed shapes when you release the mouse button. The lasso on the left side of Figure 2-7 will produce the selection on the right, in which only the octagon and circle are selected.

> ✓ **TIP** To ensure that you select the shapes you want while using Lasso Select, be sure to release the mouse button very close to the beginning of the "rope." You aren't required to end at exactly the same place, and in some cases, a partially closed loop will still select some shapes, but it is best to end very near where you started.

> ✓ **TIP** You can change selection behavior in Visio so it will select shapes that are partially enclosed by a bounding box or lasso. Click the File tab to display the Backstage view, click Options in the left pane, and click Advanced. Then click the Select Shapes Partially Within Area check box.

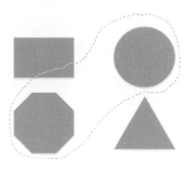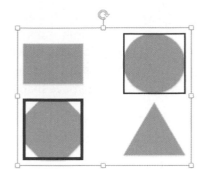

Figure 2-7 *A lasso used to select shapes*

> ✓ **TIP** You can combine either area or lasso selection with click selection to produce the result you want.

To select one shape

1. Click on the shape once.

To select multiple shapes by clicking

1. Click once to select the first shape.

2. Hold down either the **Shift** key or the **Ctrl** key while clicking additional shapes.

To select one or more shapes by using Area Select

1. Click once on the drawing page and drag to create a bounding box around the shape or shapes you want.

To change from Area Select to Lasso Select

1. On the **Home** tab, in the **Editing** group, click the **Select** button, and then click **Lasso Select**.

To create a lasso selection

1. Hold down the mouse button and drag a lasso around the shape or shapes you want, being certain to end the lasso near its beginning.

To revert to using bounding boxes

1. Click the **Select** button, and then click **Area Select**.

To combine area or lasso selection with click selection

1. Do either of the following:

   - Select one or more shapes by clicking them, and then add additional shapes by holding down **Shift** or **Ctrl** while drawing a bounding box or lasso loop.

   - Start with a bounding box or lasso selection, and then add additional shapes by holding down **Shift** or **Ctrl** as you click the shapes you want.

To remove shapes from a selection

1. Hold down the **Shift** key or the **Ctrl** key while clicking shapes.

To select all shapes on a page

1. Press **Ctrl+A**.

Copy, paste, and duplicate shapes

Prior to the 2010 version, Visio always pasted shapes into the center of the drawing window. Occasionally, this was what you wanted, but as often as not, this placement required additional dragging and nudging. Visio 2016, like its two immediate predecessors, works more logically. If you copy one or more shapes from Page-1 and then paste them onto Page-2, Visio will paste them into the same position on Page-2 that they occupied on Page-1, even if that part of the page is not visible when you paste.

Pasting shapes to the same page from which they were copied works slightly differently:

- If the copied shapes are visible in the drawing window when you paste, the pasted shapes will be located at a small offset below and to the right of the original shapes.

- If the copied shapes are not visible in the drawing window when you paste, Visio will paste the shapes into the center of the drawing window.

You can paste shapes to a specific location, whether on the page from which they were copied or another page, and you can duplicate shapes as an alternative to copying and pasting. Duplicated shapes are placed at a small offset below and to the right of the original shapes, as shown in Figure 2-8.

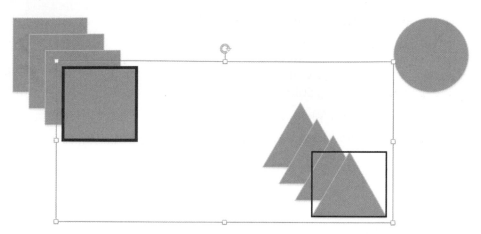

Figure 2-8 *Two shapes that have been duplicated three times*

> ✓ **TIP** You can both duplicate shapes and constrain how they are positioned by combining two keyboard-mouse shortcuts. Pressing Shift while dragging constrains movement to either vertical or horizontal so that shapes remain aligned on one axis. Pressing Ctrl and Shift while dragging duplicates selected shapes and keeps them aligned with the originals.

Duplicating shapes offers one advantage over copying: it doesn't use the Clipboard. Consequently, if you have shapes or data on the Clipboard that you want to preserve, but you also want to clone one or more shapes, the original data will remain on the Clipboard if you duplicate the shapes rather than copy them.

To copy shapes

1. Select the shapes you want to copy, and then press **Ctrl+C**.

To paste shapes onto the same page and let Visio choose the placement

1. Do either of the following:

   - Copy two or more shapes, and then press **Ctrl+V** to paste the shapes onto the same page. Note that Visio places the pasted shapes at a small offset from the original shapes.

   - Scroll until the original shapes are no longer on the screen, and then press **Ctrl+V** to paste the shapes. Notice that Visio pastes them in the center of the drawing window.

2

Notice, also, that if the drawing page is not large enough to contain the pasted shapes, Visio either expands the size of the page if Auto Size is on, or places them on the canvas if it is not.

 SEE ALSO For information about the Auto Size function that automatically expands and contracts Visio pages, see Chapter 3, "Manage text, shapes, and pages."

To paste shapes onto a different page and let Visio choose the placement

1. Copy two or more shapes.

2. At the bottom of the drawing window, click a page name tab to switch to a different page.

   Or

   Click the **Insert Page** button (the + sign) to add a page to the diagram.

3. Press **Ctrl+V** to paste the copied shapes onto the page. Notice that Visio places them in the same location on the new page that they occupied on the original page.

To paste shapes to a specific location on a page

1. Right-click the place on the page where you would like the copied shapes to appear, and then click **Paste**.

To duplicate one or more selected shapes

1. Do either of the following:

   • Press **Ctrl+D**.

   • Drag the shapes while holding down the **Ctrl** key, and then release the mouse button at the target location.

Position shapes by using rulers and guides

As described earlier in this chapter, you can align shapes by using the Dynamic Grid feature of Visio 2016. However, the Dynamic Grid doesn't always do what you need. For example, if there are shapes between the two you are trying to align, the Dynamic Grid doesn't help. In other cases, you might want to align shapes in ways that the Dynamic Grid can't.

Use rulers to align and size shapes

The Visio ruler provides valuable assistance for shape positioning and sizing. One ruler appears on the left edge of the drawing window, and another is located across the top. If you create a diagram by using a US Units template, which is the selected template type in Figure 2-9, the ruler will be delineated in feet and inches. If you click Metric Units, shown in Figure 2-9, the ruler will be marked in meters, centimeters, or millimeters.

 TIP If the ruler is not visible, or if it is and you would like to hide it, on the View tab, in the Show group, select or clear the Ruler check box.

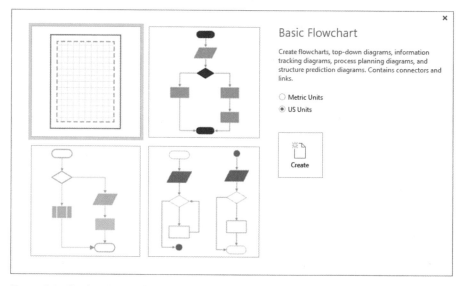

Figure 2-9 *The description of the Basic Flowchart template includes a choice between Metric Units and US Units*

As you drag shapes on the drawing page, Visio provides visual location information on the ruler in the form of dashed lines. The lines on the top ruler in Figure 2-10 mark the left, center, and right of the octagon; the lines on the side ruler denote the top, middle, and bottom of the shape.

You can use the lines on the rulers to position shapes as you move them.

When you drag a side handle to resize a shape in either the horizontal or vertical dimension, a single dashed line will appear on the corresponding ruler. If you drag a corner handle to resize a shape in both dimensions, a single line will appear on each ruler.

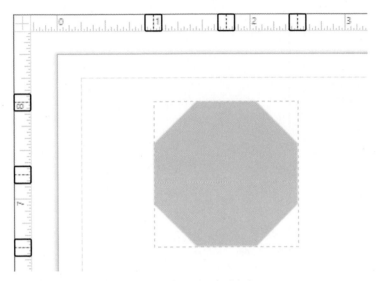

Figure 2-10 *Dashed lines on the left and top rulers show the position of a shape*

To position shapes by using the ruler

1. While dragging the shape in any direction, use the dashed position indicator lines on the vertical and horizontal rulers to position the shape exactly where you want it.

Use guides to align and size shapes

A guide is a tool for aligning shapes, but it also allows you to move shapes as a unit after you have aligned them. You create guides by clicking a ruler and then dragging to the drawing page. You can add as many horizontal or vertical guides to the page as you want.

Guides are useful in many circumstances, but they are especially helpful in a situation like the one depicted in Figure 2-11. The two stars in this diagram cannot be aligned by using the Dynamic Grid because of the intervening horizontal rectangle. Consequently, a vertical guide has been dragged onto the page.

 TIP If you can't see the guides on a page, or if they are visible but you would like to hide them, on the View tab, in the Show group, select or clear the Guides check box.

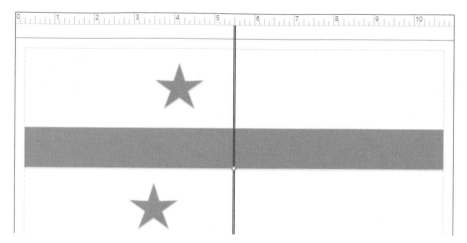

Figure 2-11 *A vertical guide can be used to align two shapes*

You can glue a shape to a guide at the shape's edges or center by dragging it toward the guide, as shown in Figure 2-12.

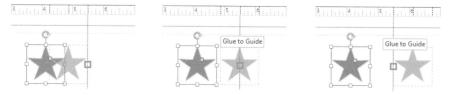

Figure 2-12 *Gluing a shape to a guide*

In Figure 2-13, the two stars are now precisely aligned at their centers, despite the intervening shape.

It's important to realize that the stars are actually glued to the guide. If you move the guide, the stars will move also. However, if you no longer need the guide, perhaps because you don't need to move the aligned shapes as a unit, you can delete the guide as you would any other shape.

 TIP Guides appear on the drawing page but do not print.

2

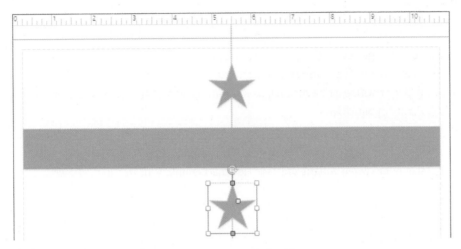

Figure 2-13 *Two stars glued at their centers to a vertical guide*

To align shapes by using a guide

1. Place two shapes on the drawing page.

2. Click either ruler, and then drag a guide onto the page.

3. Drag the first shape to the guide and glue it at the center or an edge.

4. Drag the second shape to the guide and glue it the same way that you glued the first shape.

To move shapes that are glued to a guide

1. Glue two or more shapes to a guide as described in the preceding procedure.

2. Drag the guide to a new location and note that all aligned shapes move with the guide.

To delete a guide

1. Click to select the guide, and then press the **Delete** key.

Resize, reposition, and reorient shapes

After you've placed shapes onto the drawing page, you might need to move or resize some of them. Visio provides a variety of techniques for doing so. You can alter shapes by using your mouse or keyboard, or a combination of the two. You can also use the Size & Position window.

> **TIP** The shapes shown in the figures in this topic are from the Basic Flowchart Shapes stencil that opens when you use the Basic Flowchart template located in the Flowchart template group.

Use control handles

When you select a shape, a set of white squares appear. These squares are referred to as selection handles, resize handles, or just handles. Pictured on shapes A and B in Figure 2-14, the handles allow you to alter a shape in the following ways:

- Dragging the square handles in the center of each edge alters the width or height of the shape.

- Dragging the square handles on the corners adjusts the width and height proportionally.

Occasionally, you might notice that you are unable to drag one or more handles on a shape. This is usually an indication that the shape designer has locked one or more attributes of the shape. Shape B, on the right side of Figure 2-14, displays diagonal slashes through the top and bottom handles, indicating that the height of the shape is locked. Note, too, that there are slashes through the corner handles: if you can't adjust the height, you can't change both dimensions at the same time by using a corner handle.

Figure 2-14 *Comparison of shapes with locked attributes and unlocked attributes*

TIP Previous versions of Visio displayed locked handles with a different color than unlocked handles. In Visio 2016, the distinction is more subtle and relies on the diagonal lines described in conjunction with Figure 2-14.

In addition to the side and corner handles, a circular arrow appears at the top center of most selected shapes. This is the rotation handle and it is visible above shape B on the right side of Figure 2-14. (Shape A does not display a rotation handle on the left side of Figure 2-14 because rotation has been locked for that shape.) Clicking and dragging the rotation handle rotates the shape around its pin position.

TIP You can control the precision of shape rotation by moving the pointer farther from, or closer to, the rotation handle. For example, if the pointer is near the rotation handle, the shape will rotate in 15-degree increments. If you move the pointer out, the shape will rotate in increasingly smaller increments until you are rotating it fractions of a degree at a time. As you rotate a shape, you can view the incremental change in rotation angle in the Size & Position window.

SEE ALSO For information about how to view the angle of a shape in the Size & Position window, see "Use the Size & Position window" later in this chapter.

In addition to resize and rotation handles, you might encounter a yellow control handle on some Visio shapes. Control handles allow shape designers to give the user control of various shape properties. You will find control handles that adjust the location of interior or exterior lines, the position of text on the shape, the size of the shape, or any number of other shape attributes. As an example, you can use the control handle on shape D in Figure 2-15 to move the interior vertical lines within the shape, as shown in the left and right views of shape D.

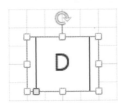 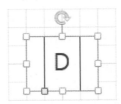

Figure 2-15 *A control handle that adjusts interior line position in a shape*

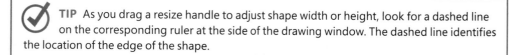

> **✓ TIP** Yellow control handles appear on a variety of the shapes in Visio stencils. Whenever you select a shape and notice a yellow handle, it's worth experimenting with it to learn how you can use it to alter the shape's appearance. If you make a change that you don't like, simply press Ctrl+Z to undo the modification.

To adjust shape height and width

1. Select a shape, and then drag any of the side or corner handles to resize the shape.

> **✓ TIP** As you drag a resize handle to adjust shape width or height, look for a dashed line on the corresponding ruler at the side of the drawing window. The dashed line identifies the location of the edge of the shape.

To rotate a shape

1. Select a shape, and then drag the rotation handle.

2. Move the pointer closer to, and then farther away from, the shape as you drag across the screen to observe the differences in rotation increment.

Use the Size & Position window

The Size & Position window serves two purposes in Visio: you can use it to view the values of six shape attributes—X coordinate, Y coordinate, width, height, angle, and pin position—for a two-dimensional shape, and you can use it to change those same six values.

For example, if the Size & Position window shows that a shape is 2 inches wide, like the shape on the left in Figure 2-16, and you enter *3.5* in the Width cell, the shape width will change immediately. Similarly, if the Y position of a shape on a page is 50 mm and you enter *125* in the Y cell, the shape will move up the page to the new position.

One-dimensional Visio shapes display properties that are appropriate for a line, including the beginning and ending coordinates and the length, in the Size & Position window, as shown on the right in Figure 2-16.

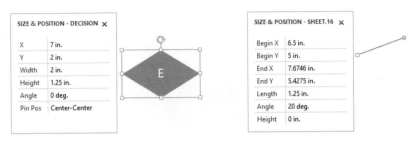

SIZE & POSITION - DECISION ✕	
X	7 in.
Y	2 in.
Width	2 in.
Height	1.25 in.
Angle	0 deg.
Pin Pos	Center-Center

SIZE & POSITION - SHEET.16 ✕	
Begin X	6.5 in.
Begin Y	5 in.
End X	7.6746 in.
End Y	5.4275 in.
Length	1.25 in.
Angle	20 deg.
Height	0 in.

Figure 2-16 *The Size & Position window shows values for selected shapes*

If you enter a value into a cell in the Size & Position window and do not include units, Visio will default to using whatever units were displayed for that cell before you made the change. However, you can specify units when you enter values. For example, if the Y value is 60 mm and you enter either *12 cm* or *12 centimeters*, Visio will convert and apply the value; in this case the result will display as 120 mm.

Visio will even convert across measurement systems. Continuing the example in the previous paragraph, if you enter either *3 in* or *3 inches*, Visio will move the shape and then display the result as 76.2 mm.

The purpose of the first five rows in the Size & Position window for two-dimensional shapes is reasonably obvious, but the sixth row requires additional explanation. Pin Pos, short for *pin position*, is the center of rotation for a shape. The default Pin Pos for most shapes is Center-Center, as shown for the shape in Figure 2-16, which means that the shape will rotate around its center.

> ✓ **TIP** To envision the purpose of the pin position, imagine that a shape is a piece of paper you've stuck on your wall with a pin. If you rotate the piece of paper, it will rotate around the pin.

You can change the Pin Pos to rotate the shape around a different point. In Figure 2-17, shape E is being rotated around its lower-left corner.

> ✓ **TIP** When you change the Pin Pos for a shape, the location of the shape on the page will change. This is because the X and Y coordinates of the shape actually specify the location of the pin and not the coordinates of the center of the shape. Because you have moved the pin within the shape, the location of the shape on the page will change.

SIZE & POSITION - DECISION ✕	
X	7 in.
Y	4.25 in.
Width	2 in.
Height	1.25 in.
Angle	40 deg.
Pin Pos	Bottom-Left

Figure 2-17 *A shape being rotated around its lower-left corner*

You can also view three attributes of a two-dimensional shape, or two attributes of a line, without opening the Size & Position window. Visio displays either two or three attributes of a selected shape on the status bar at the bottom of the Visio window, as shown in Figure 2-18. The image on the bottom is for a two-dimensional shape; the one on the top is for a line.

> ✓ **TIP** Clicking the Length, Width, Height, or Angle buttons on the Visio status bar opens the Size & Position window.

| Page 1 of 1 | Length: 2.5 in. | Angle: 20° | English (United States) |

| Page 1 of 1 | Width: 2 in. | Height: 1.25 in. | Angle: 40° | English (United States) |

Figure 2-18 *Status bar display of shape properties for a two-dimensional shape on the bottom and a line on the top*

To open the Size & Position window

1. Do either of the following:

   - On the **View** tab, in the **Show** group, click **Task Panes**, and then click **Size & Position**.

   - With a shape selected, click either the **Length**, **Width**, **Height**, or **Angle** button on the status bar at the bottom of the Visio window.

To view changes to shape attributes

1. Select a shape.

2. Open the **Size & Position** window (optional).

3. Drag the shape to a new location on the page.

   Or

   Use the resize handles to change the shape's width or height.

   Or

   Use the rotation handle to rotate the shape.

4. While making any of the changes in the preceding step, note the new values that are displayed on the Visio status bar or in the **Size & Position** window.

To adjust shape properties by using the Size & Position window

1. Select a shape, and then open the **Size & Position** window.

2. Enter a new value for any shape attribute and note the change in the shape.

Connect shapes by using lines

Visio shapes are either one-dimensional (1-D) or two-dimensional (2-D). 1-D shapes act like lines with endpoints that can be attached to other shapes. 2-D shapes behave like polygons with edges and an interior. However, appearances can be deceiving, because some shapes that appear to be two-dimensional might actually be 1-D shapes in Visio; there's an example in the topic titled, "Add equipment to rack diagrams" in Chapter 7 , "Create network and datacenter diagrams." The reverse can also be true.

This topic describes a category of 1-D shapes referred to as *lines*. The topic "Connect shapes by using dynamic connectors" later in this chapter describes a special type of 1-D shape known as a dynamic connector.

One way to create a line in Visio is to use the Line tool. The Line tool is one of six tools available from the drawing tools button, which is immediately to the right of the Pointer Tool in the Tools group on the Home tab. On the left side of Figure 2-19, the pointer is on top of the drawing tools button, and the ScreenTip describes the active drawing tool.

If you want to use the Line tool but it isn't visible, click the arrow next to whichever tool is displayed on the button, and then select the tool you want. The result of selecting the Line tool appears on the right side of Figure 2-19.

> **TIP** You can also access the drawing tools on the mini toolbar, as shown in Figure 2-4. When you select the Line tool by using this technique, as soon as you've drawn one line, the pointer reverts to the Pointer Tool.

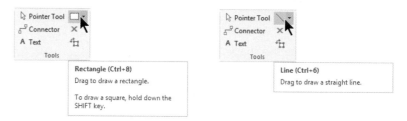

Figure 2-19 *The Rectangle and Line tools on the Home tab*

When the Line tool is active, the cursor changes to a plus sign with a diagonal line to its lower right, as shown in the left graphic in Figure 2-20. In that same graphic on the left, there are multiple dark gray squares, known as connection points. Connection points on a shape are normally invisible in Visio 2016, but they appear whenever you move the Line tool near the shape.

> **IMPORTANT** Not all shapes contain connection points. If you don't see gray squares anywhere on a shape when you approach it with the Line tool, the shape might not include any connection points.
>
> There is one other possibility: the shape might contain connection points, but the global option setting to view connection points might be turned off. To verify whether connection point viewing is on or off, examine the Connection Points check box in the Visual Aids group on the View tab.

When you move the Line tool close enough to a specific connection point, a green square surrounds the connection point, as shown in the graphic on the right in Figure 2-20. Clicking the connection point glues the line to the shape.

Figure 2-20 *The Line tool interacting with nearby shapes*

The image on the left in Figure 2-21 shows a line that has been glued at both ends and that the line is still selected. Notice that the left end of the line, which was the first to be glued, displays a green circle. The originating end of a line is often referred to as the "from" end. The destination end of the line, also known as the "to" end, displays a white circle with a green dot in the center.

In the image on the right in Figure 2-21, a line above the rectangle has not been glued to any shapes. This line displays a white square on the "from" end and a gray square on the "to" end.

Figure 2-21 *Shapes connected by a line and a line that is not glued to any shapes*

The color distinction between the glued and unglued line ends in Figure 2-21 is an important one in Visio. Although the difference is quite obvious in Figure 2-21 because you can see exactly what is connected where, the paragraphs that follow include an example in which the color of the line end is very helpful in determining connectedness.

If you attempt to glue one end of a line to shape that doesn't contain connection points, you will be able to drop the end of the line inside or on the edge of the shape; however, it will not be glued. The left side of Figure 2-22 is an example of this situation; note that the "from" end of the line is glued to the center of the octagon, but you can tell from the gray square that the "to" end is unglued even though it is sitting on the edge of the long rectangle.

You can prove to yourself that the line is not glued simply by relocating the rectangle. On the right side of Figure 2-22, the rectangle has been shifted to the right and the line is no longer connected.

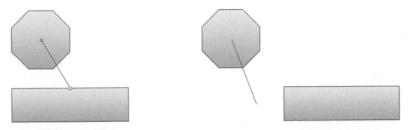

Figure 2-22 *A line drawn from an octagon to a rectangle but not glued to the latter shape*

Four different tools are available for drawing lines:

- **Line tool** Draws straight lines

- **Arc tool** Draws arcs

- **Freeform tool** Draws lines that have as many bends as you want

- **Pencil tool** Draws curved and straight lines, but can also be used to deform or reshape existing 1-D and 2-D shapes

Figure 2-23 includes an arc between the rectangle and the circle, and a freeform line from the center of the circle to the edge of the square.

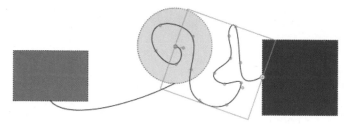

Figure 2-23 *An arc and a freeform line*

 TIP Blue circles are at the key points of curvature along the freeform line in Figure 2-23. These circles are actually handles that you can drag to reshape the line.

The blue circles are only visible if you select the shape with one of the line tools (Line, Freeform, Arc, or Pencil). If you select it with the Pointer Tool or the Rectangle or Ellipse tool, only the endpoints will be visible.

An important feature of all four line types is that they retain their form when you move the shapes to which they are glued. If a line begins as a straight line, it will always be a straight line; if it starts as a squiggly line, it will always look that way. This behavior is in marked contrast to the dynamic connector that is described in the topic that follows.

To use the Line, Arc, Freeform, or Pencil tool

1. On the **Home** tab, in the **Tools** group, click the drawing tools button, and then select the tool you want.

   Or

Right-click the drawing page, click the **Drawing Tools** button in the upper-left corner of the mini toolbar, and then select the tool you want.

2. Drag to create a line.

To glue a line to a shape

1. Select the line tool you want.

2. Move the pointer near a shape until the connection points appear.

3. Click a connection point, and then drag the other end of the line onto a connection point on the same or another shape.

To return to the Pointer Tool after selecting one of the line tools from the Home tab

1. Do either of the following:

   • In the **Tools** group, click the **Pointer Tool** button.

   • Press **Ctrl+1**.

Create 2-D shapes by using the line tools

The various line drawing tools are not limited to creating 1-D shapes. You can create a 2-D shape simply by finishing where you start; that is, either draw a set of connected segments or draw a continuous line that ends where it begins. The amoeba-like shape in Figure 2-24 was created by using the Freeform tool.

Figure 2-24 *2-D shape drawn by using the Freeform tool*

Connect shapes by using dynamic connectors

The 1-D shapes described in the preceding topic can contain bends, curves, or corners, but only if you place them there or you use a tool specifically designed for that purpose. A dynamic connector, also referred to simply as a connector, is a 1-D shape to which Visio automatically adds and removes corners or bends based on the relative positions of the shapes to which it's glued.

As a result, dynamic connectors are an essential component of many connected diagrams—flowcharts, organization charts, and network diagrams, for example—because you can use them to concentrate on positioning the 2-D shapes while Visio takes care of organizing the 1-D shapes. There will, of course, be situations in which you will need to override the choices made by Visio, or even change the settings that control Visio choices. Much of the time, however, letting Visio position and route dynamic connectors works just fine.

You can elect to use a dynamic connector in several ways, just as was true for the various line tools:

- Click the Connector tool in the Tools group on the Home tab. When you use this technique, the Connector tool remains active until you select a different tool.

- Right-click the drawing page or a shape, and then click the Add One Connector To The Page button. Just as the name suggests, using the mini toolbar technique draws exactly one connector, and then the pointer reverts to the Pointer Tool.

- Use the AutoConnect feature that is described in the topic "Use AutoConnect and Quick Shapes" later in this chapter.

Connect to shapes that contain connection points

When the Connector tool is active, the pointer changes to a black arrow; beneath it is an arrow that has two right-angle bends. Both parts of Figure 2-25 include an active Connector tool.

Figure 2-25 *The Connector tool interacting with nearby shapes*

As was true with the line tools described in the preceding topic, when you move the Connector tool close enough to a specific connection point, a green square surrounds the connection point. See the right side of Figure 2-25 for an example.

Clicking a connection point glues the line to the connection point. When you then drag to a different connection point and release the mouse button, you create static glue between the two connection points. Regardless where you move the glued shapes, the connector will always be attached at the same two points.

> **TIP** Visio uses the same circle symbols to identify glued dynamic connectors that were used to identify glued lines.

In the graphic on the left in Figure 2-26, notice that the "to" end of the connector includes an arrowhead. Although the arrowhead is largely obscured by the green handle in this image, when the dynamic connector is deselected, as it is in the right side of Figure 2-26, the arrowhead is visible. Although you can add arrowheads and other types of line ends to any 1-D shape, dynamic connectors typically include them by default.

> **TIP** Arrowheads are just one type of format that can be applied to either a line or a connector. Line formatting is described in "Apply colors and patterns" in Chapter 6, "Add style, color, and themes."

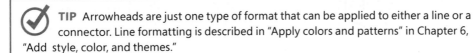

Figure 2-26 *Shapes linked with a connector and a connector that is not glued to any shapes*

In the image on the right in Figure 2-26 is a connector above the rectangle that has not been glued to any shapes. This connector displays a white square on the "from" end and a gray square on the "to" end. Even if you try to draw the connector as a straight line, notice that it appears to have a mind of its own. This will turn out to be one of the most useful characteristics of a dynamic connector, as you will discover in the remainder of this topic.

To use the Connector tool

1. On the **Home** tab, in the **Tools** group, click the **Connector** tool to select a persistent tool.

    Or

    Right-click the drawing page, and then click the **Add One Connector to the Page** button in the lower-left corner of the mini toolbar to select a one-time-use **Connector** tool.

2. Drag to create a dynamic connector.

To glue a dynamic connector to a connection point (static glue)

1. Select the persistent **Connector** tool.

    Or

    Select the one-time-use **Connector** tool.

2. Click a connection point, and then drag to another connection point.

Connect to shapes that do not contain connection points

When you drag an unglued dynamic connector end toward a shape that does not contain connection points, the reaction is very different from dragging a line end to the same shape.

On the left side of Figure 2-27, the "from" end of a connector is glued to a connection point in the center of the octagon. When you drag the other end of the connector toward the wide rectangle, which does not contain any connection points, the border of the shape lights up in bright green.

Note the location of the pointer (marked by a plus sign) inside the wide rectangle on the left side of Figure 2-27; you will notice in the image on the right that the "to" end of the arrow has been attached at a different location. In fact, Visio has established dynamic glue to the rectangle and it has chosen a contact point that is directly below the center of the octagon.

> **TIP** It's important to note that shapes with connection points react in the same way to an approaching dynamic connector as shapes without connection points. Consequently, you have two choices for attaching a connector to a shape with connection points. You can create static glue to a specific connection point, or you can establish dynamic glue to the shape as a whole simply by pointing to a part of the shape without connection points before releasing the mouse button.

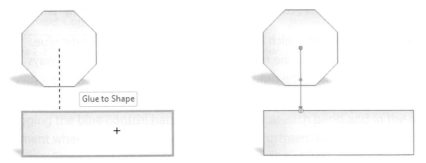

Figure 2-27 *Interaction between a dynamic connector and a shape without connection points*

To see the real power of the dynamic connector, move a shape at one end and watch how Visio adds and removes corners or bends.

It's also important to appreciate the difference in behavior between the reactions of a dynamic connector that is statically glued versus one that is dynamically glued.

Figure 2-28 illustrates how Visio adjusts a dynamically glued connector to accommodate changes in the position of one or both shapes at its ends.

- On the left side of the figure, the rectangle is moved to the right from its position in Figure 2-27 and the connector now touches the rectangle at a different place.

- On the right side of Figure 2-28, the rectangle is moved to a position above the octagon, and the connector is now attached at the bottom of the rectangle.

Through both of these changes, the connector remains in the center of the octagon because it is statically glued there.

Figure 2-32 *Fixed connection points as a result of static glue*

To create bends in a dynamic connector

1. Select a shape at one end of a dynamic connector.
2. Drag the shape to a new location on the page.

To move segments of a dynamic connector

1. Select a dynamic connector that contains at least one bend.
2. Drag one of the blue adjustment handles on the dynamic connector.

To change the style of a dynamic connector

1. Select a dynamic connector that contains at least one bend.
2. Right-click the connector and select **Right-Angle Connector**, **Straight Connector**, or **Curved Connector**.

To restore a dynamic connector to its simplest form

1. Right-click the dynamic connector, and then click **Reset Connector**.

Identifying 1-D shapes and types of glue

In the preceding topics, you learned about several types of 1-D shapes and two forms of glue. This sidebar summarizes the behavior of 1-D shapes and identifies the visual cues Visio uses to differentiate glued and unglued endpoints of 1-D shapes.

- A 1-D shape drawn with any of the line tools (Line, Freeform, Arc, or Pencil) retains its original form when the shapes at the ends are moved.

- A 1-D shape created by using the Connector tool adds or removes bends in the line to accommodate shape movements.

2

- A line or dynamic connector attached to a connection point forms static glue; the 1-D shape remains attached at that fixed point on the 2-D shape no matter how the 2-D shape is moved.

- A dynamic connector attached to a shape but not to a connection point forms dynamic glue; as the 2-D shape moves, the point at which the dynamic connector attaches to the shape changes.

- A 1-D shape whose endpoints are not glued appears with square control handles that are white on the "from" end and gray on the "to" end, as shown in Figure 2-33.

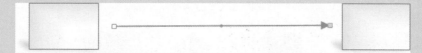

Figure 2-33 *Unglued dynamic connector*

- A 1-D shape whose endpoints are glued appears with round control handles; the "from" end is a green circle and the "to" end shows a green dot inside a white circle, as shown in Figure 2-34.

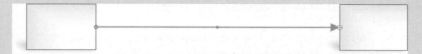

Figure 2-34 *Glued dynamic connector*

TIP In previous versions of Visio, the endpoints of 1-D shapes that were attached by using static glue looked different than endpoints that were attached by using dynamic glue. Visio 2016 no longer provides a visual distinction between the two.

Use AutoConnect and Quick Shapes

AutoConnect was introduced in Visio 2007 and provides a fast means to link shapes by using dynamic connectors. Quick Shapes were introduced in Visio 2010 and build on AutoConnect so you can create drawings even more quickly.

For many diagrams, using the Dynamic Grid is sufficient for aligning and spacing shapes as you add them to the page. However, the combination of AutoConnect and Quick Shapes in Visio 2016 is an even better choice for certain diagram types.

 TIP The shapes shown in the figures in this topic are from the Basic Flowchart Shapes stencil in the Basic Flowchart template located in the Flowchart template group.

Flowcharts provide an excellent example. If you drag a set of flowchart shapes onto the page in a configuration like the one shown in Figure 2-35, you can use AutoConnect to add dynamic connectors simply by pointing and clicking.

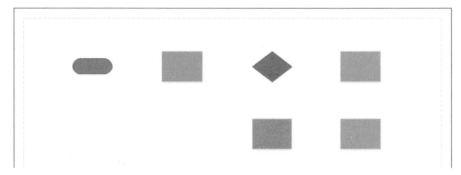

Figure 2-35 *The start of a flowchart, with no dynamic connectors*

AutoConnect arrows appear as four small blue triangles when you point to any shape on the drawing page, as shown in Figure 2-36.

⚠ **IMPORTANT** If the AutoConnect arrows don't appear when you point to a shape, it's probably because AutoConnect is turned off for this drawing. To activate AutoConnect, select the AutoConnect check box in the Visual Aids group on the View tab.

There is also an application-level setting for AutoConnect. Consequently, if the arrows still don't appear after changing the document setting, you have another recourse. In the Backstage view, click Options. In the Visio Options dialog box, click Advanced, and then verify that the Enable AutoConnect check box is selected.

Figure 2-36 *Three flowchart shapes that have the pointer on top, causing AutoConnect arrows to appear*

Clicking one of the arrows fires a dynamic connector across the gap and glues the ends dynamically to both shapes. With just three clicks, the sample diagram looks like Figure 2-37.

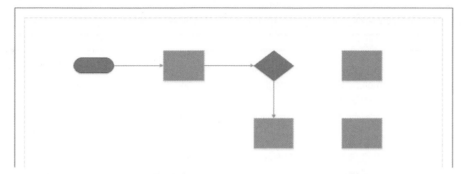

Figure 2-37 *Partially completed flowchart*

It's clear that AutoConnect makes short work of adding dynamic connectors to existing shapes. Each AutoConnect arrow seeks out a neighboring shape in the direction that the arrow points.

But what if you want to link a shape to one that is not directly in line with any of the four AutoConnect arrows? It turns out that AutoConnect also solves this problem easily: simply drag an AutoConnect arrow to any other shape.

For example, in Figure 2-37, you might want to link the decision diamond with the process shape in the lower-right corner. To do so, click the AutoConnect arrow on the right side of the diamond, and then drag it onto the process rectangle.

As you drag, the screen will look like the graphic on the left in Figure 2-38. When you release the mouse button on top of the process box, the shapes will be connected, as shown on the right.

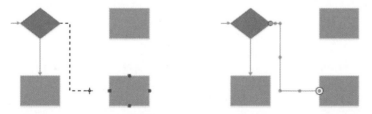

Figure 2-38 *An AutoConnect arrow used to manually link to a shape*

> **TIP** When you're using AutoConnect arrows, you might notice that they seem to appear more quickly sometimes than others. That's because Visio wants them to be available to you but only when you want them. If you've used AutoConnect recently, the arrows appear much more quickly when you pause on a shape. However, if you haven't used them recently, there is a delay before they appear so they don't get in your way.

> **TIP** On occasion, you might notice that AutoConnect arrows appear on some sides of a shape but not on all sides. This is because the arrows only appear on the sides that are not yet connected to a nearby shape.

As you use AutoConnect, you'll notice that if you point to an AutoConnect arrow for a moment before clicking, a live preview gives you a look at the result, as shown in Figure 2-39. In addition, a mini toolbar that contains four shapes appears. Although the Quick Shapes mini toolbar is of limited value when you are using AutoConnect to link existing shapes, it is of significant value for adding shapes to the page, as you will discover in the remainder of this topic.

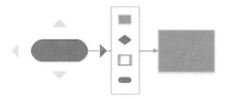

Figure 2-39 *A live preview and the Quick Shapes mini toolbar*

Figure 2-40 contains one shape—a start/end shape—on the drawing page. Pointing to the AutoConnect arrow on the right of the start/end shape reveals the Quick Shapes mini toolbar. If you leave the pointer over the AutoConnect arrow, a live preview shows a preview of the shape that is currently selected in the stencil.

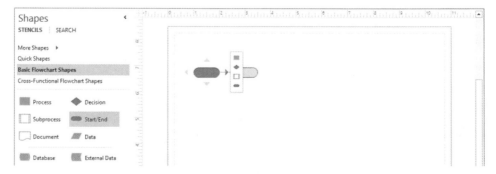

Figure 2-40 *A selected master in the stencil and the Quick Shapes mini toolbar on the drawing page*

If you want to add another start/end shape to the current drawing, a single click will accomplish that and the new shape will be automatically spaced at the default interval for this page.

However, if you want to add a different shape, Quick Shapes provide an instant solution. Every open stencil in Visio 2016 includes a Quick Shapes section at the top of the stencil window pane, and most stencils include preselected Quick Shapes. If you look closely at the Basic Flowchart Shapes in the Shapes window, you'll notice a fine gray line between the Document/Data shapes and the Database/External Data shapes.

The shapes that appear in the mini toolbar are the first four shapes in the Quick Shapes section. If you want different shapes to appear on the Quick Shapes mini toolbar, simply drag them to be among the first four shapes in the Quick Shapes section of the stencil.

 TIP You can change the order of appearance of masters in either the Quick Shapes section or in the main part of a stencil merely by dragging a master to a new location.

Point to any of the shapes in the Quick Shapes mini toolbar and notice that the live preview changes to reflect that shape, as illustrated in Figure 2-41.

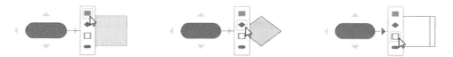

Figure 2-41 *Quick Shapes with a live preview*

Starting with a single shape on the page, as shown in Figure 2-40, three clicks on the Quick Shapes mini toolbar will build the diagram shown in Figure 2-42.

 TIP When you "shoot" shapes onto the drawing page by using AutoConnect by itself or in conjunction with Quick Shapes, new shapes are positioned by using the default spacing interval for the page. For information about changing the default spacing intervals, see Figure 2-4.

Generally, when you rotate a shape, the text in the shape rotates along with it, which is probably what you would expect to happen. Indeed, this is the default behavior for text in a Visio shape; Figure 3-6 shows an example.

Figure 3-6 *An inverted shape whose text is also upside down*

When you select more than one shape and rotate the entire selection, the text on the selected shapes might not all behave the same way. In Figure 3-7, the group of shapes on the left shows upright text on the selected shapes, one of which is a dynamic connector arrow pointing to the right. In the other two groups, the text in the circle and square is rotated with the respective shapes, whereas the connector text remains right side up. This is an example of a shape that contains formulas that cause shape text to behave differently.

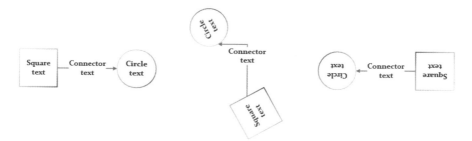

Figure 3-7 *The text on a dynamic connector does not rotate when the connector and adjacent shapes are rotated*

Other text behaviors are possible, too. For example, the Right Arrow shape shown in Figure 3-8 is from the Blocks Raised stencil in the Block Diagram template. Its text neither follows the orientation of the shape nor is always upright. Instead, a formula in the shape maintains the text at multiples of 45 degrees.

Figure 3-8 *Comparing shape rotation with text rotation when the latter is controlled by a formula in the shape*

In addition to controlling text angle with embedded formulas, you can also control the orientation of the text in a shape from the Visio user interface. The arrow shown in Figure 3-9 is the 2-D Single arrow from the Blocks stencil in the Basic Shapes template. The text on the arrow rotates with the arrow unless you take direct control by using the Text Block tool that was introduced in the preceding topic; the results of rotating just the text block are shown in Figure 3-9.

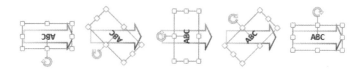

Figure 3-9 *The text can rotate while the shape remains fixed*

Remember that you can combine several text block alterations to achieve the effect you want. The two computer monitors shown on the left side of Figure 3-10 show one possibility. The text on the left monitor is in the default position; the text on the right monitor is raised and rotated to create a different effect. In the city icon, the text is rotated and styled to produce a more dramatic view.

Figure 3-10 *Text blocks can be repositioned and rotated*

Add ScreenTips and comments

You can include ScreenTips and comments in your diagrams to provide readers with supplemental, on-demand information. Although these serve similar purposes, they have very different characteristics:

- **ScreenTips** These display pop-up text when you point to a shape, but they are otherwise invisible. In fact, there is no way to know that a ScreenTip exists unless you point to a shape containing one and a ScreenTip appears.

> ⚠ **IMPORTANT** ScreenTips are part of a shape. Consequently, they move with a shape and are deleted when you delete a shape.

- **Comments** These indicate their presence with a special icon but require that you click the icon in order to view the comment text. Each comment shows the name of the comment author and the date when it was created. Beginning with Visio 2013, one comment shape can contain threaded comments from multiple authors; individual entries are displayed in chronological order.

> ⚠ **IMPORTANT** If you select exactly one shape and add a comment, the comment will be attached to that shape. If you select two or more shapes and then add a comment, the comment will be attached to the anchor shape. (Anchor shapes are explained in Chapter 6, "Add style, color, and themes.") If you add a comment when no shapes are selected, the comment will be attached to the drawing page.

> ✓ **TIP** Prior to Visio 2013, comments were always attached to a page and never to a shape. If you have an older version of Visio and move a shape that happens to have a comment near it, you will successfully move the shape, but the comment will not move. For more information about commenting, see Chapter 15, "Collaborate and publish diagrams."

When deciding whether to use ScreenTips or comments, consider the following:

- Use ScreenTips to provide useful but noncritical information about a shape; however, understand that readers might not discover the existence of a ScreenTip.

- Use comments when it's important for readers to see that a comment exists, when you expect multiple people to exchange ideas as threaded comments, and when it's helpful to know the author, date, and time for each annotation.

 TIP Callouts provide a third, and more visible, method for adding annotations to shapes. You will work with callouts in Chapter 13, "Add structure to your diagrams."

An example of a ScreenTip and a comment is shown in Figure 3-12. The ScreenTip appears across the chair shape because the pointer is positioned on the chair shape. A comment balloon above the upper-right corner of the sofa shape indicates the presence of a comment; the word *Comments* appears because the pointer is located near the comment indicator.

Figure 3-12 *ScreenTips and comments appear in different ways*

Clicking a comment indicator displays the text of the most recent comments, as shown in Figure 3-13.

TIP You can delete individual comments by clicking the stylized letter *X* located to the right of the first comment and any other comment to which you point.

Figure 3-13 *In addition to comment text, a comment box displays the author's name and the time when the comment was entered*

Comments added by a different author are clearly marked, as shown in Figure 3-14. When a shape contains multiple comments, you can collapse individual comments, as shown for the first comment in Figure 3-14.

Figure 3-14 *Threaded comments make it easy to follow a conversation*

 TIP In addition to adding comments to shapes, you can also add comments to a page. If you do, Visio places a comment indicator in the upper-left corner of the page.

If you would like to see all comments in a document in one place, Visio provides a Comments pane, as shown in Figure 3-15. Clicking a comment in the pane highlights the shape containing the comment. If you click a comment for a shape on the current page, Visio will move the shape into view (if it wasn't already), and then highlight the comment indicator in blue. If you click a comment for a shape on a different page, Visio will switch to that page to make the commented shape visible.

Figure 3-15 *All comments in a diagram are accessible in the Comments pane*

> ✅ **TIP** In Visio 2016, comments can be entered by Visio users or by people who do not have Visio. Consequently, Visio users and non-users can collaborate on the same diagram. This feature, which requires Microsoft SharePoint and Visio Services, is described in Chapter 15, "Collaborate and publish diagrams."

To add a ScreenTip

1. Select a shape, and then on the **Insert** tab, in the **Text** group, click the **ScreenTip** button to open the **Shape ScreenTip** dialog box.

2. In the **Shape ScreenTip** dialog box, enter text, and then click **OK**.

To open or close the Comments pane

1. On the **Review** tab, in the **Comments** group, click the upper half of the **Comments Pane** button.

To add a comment to a shape

1. Select a shape, and then on the **Review** tab, in the **Comments** group, click the **New Comment** button.

   Or

   Select a shape, and then in the **Comments** pane, click the **New Comment** button.

   Or

   Right-click a shape, and then click **Add Comment**.

2. Enter text, and then click outside the comment box.

To add a comment to a page

1. Ensure that nothing is selected, and then on the **Review** tab, in the **Comments** group, click the **New Comment** button.

   Or

   Right-click a blank area of a page, and then click **Add Comment**.

2. Enter text, and then click outside the comment box.

To reply to a comment

1. If the **Comment** pane is closed, click the comment indicator on a shape or a page, and then click **Reply**.

   Or

   If the **Comment** pane is open, locate the comment you want, and then click **Reply**.

2. Enter your reply text, and then click outside the comment box.

To show or hide comment indicators

1. On the **Review** tab, in the **Comments** group, click the **Comments Pane** arrow (not its button), and then click **Reveal Tags**.

Insert pictures

In Chapter 2, "Create diagrams," and earlier in this chapter, you explored techniques for creating a shape by dragging a master from a stencil and by creating a text box. At times, however, you might want to create a shape by using an image.

Fortunately, Visio makes that easy to accomplish. You can import a photograph or an image in any common file format from a computer, and you can search for pictures from various online sources. Figure 3-16 shows available sources for the author's computer.

Figure 3-16 *Pictures can be inserted from multiple online locations*

Figure 3-17 combines a photograph, a clip art icon, and a flag image retrieved by searching the Internet.

Figure 3-17 *You can combine a variety of image types in a single graphic*

To insert an image from a computer or network drive

1. On the **Insert** tab, in the **Illustrations** group, click the **Picture** button.

2. Browse to the location you want, select the image file, and then click **Open**.

To insert an image from an online search

1. On the **Insert** tab, in the **Illustrations** group, click the **Online Pictures** button.

2. Enter search terms in the **Bing Image Search** text box.

   Or

   Click **OneDrive** or another image source.

3. Select the image you want, and then click **Insert**.

Replace shapes

Since the early days of Visio, users have wanted to be able to replace a shape on the drawing page with an entirely different shape, and yet retain the key attributes of the original shape. That capability finally arrived with Visio 2013 and is an important feature to know about in Visio 2016.

Figure 3-18 provides a good first example to understand the power of the replace shape feature. The diagram in Figure 3-18 was created by using the Directional Map template (not the Directional Map 3D template) in the Maps And Floor Plans template category.

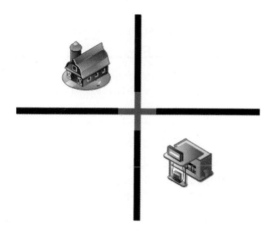

Figure 3-18 *A representation of an intersection in a map drawn with Visio*

By using the replace shape feature, you can do something straightforward like swap the barn for a stadium, or perform a more complex swap, such as replacing the four-way intersection with a full-scale, highway cloverleaf (both shown in Figure 3-19). Although both changes required just a single click from the user, the new intersection involved more sophisticated changes behind the scenes. The cloverleaf retains the color of the previous intersection shape, and despite being quite a bit larger than the old intersection, it is still glued to all four road segments.

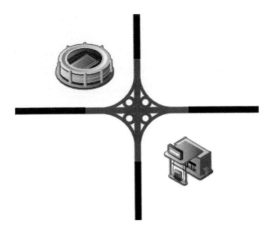

Figure 3-19 *Visio automatically adjusted the lengths of the road segments to fit the new shape*

 TIP If you replace shapes that contain data, text, comments, and other customizations, most are preserved in the new shapes. See Chapter 8, "Work with shape data," for more information about data in shapes.

When you click the Change Shape button, Visio presents the shapes in the currently active stencil. However, Visio also provides a menu from which you can select shapes from any other open stencil. Figure 3-20 shows the Landmark Shapes from the currently active stencil, in addition to the names of additional stencils.

If the shape you want is not in one of the open stencils, simply open the stencil you want before clicking the Change Shape button. As a result, you can replace a shape in a drawing with any of tens of thousands of other shapes.

TIP If you select multiple shapes before clicking Change Shape, you can replace all of them at once.

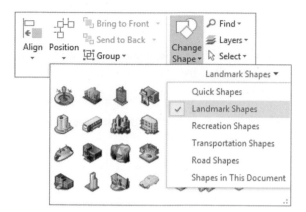

Figure 3-20 *You can access shapes from multiple stencils on one menu when you have multiple stencils open*

To replace shapes

1. Select one or more shapes, and then on the **Home** tab, in the **Editing** group, click the **Change Shape** button.

   Or

   Right-click a shape, and then on the mini toolbar, click the **Change Shape** button.

2. Click the replacement shape you want.

To replace shapes by using a master from a different stencil

1. (*Optional*) If the stencil you want isn't open, in the **Shapes** window, click the **More Shapes** button, and then click the name of the stencil you want to open.

2. Click the **Change Shape** button.

3. Click the down arrow to the right of the name of the active stencil.

4. Click the name of the stencil you want, to display a gallery of its shapes.

5. Click the replacement shape you want.

Group shapes

So far, you have primarily learned about working with simple, individual shapes. However, sets of shapes that have been grouped together are very common in Visio for a variety of reasons, such as the following:

- It's easier to move or perform an operation on a set of shapes in a group than it is to do the same thing with multiple, discrete shapes.

- Shape designers need to create a more sophisticated appearance or behavior for a variety of reasons, such as:

    - To display text in multiple places on the shape.

    - To display different colors on different parts of the grouped shape.

    - To allow different parts of the shape to respond differently to external changes.

    - To protect the alignment of subshapes within the group.

The first case is illustrated in Figure 3-21, which shows four shapes from the Department stencil in the Work Flow Diagram template, that have been grouped on the drawing page. The four out-of-the-box shapes are on the left side of the diagram. In the center, the fill color of all four shapes has been changed with a single click. On the right, the color has been changed with another click, and all four shapes have been resized by dragging one handle on the group. Similarly, you can move, copy and paste, or delete all four shapes simply by performing those operations on the group shape.

 TIP Like the individual shapes that comprise it, a group is also a shape. You can apply borders or fills, add fields and text, and add shape data—in short, you can do anything with a group shape that you can with any other shape.

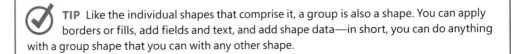 **TIP** Selecting a shape within a group requires two clicks; the default behavior in Visio is that the first click selects the group.

Evidence of using groups to create more-sophisticated shapes is shown in Figure 3-21; some of the department shapes are groups themselves. The designers of those shapes created them by combining multiple objects or images.

Figure 3-21 *You can change properties of multiple shapes at one time when they have been grouped*

Figure 3-22 provides another example of sophisticated shape design. The shapes on the left are from the Furniture stencil (the Maps And Floor Plans template group); the shapes on the right are from the Compliance Shapes stencil (the Business template group). Like these seven shapes, many of the masters in Visio stencils consist of grouped shapes.

> ⚠ **IMPORTANT** You should be cautious if you are thinking about ungrouping a shape that you didn't design. The reason? In many grouped shapes, the attributes of the subshapes are derived from properties of the group. For example, the size, color, or position of a subshape might depend on a value in the group. When you ungroup a shape, all of its properties—shape geometry, shape data, everything—disappears. Consequently, ungrouping can be destructive unless you know what you're doing.

Figure 3-22 *Examples of grouped shapes from Visio stencils, including some new shapes in Visio 2016*

Organizing collections of shapes into groups has many advantages, but also has some disadvantages. You will learn more about both in the topic, "Compare containers and groups," in Chapter 13, "Add structure to your diagrams."

To group a selection of shapes

1. Do one of the following:

   - On the **Home** tab, in the **Arrange** group, click the **Group** button, and then click **Group**.

   - Right-click any of the selected shapes, click **Group**, and then click **Group**.

   - Press **Ctrl+G**.

   - Press **Ctrl+Shift+G**.

To ungroup a selection of shapes

1. Do one of the following:

   - On the **Home** tab, in the **Arrange** group, click the **Group** button, and then click **Ungroup**.

   - Right-click any of the selected shapes, click **Group**, and then click **Ungroup**.

   - Press **Ctrl+Shift+U**.

To select a shape within a group

1. Click the group shape to select the group.

2. Click the shape you want.

Understand and use layers

You can put Visio shapes on layers to organize and control various properties of the set of shapes. Unlike some drawing programs, Visio layers are not "in front of" or "behind" other layers. Instead, shapes are assigned to layers to give you control over things like whether layer members are printable, visible on the drawing page, or selectable.

In a floor plan, for example, you might put furniture on one layer, walls and building infrastructure on another layer, and electrical wiring on a third layer. You could then use layer properties to perform tasks like the following:

- Lock the infrastructure and wiring layers as you rearrange the furniture.

- Hide the layer containing furniture when you want to view the full, open space.

- Leave the electrical wiring visible on the screen but set the properties of its layer so the wiring doesn't print.

- Select all shapes on a specific layer or layers.

Using layers can be extremely helpful because they provide considerable flexibility in managing the components of a sophisticated drawing. However, you might want to plan your layer scheme ahead of time because of the potential complexity: a drawing page can have multiple layers; each layer has seven properties; and a shape can reside on multiple layers, one layer, or none.

 TIP Every layer belongs to exactly one page. If you use the same layer name on two or more pages, each of those layers is unrelated to the others.

The seven properties of a layer are shown in Figure 3-23 and are described in the following text.

Many Visio templates include predefined layers, and shapes from the corresponding stencils are added to those layers automatically. The layers in Figure 3-23 were added to the diagram simply by dragging shapes from the Furniture stencil in the Maps And Floor Plans group. Similar, predefined layers are available in the Flowchart and Engineering templates, among others.

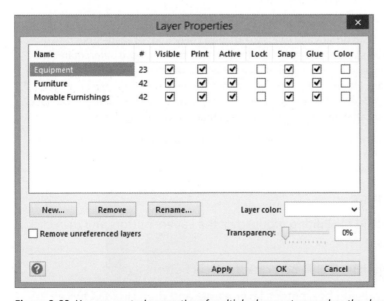

Figure 3-23 *You can control properties of multiple shapes at once when the shapes are on layers*

The seven properties in the Layer Properties dialog box are:

- **Visible** Controls whether the shapes on a layer are visible on the drawing page.

- **Print** Includes or excludes the members of a layer from printing.

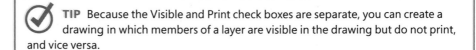

> **TIP** Because the Visible and Print check boxes are separate, you can create a drawing in which members of a layer are visible in the drawing but do not print, and vice versa.

- **Active** Causes all new shapes added to the page to be added to the layer. More than one layer can be active at once, in which case new shapes are added to all active layers.

- **Lock** Prevents you from selecting, moving, or editing any shapes on the layer. In addition, you cannot add shapes to a locked layer.

- **Snap and Glue** Allows and disallows snapping or gluing other shapes to the shapes on this layer.

- **Color** Temporarily overrides the colors of all objects on a layer; clearing this option returns layer members to their original colors. When you select the Color property for a layer, the Layer Color and Transparency settings in the lower right of the dialog box are activated.

> **TIP** You can use both groups and layers to organize collections of shapes, but it's important to understand that they serve different purposes and have different behaviors. For example, when you select a group and then move it or resize it, the changes affect all of the shapes in the group. However, if you select and then move or resize a shape on a layer, your action has no effect on any other shapes. By using a layer, on the other hand, you can lock, hide, and otherwise affect all shapes on the layer in ways that you cannot with a group.
>
> It's also important to realize that groups and layers are not mutually exclusive—there are often good reasons to use both in the same drawing.

To create a layer on a page

1. On the **Home** tab, in the **Editing** group, click the **Layers** button, and then click **Layer Properties**.

2. In the **Layer Properties** dialog box, click the **New** button.

3. In the **New Layer** dialog box, enter a layer name, and then click **OK** twice.

Or

1. Select a shape.

2. On the **Home** tab, in the **Editing** group, click the **Layers** button, and then click **Assign to Layer**.

3. In the **Layer** dialog box, click the **New** button.

4. In the **New Layer** dialog box, enter a layer name, and then click **OK** twice.

Or

1. Copy a shape that is assigned to a layer on one page, and then paste it to another page. (If a layer of the same name already exists on that page, the copied shape will be added to the existing layer.)

Or

1. Drag a shape onto the drawing page from one of the stencils in the **Basic Flowchart** template, or another template that contains built-in layers.

To remove a layer from a page

1. On the **Home** tab, in the **Editing** group, click the **Layers** button, and then click **Layer Properties**.

2. In the **Layer Properties** dialog box, select the name of the layer you want to delete.

3. Click the **Delete** button, and then respond to the warning message shown in Figure 3-24.

Figure 3-24 *Deleting a layer might delete all shapes on the layer*

> **TIP** The warning message shown in Figure 3-24 can be misleading. If a shape is a member of the layer you are deleting but is also a member of another layer, the shape will not be deleted.

4. Click **OK** to close the **Layer Properties** dialog box.

To change layer properties

1. Open the **Layer Properties** dialog box, select or clear the layer properties you want to change, and then click **OK**.

To assign a shape to a layer

1. On the **Home** tab, in the **Editing** group, click the **Layers** button, and then click **Assign to Layer**.

2. In the **Layer** dialog box, select the layer or layers to which you want to assign the shape, and then click **OK**.

Or

1. Drag a shape onto the drawing page from one of the stencils in the **Basic Flowchart** template, or another template with built-in layers.

To remove a shape from a layer

1. On the **Home** tab, in the **Editing** group, click the **Layers** button, and then click **Assign to Layer**.

2. In the **Layer** dialog box, clear the check box in front of the layer or layers from which you want to remove the shape, and then click **OK**.

To select all shapes on a layer

1. On the **Home** tab, in the **Editing** group, click the **Select** button, and then click **Select by Type**.

2. In the **Select by Type** dialog box, click **Layer**, select the check box for the layer you want, and then click **OK**.

Manage pages

Pages in a Visio drawing are independent of each other, so any one page can have dimensions, measurement units, and other characteristics that are different from any other page. Consequently, you can mix larger and smaller pages, and even portrait and landscape pages, within the same diagram.

Within any one page, Visio maintains separate settings for the on-screen drawing page and the physical page on which it will print. You can take advantage of this difference to do things such as the following:

- Compress a large drawing to fit on a smaller sheet of paper.

- Print a drawing on a large sheet of paper.

- Print a drawing across multiple sheets of paper.

At a high level, Visio pages fall into two categories:

- **Foreground pages** These contain the active drawing content and are typically the pages that are printed or published in some form.

- **Background pages** These contain shapes and page elements that can be configured to appear on one or more pages. However, objects located on background pages cannot be selected or edited unless the background page is the active page.

Background pages are valuable because you can link other pages to them. When you have done that, all text and graphics on the background pages appear on the linked pages.

A common scenario is to place a border, a page number, a page name, and possibly a watermark or other design element on a background page so all of those appear automatically on every foreground page in a consistent location.

Another common use case is to populate a background page with the company logo, a legal notice, and any other graphic or text you want to have appear on multiple pages.

As you plan a new diagram, especially if it will have multiple pages, remember that a diagram can also have multiple background pages. Consequently, some foreground pages might exhibit content from one background page, whereas other pages might use different background pages and look entirely different.

> **TIP** Although linking a foreground page to a background page is the most common scenario, you can also link background pages to each other, creating a hierarchy of page content that can be shared across multiple foreground pages in creative and effective ways.

Work with foreground pages

The key to working with foreground pages is the set of page name tabs at the bottom of the drawing window. You can right-click an existing page name tab to perform any of the tasks in the shortcut menu shown in Figure 3-25.

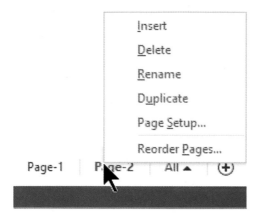

Figure 3-25 *You can add, remove, and alter page properties from the page tab shortcut menu*

When you add a foreground page to a diagram, Visio uses the properties of the current, active page to set the attributes for the new page. For example, if Page-3 has a landscape orientation with metric measurement units and is linked to a background page, your new page will inherit those attributes, including the link to the background page.

If all of the pages in your diagram are configured the same way, then adding a new page is straightforward. However, if your diagram contains foreground pages with differing orientations, measurement units, background pages, or printer paper settings, you should select the current page that is most like the page you want to add, before you click Insert.

In addition to copying the attributes of a page, Visio can duplicate the contents of a page. First introduced with Visio 2013, the duplicate page feature satisfies a long-standing request from Visio users.

To add a foreground page immediately after the current foreground page

1. Right-click the page name tab, and then click **Insert**.

2. In the **Page Setup** dialog box, on the **Page Setup** tab, click **Foreground** if it's not already selected.

3. Change the name of the page, if you want.

4. Click **OK**.

To add a foreground page after all current foreground pages

1. Do one of the following:

   • Click the **Insert Page** (+) button.

   • On the **Insert** tab, in the **Pages** group, click the **New Page** button (not its arrow).

   • On the **Insert** tab, in the **Pages** group, click the **New Page** arrow, and then click **Blank Page**.

To rename a page

1. Double-click the page name tab you want to change, and then enter a new name.

2. Press **Enter**.

   Or

   Click anywhere outside the page name tab.

Or

1. Right-click a page name tab, and then click **Page Setup.**

2. In the **Page Setup** dialog box, enter a new name in the **Name** box, and then click **OK**.

To move a page

1. Drag a page name tab left or right to a new location.

> ✓ **TIP** Dragging page name tabs is an easy way to resequence pages when the destination tab location for your page is visible at the bottom of the drawing window. However, if your diagram contains many pages and the destination tab is not visible, the following method might be easier to use.

Or

1. Right-click a page name tab, and then click **Reorder Pages**.

2. In the **Reorder Pages** dialog box, shown in Figure 3-26, click the name of the page you want to move, and then click either the **Move Up** or **Move Down** button until the page is in the location you want.

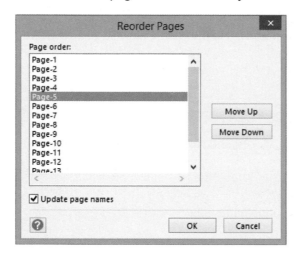

Figure 3-26 *Moving pages in a large diagram is easier by using the Reorder Pages dialog box*

3. Click **OK**.

To duplicate a page

1. Do one of the following:

   - Right-click a page name tab, and then click **Duplicate**.

   - On the **Insert** tab, in the **Pages** group, click the **New Page** arrow, and then click **Duplicate This Page**.

To delete a page

1. Right-click a page name tab, and then click **Delete**.

Configure foreground pages

Most page configuration functions are located on one of five tabs in the Page Setup dialog box. When you open the Page Setup dialog box, the Page Properties tab is displayed, as shown in Figure 3-27.

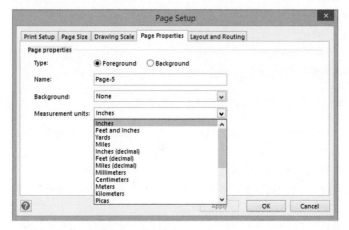

Figure 3-27 *You set key properties of a foreground page by using settings on the Page Properties tab*

On the Page Setup tab, you can change the page type, enter a different page name, select a background page, or change the measurement units for the page. Be sure to notice the scroll bar in the Measurement Units menu—you have 20 choices. If you change the measurement units, the result is visible in the rulers on the top and left of the drawing page.

You use the options on the Print Setup tab, shown in Figure 3-28, primarily to affect the size and layout of the physical page on which you will print.

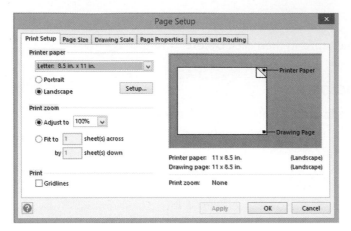

Figure 3-28 *Printer paper settings are distinct from drawing page settings*

On the Print Setup tab, you can change settings for the following:

- **Printer paper** Choose the paper size for your printer. Most US Units templates default to letter-sized paper, as shown in Figure 3-28. Metric templates typically default to A4. Regardless of the default, there is a long list of alternate, predefined paper sizes available. You can also select Portrait or Landscape orientation.

- **Print zoom** The default zoom for many templates defaults to Adjust To 100%, but you can select a different zoom level if you want your drawing to print larger or smaller than normal. Choose a zoom setting greater than 100% in order to split your drawing across multiple sheets of paper; choose a setting less than 100% to scale your diagram down to fit onto a portion of the printer paper.

- **Fit to** Use this setting as an alternative method to scale your drawing for printing.

- **Print** The single setting in this section includes or excludes gridlines from printed output. The default in most templates is to exclude gridlines.

The preview pane on the right side of the Print Setup tab changes dynamically to reflect your current print settings and displays them in both visual and text form.

On the Page Size tab, shown in Figure 3-29, you can change attributes of the drawing page; changes you make on this tab do not directly affect the printed page.

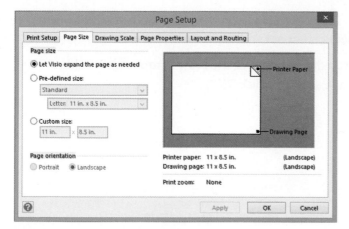

3

Figure 3-29 *Drawing paper settings can mimic those of the printer paper, or can be set independently*

The Page Size tab includes two configuration sections plus a preview pane:

- **Page size** The first option in this section enables dynamic **Auto Size** behavior. As an alternative, you can use the second and third options to set a fixed page size, either from a list of preset sizes or by entering specific dimensions.

- **Page orientation** The options in this section are active only if you choose Pre-Defined Size or Custom Size in the Page Size section. You can use these options to set a different orientation for the physical page than the one that is set for the drawing page.

 SEE ALSO For information about the Drawing Scale tab, see "Change the drawing scale," in Chapter 7, "Create network and data center diagrams."

To configure printer paper settings

1. Right-click a page name tab, and then click **Page Setup.**

2. In the **Page Setup** dialog box, click the **Print Setup** tab.

3. Make the changes you want, and then click **OK.**

To change page orientation

1. Do one of the following:

   - On the **Design** tab, in the **Page Setup** group, click the **Orientation** button, and then click either **Portrait** or **Landscape**.

   - Open the **Page Setup** dialog box, click the **Print Setup** tab, click either **Portrait** or **Landscape**, and then click **OK**.

To change the drawing page size

1. In the **Page Setup** group, click the **Size** button, and then click the page size you want.

Or

1. Open the **Page Setup** dialog box, and then click the **Page Size** tab.

2. Click **Pre-defined size**, choose one of the standard paper sizes, and then click **OK**.

   Or

   Click **Custom size**, enter a page width and height in the appropriate boxes, and then click **OK**.

Manage Auto Size

Auto Size is a page configuration setting that can be either helpful or annoying. The purpose of Auto Size is to extend the size of the drawing page automatically if you drag a shape on the canvas beyond the current page boundaries. In Figure 3-30, a circle is being dragged off the page to the right. Its former location is shown as a selected shape, and its current location is under the pointer. Visio is in the process of adding a new page, identifiable by the white page-sized rectangle against the gray canvas. When you place the circle on the new page, Visio will complete the addition of the page.

The reverse is also true: when you delete or drag the last shape from an extended section of the drawing page, Visio will remove the extended page.

 TIP Auto Size works both horizontally and vertically: if you add or drag shapes above or below the current page, Visio will add the required pages there also.

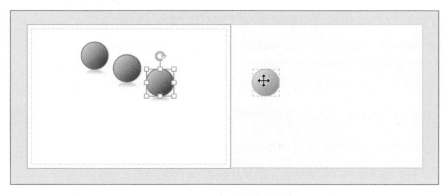

Figure 3-30 *Auto Size is extending the drawing page to the right*

As shown in Figure 3-31, when Auto Size is off, Visio does not extend the drawing page. Auto Size is turned on in some templates but is off in others. However, you can change the Auto Size setting.

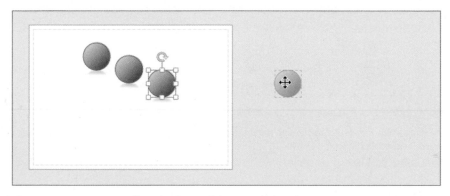

Figure 3-31 *Auto Size is off, so the dragged shape resides on the canvas*

 TIP The Auto Size option is applied per page. Consequently, changing the setting for the current page does not affect other pages.

To turn Auto Size on or off

1. On the **Design** tab, in the **Page Setup** group, click the **Auto Size** button.

Or

1. Right-click a page name tab, and then click **Page Setup**.
2. In the **Page Setup** dialog box, click the **Page Size** tab.
3. Click **Let Visio expand the page as needed** or one of the other **Page size** options, and then click **OK**.

Work with background pages and borders

Several of the features discussed in this section create background pages for you automatically. You can also create background pages manually. In either case, background pages exist so you can consolidate text and graphics that need to appear on multiple pages.

Apply backgrounds and borders automatically

Two buttons in the Backgrounds group on the Design tab, shown in Figure 3-32, are the key to automatic creation of background pages:

- **Backgrounds** This button provides a gallery of images that can be used on background pages.

- **Borders & Titles** This button includes a gallery of border designs that are accompanied by a text block for a title; most also include a page number and some include a date.

Figure 3-32 *The Backgrounds group of the Design tab includes two buttons for creating background pages*

When you click a button in either gallery, Visio does three things:

- Adds a background page with a name in the format of *VBackground-1*

- Inserts the selected border and title or image onto the background page

- Links the background page to the currently active foreground page

The result of adding the Flow background image to a foreground page containing three square shapes is shown in Figure 3-33.

 SEE ALSO For information about using themes, see Chapter 6, "Add style, color, and themes."

 TIP Backgrounds and borders are not mutually exclusive. You can include both on the same background page.

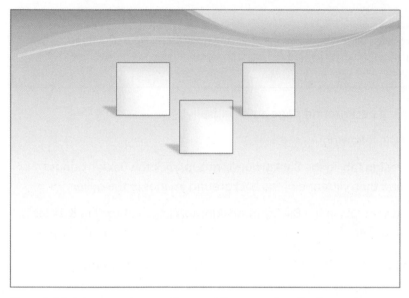

Figure 3-33 *A foreground page with content from an assigned background page*

In Figure 3-34, the background image has been replaced by the Civic border and title background page. Unrelated to the new border and title, Variant 2 of the Gemstone theme has also been applied to Figure 3-34 to provide additional visual enhancement.

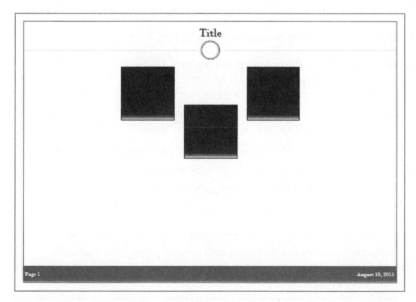

Figure 3-34 *The Civic border and title background page applied to a foreground page*

> ⚠ **IMPORTANT** To change the title in a title block on a background page, you must browse to the background page. Although you can see the word *Title* in Figure 3-34, you cannot edit it because you are viewing the foreground page; background page elements are read-only when viewed on foreground pages.

To create and apply a background page automatically

1. Do either of the following:

   - On the **Design** tab, in the **Backgrounds** group, click the **Backgrounds** button, and then click one of the background images in the gallery.

   - On the **Design** tab, in the **Backgrounds** group, click the **Borders & Titles** button, and then click one of the border/title combinations in the gallery.

To delete an automatically assigned background page from a diagram

1. Do either of the following:

   - Click the **Backgrounds** button, and then click the **None** thumbnail at the top of the gallery.

   - Click the **Borders & Titles** button, and then click the **None** thumbnail at the top of the gallery.

To remove an automatically assigned background page from a foreground page

1. Right-click a page name tab, and then click **Page Setup**.

2. On the **Page Setup** tab of the **Page Setup** dialog box, in the **Background** list, select **None**, and then click **OK**.

Apply background pages manually

You can add a background page manually in the same way that you add foreground pages; however, you must be certain to set the page type to background at the appropriate time. When you create a manual background page, Visio assigns a page name in the format *Background-1*.

> ✓ **TIP** You can distinguish automatically created background pages from manually created background pages by their names. Visio begins each automatically generated page name with the letter *V*, whereas manually created background pages do not contain the *V*.

Figure 3-35 shows the top part of a newly created background page with two elements. In a real diagram, the text box might contain a company name, a legal notice, an author's name, or any other text you want to be visible on foreground pages. The sun icon represents a company logo or other important graphic element.

Figure 3-35 *An example of a manually created background page*

Having created a background page, you can then assign it to one or more existing pages. Note that you can link a background page to only one page at a time.

> ✓ **TIP** All page attributes, including background page assignments, are copied when you insert a new page. If you want to assign the same background page to multiple new pages, assign it to one page first, and then use that as the active page when you insert additional pages.

Figure 3-36 shows the top part of a foreground page containing a set of triangles. The page has been linked to the background page shown in the preceding figure.

Figure 3-36 *An example foreground page with content from the background page shown in the previous figure*

To create a background page manually

1. Right-click any page name tab, click **Insert**, and on the **Page Setup** tab in the **Page Setup** dialog box, click **Background**.

    Or

    On the **Insert** tab, in the **Pages** group, click the **New Page** arrow (not its button), and then click **Background Page**.

2. Change the name of the background page, if you want.

3. Click **OK**.

To assign a background page manually

1. Activate the foreground page that you want to assign a background to, and then open the **Page Setup** dialog box to the **Page Setup** tab.

2. Select a page from the **Background** list, and then click **OK**.

To remove a manually assigned background page from a foreground page

1. In the **Page Setup** dialog box, on the **Page Setup** tab, select **None** from the **Background** list, and then click **OK**.

Skills review

In this chapter, you learned how to:

- Manage shape text
- Create and format text boxes
- Add ScreenTips and comments
- Insert pictures
- Replace shapes
- Group shapes
- Understand and use layers
- Manage pages

Practice tasks

There are no practice files for this chapter.

Manage shape text

Start Visio, click the General template category thumbnail, double-click the Basic Diagram template, and then perform the following tasks:

1. Drag six shapes to the drawing page.

2. Add text to all six shapes.

3. Move the text block for the first shape so the text is centered above the shape.

4. Decrease the size of the text block on another shape so the text block is smaller than the shape.

5. Align the text in a third shape to the upper-left corner.

6. Rotate the text in the fourth shape 180 degrees.

7. Select the fourth and fifth shapes, and then rotate them clockwise by 90 degrees.

8. Rotate the text block in shape six so it is at a 45-degree angle to the shape.

9. Leave the diagram open if you're continuing to the next practice task.

Create and format text boxes

Continue working with the diagram from the preceding practice task or create a new diagram from the Basic Diagram template, and then perform the following tasks:

1. Activate the **Text** tool, draw a rectangle, and then enter text into the text box.

2. Change the font and font size.

3. Rotate the text box by 45 degrees in either direction.

4. Leave the diagram open if you're continuing to the next practice task.

Add ScreenTips and comments

Continue working with the diagram from the preceding practice task or create a new diagram from the Basic Diagram template, and then perform the following tasks:

1. Use an existing shape or add several new shapes to the page.
2. Add a ScreenTip to a shape, and then enter **This is an example of ScreenTip text**.
3. Point to the shape until the ScreenTip appears.
4. Select a different shape and enter a comment.
5. Click the comment indicator to see the text of the comment.
6. Reply to the comment with additional text.
7. Open the **Comments** pane to see how the comments appear there.
8. Ensure that no shapes are selected, and then add a comment to the page.
9. Hide the comment indicators, and then show them again.
10. Leave the diagram open if you're continuing to the next practice task.

Insert pictures

Continue working with the diagram from the preceding practice task or create a new diagram from the Basic Diagram template, and then perform the following tasks:

1. Import a picture from your hard drive or a network drive.
2. Import an online image by searching Bing.
3. Leave the diagram open if you're continuing to the next practice task.

Replace shapes

Continue working with the diagram from the preceding practice task or create a new diagram from the Basic Diagram template, and then perform the following tasks:

1. Use existing shapes or add several new shapes to the page.
2. Select any shape and replace it with another shape from an open stencil.
3. Select any shape and replace it with a shape from the **Workflow Objects** stencil in the **Flowcharts** group.
4. Leave the diagram open if you're continuing to the next practice task.

Group shapes

Continue working with the diagram from the preceding practice task or create a new diagram from the Basic Diagram template, and then perform the following tasks:

1. Select several shapes and group them.

2. Click outside the group to deselect it, and then select one of the shapes inside the group.

3. Ungroup the group.

Understand and use layers

Create a new diagram from the Basic Flowchart template, and then perform the following tasks:

1. Add several flowchart shapes to the page.

2. Add a new layer named Step by Step to the page.

3. Use the drawing tools to add a rectangle and a circle to the page.

4. Add the rectangle and circle to the **Step by Step** layer.

5. Hide all shapes on the **Step by Step** layer.

6. Remove the circle from the **Step by Step** layer.

7. Delete the **Step by Step** layer.

8. Select all shapes on the **Flowchart** layer, and then lock the layer.

9. Leave the diagram open if you're continuing to the next practice task.

Manage pages

Continue working with the diagram from the preceding practice task or create a new diagram from the Basic Flowchart template, and then perform the following tasks:

1. Add multiple foreground pages to the diagram by using several techniques.

2. Rename one of the pages to Special.

3. Move the **Special** page to a new location.

4. Add several shapes to the **Special** page, and then duplicate the page.

5. Change the **Special** page settings to use a different printer paper size.

6. Change the page orientation for the **Special** page.

7. If **Auto Size** is on, drag or add a shape to extend the drawing page size; if **Auto Size** is off, turn it on, and do the same.

8. Delete or move the shape back to the original page to remove the extra page or pages.

9. Increase the size of the drawing page by selecting a standard size or by entering a custom size.

10. Add the **World** background to the **Special** page.

11. Add the **Blocks** border and title to the **Special** page.

12. Create your own background page and add several shapes or text boxes to it.

13. Assign your background page to any foreground page in the diagram.

14. Remove the **World** background from the **Special** page.

15. Delete the **Special** page.

Create business process diagrams

4

The first three chapters described many of the basic capabilities of Visio. This is the first of several chapters in which you'll apply that knowledge to creating real-world diagrams.

Using a flowchart template to create a business process diagram is a logical place to start, because Microsoft estimates that nearly one-third of all Visio diagrams are created by using a template in the Flowchart category. In this chapter, you will create three types of business process diagrams by using the most common templates: a flowchart, a swimlane diagram, and a Business Process Model and Notation (BPMN) diagram.

If your goal is not to document a business process but to draw the logic of a software module instead, the diagram creation techniques that follow will still apply.

This chapter guides you through procedures related to selecting a flowchart template, creating flowcharts, understanding and building swimlane diagrams, understanding and designing BPMN diagrams, and creating subprocesses.

> ✓ **TIP** All of the flowchart and BPMN shapes used in this chapter contain data fields. Although you will not explore shape data in this chapter, it is an essential part of the shapes used in business process diagrams and is covered in Chapter 8, "Work with shape data."

In this chapter

- Select a flowchart template
- Create flowcharts
- Understand swimlane diagrams
- Build swimlane diagrams
- Understand BPMN
- Design BPMN diagrams
- Create subprocesses

Practice files

For this chapter, use the practice file from the Visio2016SBS\Ch04 folder. For practice file download instructions, see the introduction.

Select a flowchart template

The Standard edition of Visio provides a set of basic flowchart templates, and the Professional edition includes more than twice as many.

Visio Standard

In this chapter, you will work with two of the four templates that are included in the Flowchart template group in Visio Standard 2016: Basic Flowchart and Cross-Functional Flowchart. The Flowchart group, shown in Figure 4-1, also includes the Work Flow Diagram and Work Flow Diagram – 3D templates. The former is a theme-compatible diagram type that was introduced in Visio 2013 for mapping workflows; its stencils include updated, modern shapes. The latter is available if you prefer the older style of workflow diagrams that was bundled with previous versions of Visio.

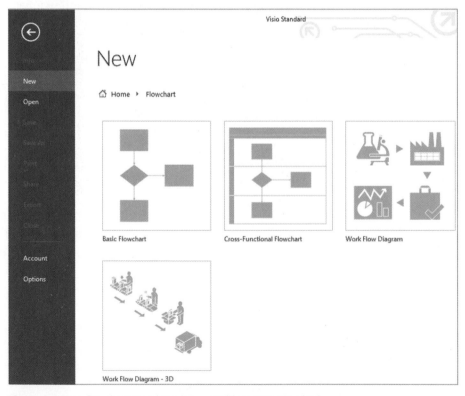

Figure 4-1 *Four flowchart templates are available in Visio Standard*

Visio Professional

The Professional edition of Visio 2016 includes the four templates that are part of the Standard edition, plus five additional templates, shown in Figure 4-2: BPMN, IDEF0, SDL, and two variations of Microsoft SharePoint Workflow, one for SharePoint 2010 and one for SharePoint 2016.

 SEE ALSO For information about IDEF0, go to *en.wikipedia.org/wiki/IDEF0*. For information about SDL, go to *en.wikipedia.org/wiki/Specification_and_Description_Language*.

4

Figure 4-2 *Nine flowchart templates are available in Visio Professional*

>  **TIP** The default font size on flowchart shapes is 8 pt. To improve the readability of the figures in this chapter, the shapes in most screen shots use a larger font size. Consequently, the text in the shapes on your drawing page might appear smaller than in the figures in this chapter.

Vertical or horizontal?

People who create flowcharts have debated for years whether flowcharts should be drawn with a vertical (portrait) or horizontal (landscape) orientation. Advocates of the vertical approach like the top-to-bottom layout, whereas horizontal devotees find the left-to-right (or right-to-left) approach to be easier to read.

You can create either style of flowchart in Visio, but the default layout is landscape, most likely because most modern monitors are widescreen. Prior to Visio 2010, the flowchart default was portrait orientation.

Create flowcharts

This topic explores the techniques for building a diagram from the Basic Flowchart template. With the information and procedures presented in this topic, you can create flowcharts such as the human resources recruiting process shown in Figure 4-8.

> **TIP** The flowchart in this topic was formatted by using variant 2 of the Gemstone theme. For information about themes and variants, see Chapter 6, "Add style, color, and themes."

One of the things you will discover very quickly when you work with flowcharts is that they are perfect candidates for using the AutoConnect and Quick Shapes features that were described in Chapter 2, "Create diagrams." Although those features are helpful in a variety of diagram types, they are particularly well suited for flowcharts.

You start a flowchart by using a start/end shape. From the Quick Shapes menu, you can quickly add process shapes like those shown in Figure 4-3. Each process box represents one step in the overall process.

Figure 4-3 *The first row of a flowchart*

Figure 4-4 shows how easy it is to position the first shape in the second row of a flowchart by using the Dynamic Grid to align the new shape with an existing process shape.

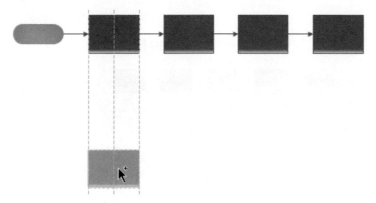

Figure 4-4 *The Dynamic Grid lines that connect the lower process shape with the upper one emphasize that the two shapes are aligned and are the same width*

Completing the second row, shown in Figure 4-5, is just as easy as the first, by using the Quick Shapes mini toolbar to place shapes onto the page. The second row includes a decision diamond, in addition to a second start/end shape that concludes the process flow.

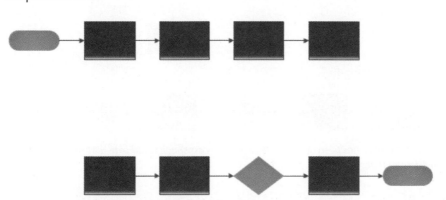

Figure 4-5 *Two rows of flowchart shapes that represent multiple tasks and one decision*

Figure 4-6 shows an interesting alternative for adding a document shape. Clicking the AutoConnect arrow beneath a shape causes Visio to place onto the page a copy of whichever master is selected in the stencil.

Prior to clicking the AutoConnect arrow, Visio displays a live preview to show you a semitransparent view of the shape that will be added to the diagram, as shown in Figure 4-6.

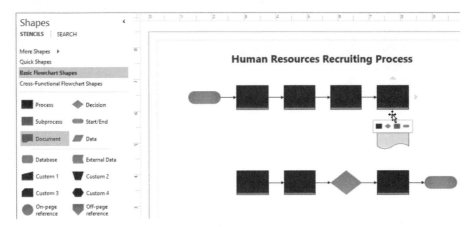

Figure 4-6 *You can place a shape onto the page by selecting a master in the stencil*

Figure 4-7 shows the state of the flowchart after adding the document shape.

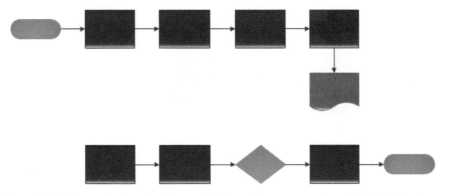

Figure 4-7 *A document shape has been added beneath one process shape to indicate that supporting documentation exists for that step*

To complete a flowchart, follow these guidelines:

- If your flowchart has more than one row, link the last shape in the upper row with the first shape in the lower row.

- Add a second outcome path to any decision diamonds you include. (You can add additional outcomes if a decision has more than two potential results.)

- Add text to each shape.

In the final version of the flowchart shown in Figure 4-8, the dynamic connector from upper right to lower left was attached to both shapes by using static glue for reasons described in the "Dynamic or static glue?" sidebar on the next page. You can use either dynamic or static glue to draw the second decision outcome at the bottom of the page. Adding text to shapes is simply a matter of selecting shapes and typing.

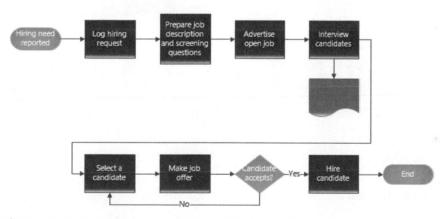

Figure 4-8 *A completed human resources recruiting process flowchart*

To build a flowchart quickly

1. Drag a **Start/End** shape onto the page.

2. Use AutoConnect arrows to add additional shapes in the same row.

3. Drag a shape onto the page to begin the lower row and use the Dynamic Grid to position it below a shape in the upper row.

4. Use AutoConnect arrows to add additional shapes in the second row.

Dynamic or static glue?

When you need to link two shapes with a connector, your choice of static versus dynamic glue might depend partly on the positions of the two shapes on the page. Using Figure 4-7 as an example, you could use one of the techniques that produce dynamic glue to link the process box in the upper right with the one in the lower left. Although the result in Figure 4-9 is a perfectly valid flowchart, it is better to avoid overlapping connectors if there is a reasonable alternative.

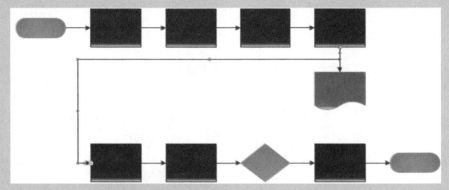

Figure 4-9 *A dynamically glued connector from below the upper-right shape to the lower-left shape takes a less than optimal path*

Using static glue from the connection point on the right side of the upper-right shape to the connection point on the left side of the lower-left shape produces a more satisfactory result, as seen in Figure 4-10.

TIP Most flowchart shapes are preconfigured with connection points in the middle of the top, bottom, left, and right edges.

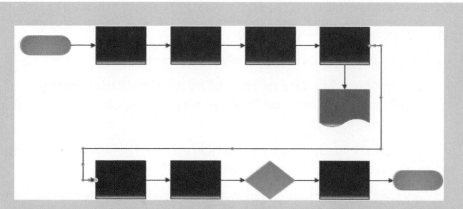

Figure 4-10 *A statically glued connector from the upper-right shape to the lower-left shape takes the desired path*

In contrast, either dynamic glue or static glue will suffice for the second decision outcome that has been added to the bottom of the diagram in Figure 4-11.

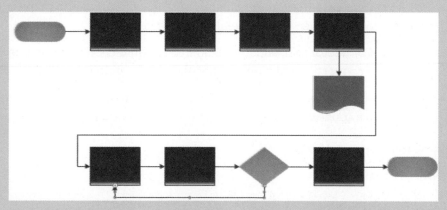

Figure 4-11 *A second decision outcome path has been added because every decision should have at least two outcomes*

To add shapes to a flowchart

1. Use any combination of the following:

   - Drag a shape from the **Basic Flowchart Shapes** stencil.

   - Use AutoConnect to place the selected master in the **Basic Flowchart Shapes** stencil onto the page. The new shape connects to the preceding shape automatically.

   - Use the Quick Shapes mini toolbar to add a shape. The new shape connects to the preceding shape automatically.

   - Click the **Connector** tool, and then drag a shape from the **Basic Flowchart Shapes** stencil. The new shape connects to the preceding shape automatically.

To connect existing shapes in a flowchart by using dynamic connectors

1. Use any combination of the following:

   - Click the **Connector** tool, and then drag from the interior of one shape to the interior of another, thereby creating dynamic glue.

   - Click the **Connector** tool, and then drag from a connection point on one shape to a connection point on another, thereby creating static glue.

   - Drag an AutoConnect arrow from one shape either to the interior (dynamic glue) or to a connection point (static glue) of another shape.

To add text to flowchart shapes

1. Do any of the following:

   - Click a shape, and then enter text.

   - Double-click a shape, and then enter text.

   - Click a shape, press F2 to switch to edit mode, and then enter text.

To exit text entry mode

1. Do any of the following:

   - Click anywhere outside the shape being edited.

   - Press the **Esc** key.

   - Press **F2**.

Understand swimlane diagrams

One drawback of a flowchart is that it doesn't show who is responsible for each of the tasks and decisions in a process. You will discover in Chapter 8, "Work with shape data," that flowchart shapes contain data fields that can be used to store this information. However, there is nothing about the layout or appearance of a flowchart that identifies the responsible parties.

A closely related alternative to a flowchart, called a swimlane diagram, solves this problem. Each process step in a swimlane diagram is placed into a specific lane, and each lane represents one role, function, or department. For example, a swimlane diagram with a focus on roles might include lanes marked *Flight Attendant, Pilot,* and *Baggage Handler*. Similarly, a department-focused chart might show lanes labeled *Flight Operations, Maintenance,* and *Catering*.

A swimlane diagram is also known as a cross-functional flowchart because it shows work steps as they cross the functional boundaries in an organization. In this context, each swimlane is usually referred to as a functional band.

Add-in tabs

Some Visio templates require additional software to provide their unique features. This is true for add-ins like the cross-functional flowchart template that is included with Visio. It is also true for TaskMap (*www.taskmap.com*) and other third-party add-ins that you acquire separately.

Like many add-ins, regardless of source, cross-functional flowcharts present a custom tab on the ribbon, as shown in Figure 4-12.

Figure 4-12 *The add-in tab for cross-functional flowcharts*

The Cross-functional Flowchart tab includes three groups. From the Insert group, you can add a swimlane, a separator, or a new page. In the Arrange group, you change the orientation, direction, and margins of swimlanes. The Design group includes a selection of styles, an option to rotate swimlane labels, and check boxes that you can select to display the title bar and swimlane separators.

Swimlane diagrams can be drawn with either horizontal or vertical lanes. You choose the orientation you prefer at the time you start a new diagram by using the Cross-functional Flowchart dialog box shown in Figure 4-13. Note that this dialog box appears only the first time you create a swimlane diagram; your selection in this dialog box becomes the default for future diagrams.

If you later want to change the orientation for a specific diagram, or change the default for future diagrams, you can do so from the Orientation menu on the Cross-functional Flowchart add-in tab, shown in Figure 4-14.

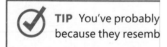

SEE ALSO For infor
framework, see "Find
diagrams."

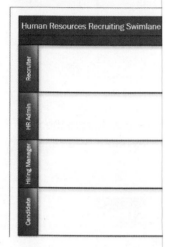

Figure 4-16 *Labeled title bar and*

TIP You've probably
because they resemb

To add flowchart shapes to
niques that were described
It's useful to know that all c
AutoConnect and Quick Sh
boundaries.

As you add shapes, Dynami
shows some familiar guidel
vertical and horizontal dasl
guideline. The dashed line
the shape being positioned

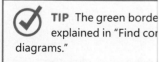

TIP The green borde
explained in "Find cor
diagrams."

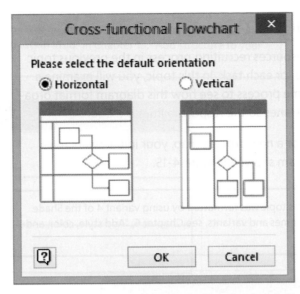

Figure 4-13 *You can choose between horizontal and vertical orientation for a swimlane diagram in the Cross-functional Flowchart dialog box*

Figure 4-14 *The Orientation button on the Cross-functional Flowchart add-in tab*

To change swimlane diagram orientation

1. On the **Cross-functional Flowchart** tab, in the **Arrange** group, click the **Orientation** button. Notice that the currently selected orientation is preceded by a check mark.

2. Click either **Horizontal** or **Vertical**.

To change the default orientation for future diagrams

1. Click the **Orientation** button, and then click **Set Default**.

2. In the **Cross-functional flowchart** dialog box, click either **Horizontal** or **Vertical**, and then click **OK**.

Build swi

The sample flowc
does not indicate
cross-functional f
nizes the work ste

If you select horiz
diagram page will

> ✓ **TIP** The sw
> theme. For
> themes.

Figure 4-15 *The initial*

The sample swimla
four roles, so two a
should be labeled
easily by using fam
shape with special

For example, one e
would any other sh
the swimlane diagr
existing lanes to sh

You can add text to
header and then ty
example shown in I

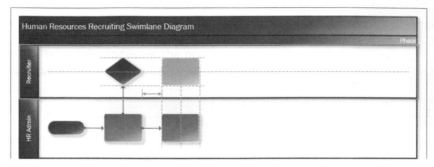

Figure 4-17 *Dynamic Grid feedback within and across swimlanes*

There isn't one correct way to build the swimlane version of the flowchart in the previous topic, but Figure 4-18 shows one example of how the shapes might be arranged in relevant lanes.

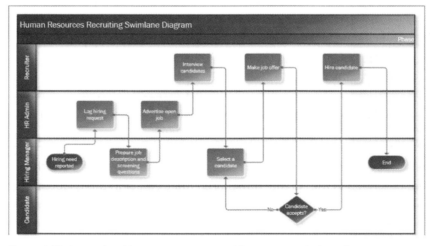

Figure 4-18 *A completed human resources recruiting process swimlane diagram*

> ✓ **TIP** Swimlane diagrams in Visio 2016 look very much like those in previous versions of Visio. However, the underlying structure is very different from pre–Visio 2013 diagrams. Current swimlanes are built on key components of Visio 2016 structured diagrams, which are described in Chapter 13, "Add structure to your diagrams."

To add a swimlane to a diagram

1. Use any combination of the following:

   • On the **Cross-functional Flowchart** tab, in the **Insert** group, click the **Swimlane** button.

- Right-click the header of an existing lane, and then click either **Insert 'Swimlane' Before** or **Insert 'Swimlane' After**.

- Drag a **Swimlane** shape from the **Cross-functional Flowchart Shapes** stencil onto the boundary between existing lanes.

- Point to the boundary between a pair of lanes with the cursor just outside the swimlane structure, and then click the blue insertion triangle.

> **SEE ALSO** For information about this method for inserting rows, see "Find containers and lists in Visio" in Chapter 13, "Add structure to your diagrams."

To label a swimlane diagram

1. Click the header that is above or beside the set of swimlanes, and then enter the text you want.

To label a swimlane

1. Click the header that is at one end of the swimlane, and then enter the text you want.

To add and connect shapes in a cross-functional flowchart

1. Use any of the techniques in the procedures at the end of the "Create flowcharts" topic earlier in this chapter.

Understand BPMN

> **IMPORTANT** The information in this topic applies only to the Professional edition of Visio 2016.

Business process experts from around the world created the Business Process Model and Notation (BPMN) standard so that a process diagram could convey more details about a process than is possible in a flowchart or a swimlane diagram. A key goal for BPMN is to improve communication about a process across all parts of an organization.

Although BPMN diagrams can improve knowledge transfer about manual processes, they can be particularly effective in enhancing communication about automated processes. Traditional flowcharts seldom contain enough detail about a process for an IT department to build systems to support the work of the business group. BPMN attempts to close that gap.

The creators of BPMN chose to use the customary flowchart shapes so that a BPMN diagram will look familiar. But they enhanced those shapes by creating multiple variations of each in order to provide additional context and meaning. For example, as shown in the figures that accompany both this topic and the following topic, most BPMN shapes can display one or more icons within the shape. The additional icons provide the reader with key details about a process step.

The BPMN templates in Visio 2016 and Visio 2013 conform to the 2.0 version of the BPMN standard. Visio 2010, which was the first version of Visio to include a BPMN template, supports BPMN 1.2.

> **SEE ALSO** For more information about the specific BPMN 2.0 features that are included with, or excluded from, the Visio 2016 and Visio 2013 BPMN template, go to *blogs.office. com/b/visio/archive/2012/11/19/introducing-bpmn-2-0-in-visio.aspx.*

BPMN uses four core shape types: Events, Activities, Gateways, and Connecting Objects, and there are multiple variations of each. Visio smart shapes are ideal for presenting shape variations visually.

The BPMN 2.0 symbol set includes the following:

- **Three types of events** Start, Intermediate, and End events appear as circles with different borders, as shown in the upper row of Figure 4-19.

  The lower row of Figure 4-19 shows one of the variations of each event type; from left to right these three images represent a timed start event, a message-based intermediate event, and an end event that results from an error.

  > **TIP** The six event shapes shown in Figure 4-19, in addition to the several dozen variations that are not shown, are actually all the same shape in Visio. The "Design BPMN diagrams" topic, later in this chapter, demonstrates a simple technique that you can use to change the shape among its many different incarnations. In drawing apps that do not have the flexibility of Visio, representing dozens of visual variations like this would require dozens of different shapes.

Figure 4-19 *BPMN event shapes*

- **Two activity types** Task and Sub-Process activities (shown in Figure 4-20) are both configured from the same Visio shape and each has multiple variations.

Figure 4-20 *An activity type with a plus sign represents a Sub-Process activity*

- **Six gateway types** Gateways are used to represent decisions, in addition to points where process paths split or join. All gateways are variations of the diamond shape shown in Figure 4-21.

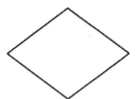

Figure 4-21 *The BPMN gateway shape*

- **Three connector types** Sequence Flow, Message Flow, and Association connectors between shapes (shown left to right in Figure 4-22), all include multiple variants.

Figure 4-22 *BPMN connector shapes*

Visio does the hard work of rearranging key diagram elements, leaving you to flesh out the remainder of new processes. In our sample process, you might add an eticketing option in a manner similar to that shown in Figure 4-31.

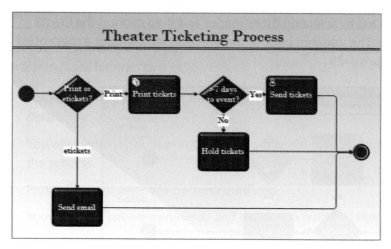

Figure 4-31 *A completed order fulfillment subprocess*

> ✅ **TIP** Automatic subprocess creation is not restricted to BPMN diagrams. You can take advantage of this feature in flowcharts and cross-functional flowcharts, too.

To create a new subprocess

1. Select a subprocess shape, and then on the **Process** tab, in the **Subprocess** group, click the **Create New** button.

To link to an existing subprocess

1. Select a subprocess shape, and then click the **Link to Existing** button.

2. Select the page you want from the menu.

To create a subprocess from existing shapes

1. Select at least two shapes, and then click the **Create from Selection** button.

2. Enter the text you want on the new subprocess shape.

3. Go to the new subprocess page and complete the definition of the subprocess.

Skills review

In this chapter, you learned how to:

- Select a flowchart template
- Create flowcharts
- Understand swimlane diagrams
- Build swimlane diagrams
- Understand BPMN
- Design BPMN diagrams
- Create subprocesses

4

Practice tasks

The practice file for these tasks is located in the Visio2016SBS\Ch04 folder. You can save the results of the tasks in the same folder.

Select a flowchart template

There are no practice tasks for this topic.

Create flowcharts

Start Visio, click the Flowcharts template category thumbnail, double-click the Basic Flowchart template, and then perform the following tasks:

1. Drag a **Start/End** shape onto the page.

2. Drag additional shapes onto the page and use either the **Connector** tool or AutoConnect arrows to link them to existing shapes.

   Or

   Use AutoConnect arrows and the Quick Shapes mini toolbar to add additional shapes and links to your flowchart.

3. Add text to each flowchart shape to describe its purpose within the process.

4. Add a description to each decision path outcome.

Understand swimlane diagrams

Start Visio, click the Flowcharts template category thumbnail, double-click the Cross-functional Flowchart template, and then perform the following tasks:

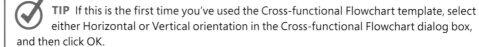

> ✓ **TIP** If this is the first time you've used the Cross-functional Flowchart template, select either Horizontal or Vertical orientation in the Cross-functional Flowchart dialog box, and then click OK.

1. Build a horizontal swimlane diagram, changing the default orientation if necessary.

Build swimlane diagrams

Create a diagram from the Cross-functional Flowchart template, and then perform the following tasks:

1. Click the heading of the swimlane structure to give the process a name.

2. Add two additional swimlanes.

3. Click the heading of each swimlane to identify the role, function, or department associated with the lane.

4. Drag a **Start/End** shape into one of the swimlanes.

5. Drag additional shapes onto the page and use either the **Connector** tool or AutoConnect arrows to link them to existing shapes.

    Or

    Use AutoConnect arrows and the Quick Shapes mini toolbar to add additional shapes and links to your flowchart.

6. Add text to each shape to describe its purpose within the process.

7. Add a description to each decision path outcome.

Understand BPMN

There are no practice tasks for this topic.

Design BPMN diagrams

 IMPORTANT The tasks in this topic can be completed only by using the Professional edition of Visio 2016.

Start Visio, click the Flowcharts template category thumbnail, double-click the BPMN Diagram template, and then perform the following tasks:

1. Add shapes and connectors to the page to lay out your process map.

2. Add a text description to each activity (task) and gateway (decision) shape.

3. Right-click each shape and select the activity, gateway, or event type, as required.

4. Right-click each task shape that represents a loop, and then set the loop type.

5. Add a **Text Annotation** to each **Start Event** and **End Event**, and to each **Task** shape that represents a loop.

6. Adjust the size and position of each text annotation.

7. Add a description to each decision path outcome.

Create subprocesses

 IMPORTANT The tasks in this topic can be completed only by using the Professional edition of Visio 2016.

Open the CreateSubprocesses diagram in Visio, and then perform the following tasks:

1. Select the **Log hiring request**, **Prepare job description and screening questions**, and **Advertise open job** shapes.

2. Create a subprocess from the selected shapes. Notice that when you create a subprocess in a swimlane diagram, Visio reproduces the swimlane structure on the new page.

Create organization charts

Chapter 4, "Create business process diagrams," introduced you to a practical, real-world application for Visio. This chapter focuses on a second common use for Visio: representing the structure of an organization in a chart that contains data about people; the chart might also contain their photographs.

In an organization chart, commonly known as an org chart, you can define reporting relationships manually by dragging smart org chart shapes onto a page and then letting Visio do the work of arranging them. Alternatively, you can point the Organization Chart Wizard at a set of data and let Visio do everything.

Regardless of the approach you take to create an org chart, Visio provides you with a multitude of options for changing the style, layout, themes, and colors of your chart.

This chapter guides you through procedures related to understanding and building organization charts, using existing data to create an organization chart, using the Organization Chart Wizard with new data, altering the layout and appearance of an org chart, and importing photographs.

In this chapter

- Understand organization charts

- Build organization charts manually

- Use existing data to create an organization chart

- Use the Organization Chart Wizard with new data

- Alter layout and appearance

- Import photographs as you create organization charts

Practice files

For this chapter, use the practice files from the Visio2016SBS\Ch05 folder. For practice file download instructions, see the introduction.

Understand organization charts

Visio org charts are well suited for the most common type of organization, in which each person has one boss. Although some organizations use matrix or other non-hierarchical structures, Visio org charts are designed for the majority of cases.

Review new features

Visio 2013 introduced a set of bold visual changes to the decade-old org chart solution, and those changes have been carried forward into Visio 2016. The most obvious visual change to org charts is the introduction of styles. Visio provides 10 styles, each of which includes six specially designed chart shapes. You will undoubtedly find that some styles are more appropriate than others are for portraying your organization's employees. With Visio, it's easy to try multiple options: you can change styles with one click.

Two other features that carried forward from Visio 2013 enhance the visual appeal of Visio org charts. Those features include the following:

■ The styled shapes use themes and shape embellishments.

 SEE ALSO For more information about using themes, see Chapter 6, "Add style, color, and themes."

■ The org chart shapes support a long-standing need for the option to import photographs automatically.

 SEE ALSO For more information about importing photographs, see "Work with pictures" and "Import photographs as you create organization charts" later in this chapter.

As mentioned about cross-functional flowcharts in Chapter 4, "Create business process diagrams," some of the magic of org charts comes from add-in software. (Also like cross-functional flowcharts, the add-in software is packaged with Visio.) The presence of the org chart add-in is visible in the same way that most add-ins are visible: by the appearance of a tab on the Visio ribbon, as shown in Figure 5-1.

Figure 5-1 *The Org Chart tab*

SEE ALSO For more information about add-in tabs, see "Understand tool tabs and add-in tabs" in Chapter 1, "Get started with Visio 2016."

The Org Chart tab retains many frequently used buttons from previous versions of Visio, including buttons to arrange, lay out, and space shapes. In Visio 2016, the tab includes buttons you can use to take advantage of styles and to import and manage pictures.

Use org chart templates

Visio 2016 provides two org chart templates in the Business category. Both templates include identical stencils and capabilities—with one difference: *Organization Chart* opens to a blank page so you can create an org chart manually; *Organization Chart Wizard* opens to the same blank page but also presents you with the first page of a wizard that steps you through the creation of a chart.

If you happen to select the Organization Chart Wizard by mistake, there's no problem: just cancel the wizard and continue without it. Similarly, if you selected the manual template but really wanted to use the wizard, it's available by clicking the Import button on the Org Chart tab.

Build organization charts manually

Although you will explore the Organization Chart Wizard in subsequent topics, it's useful to know how easy it is to create org charts manually. The good news is that even when you create an org chart by hand, Visio still does a significant percentage of the work.

For example, after you drag an Executive shape to the top of the page, you can create a view of the reporting structure simply by dragging other shapes, such as managers, employees, assistants, consultants, and vacancies, on top of the first shape. A diagram that starts with a single shape quickly becomes what is shown in Figure 5-2.

TIP If you decide after dragging a shape onto the page that it should be a different shape type, you don't need to delete and replace the shape. You can change the type by using several techniques that are included in the procedures at the end of this topic.

5

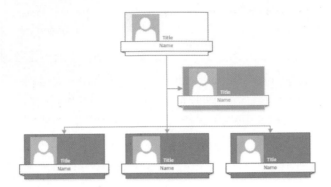

Figure 5-2 *An org chart that contains five shapes*

 TIP The Organization Chart Shapes stencil contains a special shape named *Three Positions* that makes it easy to add three employees to a chart at once.

The stencil also includes a shape called *Multiple Shapes*. Dragging this shape onto an existing org chart shape prompts you to select a shape type and then to specify how many shapes of that type you'd like to add to the chart.

Adding titles and names to the chart is as easy as entering them in two places on the shape. Click anywhere on the shape to enter the title; click the name box to enter the relevant name.

You can continue to build the chart by dragging additional shapes on top of existing shapes to show the required reporting relationships, perhaps producing a chart like the one shown in Figure 5-3.

Figure 5-3 contains at least one of each of the six primary org chart shapes. Four of the shape types are easy to identify because of their visual differences: the executive shape has a white background; manager shapes have darker backgrounds; and the vacancy shape, shown in the lower right of Figure 5-3, looks different from any other shape type.

However, the default org chart shape style (Belt) that was used in Figure 5-3 does not differentiate among assistants, positions (non-managerial employees), and consultants. Assistants like Deedee Spiros and Jason Robinson are differentiated by their physical location (offset to the right under their respective managers) but the shapes themselves look the same as those for positions and consultants.

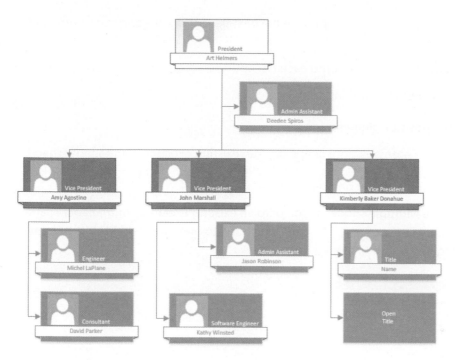

Figure 5-3 *Org chart shapes displaying names and titles*

The lack of visual distinction is merely a function of the Belt style. In the section "Change shape appearance," later in this chapter, you will discover that other styles do provide a unique appearance for each of the six shape types.

 TIP The vacancy shape is the only org chart shape that does not include a placeholder for a photograph.

To create an org chart manually

1. Display the Backstage view.

2. In the left pane of the Backstage view, click **New**.

3. On the **New** page, click **Categories**, click the **Business** thumbnail, and then double-click the **Organization Chart** template (not the Organization Chart Wizard template).

4. Drag a shape that represents the top level of your organization, such as an **Executive Belt** or a **Manager Belt** shape, onto the page.

5. Drag other shapes that represent the next tier of your organization onto the top-level shape.

6. Drag additional shapes onto each tier until your organization is represented.

7. Enter names and/or titles onto the shapes.

To add three position shapes at a time

1. Drag the **Three positions** shape onto an existing executive or manager shape.

To add multiple shapes of any type

1. Drag the **Multiple shapes** shape onto an existing executive or manager shape, or onto an unused part of the drawing page to open the **Add Multiple Shapes** dialog box, shown in Figure 5-4.

Figure 5-4 *The Add Multiple Shapes dialog box*

2. In the **Add Multiple Shapes** dialog box, enter or select a number to specify how many shapes you want to add.

3. In the **Shape** section of the **Add Multiple Shapes** dialog box, select a shape type, and then click **OK**.

To change the position type for a shape on the drawing page

1. Right-click any org chart shape, click **Change Position Type**, and then click the name of the position you want.

Or

1. Select a shape.

2. On the **Org Chart** tab, in the **Shapes** group, click the **Change Position Type** button to open the **Change Position Type** dialog box, shown in Figure 5-5.

Figure 5-5 *The Change Position Type dialog box*

3. In the **Change Position Type** dialog box, click the name of the position you want, and then click **OK**.

Or

1. Use either technique described in "Replace shapes" in Chapter 3, "Manage text, shapes, and pages."

Use existing data to create an organization chart

If the data about your organization already exists in electronic form, Visio 2016 provides a wizard that will build the org chart for you. You can begin with data that resides in any of the following repositories:

- A Microsoft Excel workbook

- A database such as Microsoft Access, Microsoft SQL Server, or other database systems

- A Microsoft Exchange Server directory

- A system that can export personnel information by generating a text file or an Excel workbook

When you build an org chart from existing data, such as the Excel data shown in Figure 5-6, you need only two key pieces of data about each employee: the employee's name and the name of the person to whom the employee reports. You can include additional data, as shown in the figure. What you include beyond the required data depends on what you would like to have available in the chart.

> ✅ **TIP** In Figure 5-6, note that Art Helmers does not report to anyone. Although another technique is described later in this topic, listing one employee without a boss is an easy way to tell the Organization Chart Wizard who is in charge.

H19	▼	:	×	✓	fx	

	A	B	C	D	E	F
1	Name	Title	Reports To	Employee Number	Extension	
2	Art Helmers	President		367911	101	
3	Amy Agostino	Vice President	Art Helmers	367929	104	
4	John Marshall	Vice President	Art Helmers	345180	125	
5	Elise Boland	Manager	John Marshall	385150	115	
6	John Goldsmith	Manager	John Marshall	367959	109	
7	Chris Hopkins	Manager	John Marshall	345138	111	
8	Senaj Lelic	Manager	Amy Agostino	367923	103	
9	Philip Choi	Manager	Amy Agostino	367965	110	
10	Krishna Mamidipaka	Manager	Amy Agostino	358132	126	

Figure 5-6 *Excel worksheet data can be used to create an org chart*

On the first page of the Organization Chart Wizard, shown in Figure 5-7, you indicate whether you want to build a chart from existing data or from data that you enter by using the wizard. The remainder of this topic displays the wizard pages that result from using existing data.

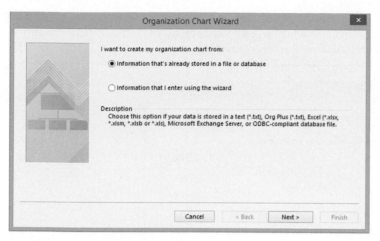

Figure 5-7 *Indicate whether data already exists*

You use the second wizard page, shown in Figure 5-8, to select the type of data source that contains your data.

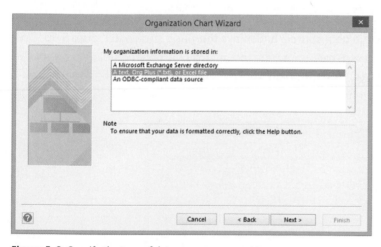

Figure 5-8 *Specify the type of data source you want to use*

If you select A Text, Org Plus (*.txt), Or Excel File as your data source, you then specify the location of the file in the next wizard page, shown in Figure 5-9.

TIP If you select either of the other two data source types, you will use different wizard pages to specify the location and access rights for the data.

Figure 5-9 *The wizard page used to specify the location of the data source*

After the wizard opens the data source, it displays the page shown in Figure 5-10. On this page, you map one field from your data to the org chart Name field, and another to the Reports To field. You can optionally specify whether your data has a separate field for employees' first names.

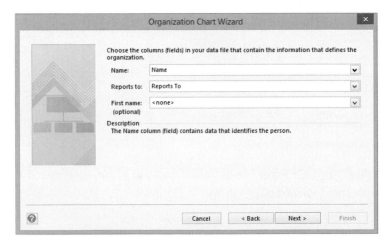

Figure 5-10 *Identify key data field names*

On the fifth page of the wizard, shown in Figure 5-11, you indicate which fields from your data you would like Visio to display on each org chart shape.

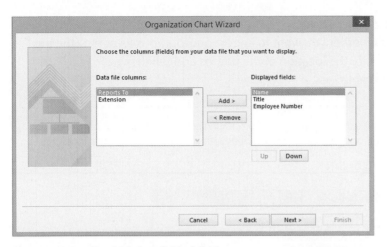

Figure 5-11 *Specify which data fields should appear on org chart shapes*

The wizard page shown in Figure 5-12 looks a lot like the previous page, but its purpose is different and unrelated. On this page, you select the fields from your data source that you would like to store as shape data in each org chart shape. By storing data inside shapes, you can run reports and use the data for other purposes without needing to revert to the original data source.

 SEE ALSO For more information about shape data and reports, see Chapter 8, "Work with shape data." For information about data visualization, see Chapter 9, "Visualize your data."

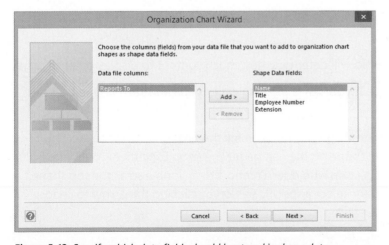

Figure 5-12 *Specify which data fields should be stored in shape data*

5

The penultimate wizard page, shown in Figure 5-13, was introduced in Visio 2013. On this page, you indicate whether you want to import photographs as part of the org chart. If you do, you specify the location of the photos and tell the wizard how to match photo files with employees.

> **SEE ALSO** For more information about incorporating photographs in your org charts, see "Work with pictures" and "Import photographs as you create organization charts" later in this chapter.

Figure 5-13 *Indicate whether you want to import pictures*

On the last page of the wizard, shown in Figure 5-14, you need to decide the following:

- Whether you or Visio will determine how much content to display on each page

  If you choose to do it yourself, a page on which you can specify page contents appears.

  If you let Visio create the pages, you can tell the program where to start by identifying the top shape on the first page. The <Top Executive> option tells Visio to select the person who doesn't report to anyone else as the top shape. Alternatively, you can select a specific person by clicking the arrow to choose anyone in your list.

- Whether to hyperlink employee shapes across pages

  If a manager's direct reports won't fit on the page with the manager, the wizard will leave the manager shape on the original page, and will also place it and the manager's direct reports on a subsequent page. If you select this option, Visio adds a hyperlink between the duplicated manager shapes.

- Whether to synchronize employee shapes across pages

  If manager shapes have been duplicated as described in the preceding bullet point, you select this check box to instruct Visio to update one shape if you make changes to the other.

5

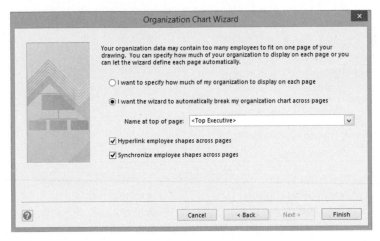

Figure 5-14 *You can provide org chart layout details on the last page of the wizard*

Using the Organization Chart Wizard saves a tremendous amount of time and work. However, the default layout and styles might not suit your needs, such as the example shown in Figure 5-15, which was created by using the wizard. You can use the techniques described in the section "Change shape appearance" later in this chapter to recast the organization chart in a variety of ways.

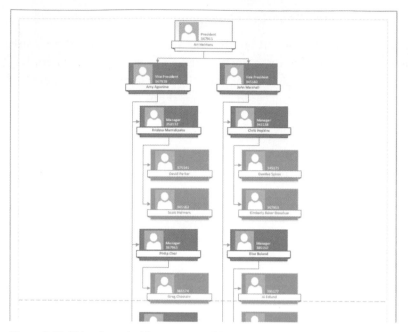

Figure 5-15 *This tall, vertical format created by using the wizard might not be ideal*

> ⊘ **TIP** Building an org chart from existing data is not the same as linking a diagram to external data. (You will explore data linking in Chapter 10, "Link to external data.") Org charts that you build from existing data are not connected to that data in any way; your org chart does not change automatically when your data does.
>
> You can use the techniques in Chapter 10 to link an org chart to your data source after using the Organization Chart Wizard. However, there are limits on what kinds of updates can be applied to the diagram automatically. For example, adding new positions or deleting employees in the data will not cause corresponding changes in your org chart. You will need to rerun the wizard to rebuild your org chart each time this type of data changes.

To start the Organization Chart Wizard

1. Do one of the following:

   - On the **New** page, click **Categories**, click **Business**, and then double-click the **Organization Chart Wizard** thumbnail.

   - With an organization chart open, on the **Org Chart** tab, in the **Organization Data** group, click the **Import** button.

Use the Organization Chart Wizard with new data

If your organization data is not in a format that Visio can read, but you would like to use the wizard, you're still in luck. The Organization Chart Wizard can help by creating a file into which you can paste or enter your data; for example, the wizard can either create an Excel workbook (Figure 5-16) or a comma-separated values (CSV) text file (Figure 5-17).

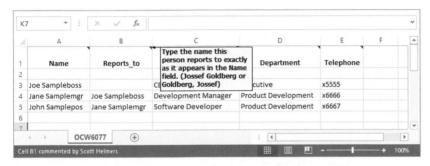

Figure 5-16 *An Excel workbook created by the Organization Chart Wizard*

Figure 5-17 *A text file created by the Organization Chart Wizard*

After creating the workbook or text file, the Organization Chart Wizard pauses until you close the file before it continues. If you don't close the file, the wizard displays a dialog box, shown in Figure 5-18, listing either excel.exe or notepad.exe, as appropriate.

 IMPORTANT If you use Excel, you must close the Excel application, not just the workbook.

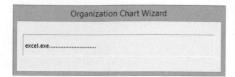

Figure 5-18 *This dialog box appears until you close the data entry file*

After you close Excel or Notepad, the wizard resumes by presenting the photo import page shown in Figure 5-13 in the preceding topic.

To create an organization data chart from data that you enter

1. Start the **Organization Chart Wizard**, and then on the first page (shown in Figure 5-7 in the preceding topic), click **Information that I enter using the wizard**.

2. On the wizard page shown in Figure 5-19, click **Excel** or **Delimited text**.

3. On the same wizard page, enter or browse to where you want to store the data file.

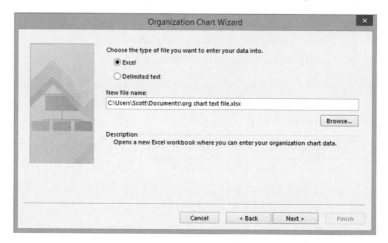

Figure 5-19 *The wizard page used to select the data file type you want to use*

4. Click **Next**.

   A dialog box appears and instructs you to type your data over the sample data.

5. Finish entering your data, click **OK** to close the dialog box, and then complete the remaining pages of the **Organization Chart Wizard** so Visio can build your org chart.

   Or

Click **OK** to close the dialog box, cancel the wizard, complete your data entry, restart the wizard, and then point it to your now-completed data file.

Alter layout and appearance

You can alter the look of your organization chart in many ways by using a broad set of enhancements that were introduced in Visio 2013. In addition, the Org Chart tab has been redesigned in Visio 2016 to make org chart customization tools more accessible.

This topic describes the functions in four of the five groups on the Org Chart tab: Layout, Arrange, Shapes, and Picture. The topic also demonstrates how Visio 2016 themes affect organization charts.

> ⚠️ **IMPORTANT** If you use the techniques described in this topic to reformat an org chart you created by using the Organization Chart Wizard, you should know this: if you subsequently import your data again with the intent of updating your org chart, all formatting will be lost. Visio creates a new org chart every time you run the wizard.

Change the layout

You use the Layout group on the Org Chart tab, shown in Figure 5-20, to adjust shape positioning on the page.

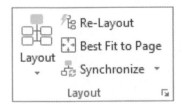

Figure 5-20 *The Layout group on the Org Chart tab*

You can make significant changes to the look of an org chart by changing to any one of 18 predefined layouts. Each layout changes the spacing and relative positions of shapes within the chart. A gallery of layout choices, shown in Figure 5-21, is displayed on a menu when you click the Layout button.

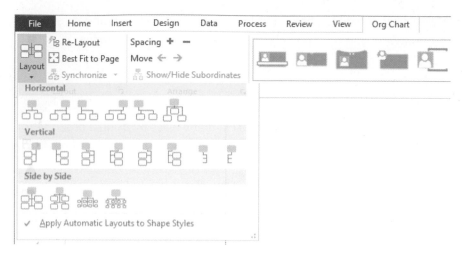

Figure 5-21 *The Layout menu*

> TIP When you select the Apply Automatic Layouts To Shape Styles check box at the bottom of the Layout menu, Visio refreshes the org chart layout every time you apply a style. You can retain your current layout when you change styles by clearing this check box. You will explore shape styles in the section, "Change shape appearance," later in the "Alter layout and appearance" topic.

If you've manually altered the size or position of any org chart shapes, your diagram might contain gaps or overlapping shapes. The org chart add-in provides a simple answer: click the Re-Layout button to restore appropriate spacing.

Another convenience feature in the Layout group is the Best Fit To Page button. Clicking this button relocates the entire org chart to fit better on the current page.

To change the layout of an org chart page

1. On the **Org Chart** tab, in the **Layout** group, click the **Layout** button.

2. Click the **Horizontal**, **Vertical**, or **Side by Side** button.

To change the layout of all, or part of, an org chart page

1. Right-click any shape that has subordinates, click **Subordinates**, and then click **Arrange Subordinates**.

2. In the **Arrange Subordinates** dialog box (shown in Figure 5-22), click one of the **Horizontal**, **Vertical**, or **Side-by-side** buttons, and then click **OK**.

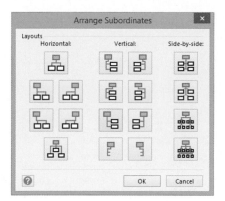

Figure 5-22 *The Arrange Subordinates dialog box*

5

To correct the spacing and positioning of all shapes in an org chart

1. On the **Org Chart** tab, in the **Layout** group, click the **Re-Layout** button.

To center an org chart on the page

1. In the **Layout** group, click the **Best Fit to Page** button.

Arrange shapes

You can use the Spacing and Move buttons in the Arrange group (Figure 5-23) to alter the vertical spacing and the location of shapes in your org chart. Note that the Spacing buttons affect every shape on the page, whereas the Move buttons operate more locally: if you select a shape that doesn't have subordinates, clicking either Move button moves only that shape; however, if you select a manager or an executive shape, that person and all subordinates will move.

Figure 5-23 *The Arrange group on the Org Chart tab*

You can also hide portions of the organization chart that are below a manager or executive. If you do, the manager or executive shape that has hidden subordinates displays an icon in the lower-right corner of the shape to indicate the presence of hidden subordinates, as shown in Figure 5-24.

Figure 5-24 *A manager shape with a collapsed subordinates icon*

To change the vertical spacing between shapes

1. On the **Org Chart** tab, in the **Arrange** group, click the **Increase the Spacing** (+) or **Reduce the Spacing** (-) button.

To move one shape

1. Select a shape that has no subordinates.

2. Click the **Move Left/Up** (←) or **Move Right/Down** (→) button.

> **TIP** In vertical layouts, the left and right arrows actually move shapes up and down.

To move a set of shapes

1. Select a shape that has subordinates.

2. Click the ← or → button.

To show or hide subordinates

1. Select a shape that has subordinates.

2. Click the **Show/Hide Subordinates** button.

Or

1. Right-click a shape that has subordinates, click **Subordinates**, and then click either **Hide Subordinates** or **Show Subordinates**.

Change shape appearance

You can use the buttons in the Shapes group, shown in Figure 5-25, to change the appearance of your organization chart. The most dramatic changes occur when you click one of the 10 org chart style buttons, each of which includes not only a different shape design, but also different layout rules. Because style changes are so easy to accomplish, you can experiment with looks that range from corporate to fanciful.

Figure 5-25 *The Shapes group on the Org Chart tab*

For example, with one click, the org chart shown in Figure 5-3 earlier in this chapter can look like Figure 5-26.

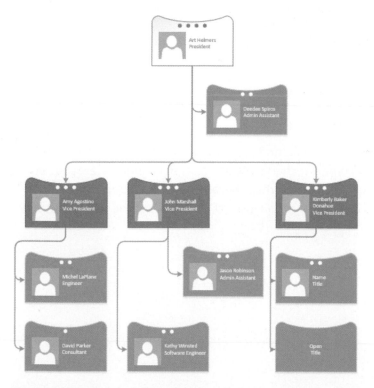

Figure 5-26 *An org chart with the Pip style applied*

> **TIP** Figure 5-3 doesn't offer any visual differentiation for position, consultant, and assistant shapes, but each of the following three figures does. Differences in chart styles are sometimes subtle, but they contain changes in geometry, adornments, or color.

With another click, the chart can look like Figure 5-27.

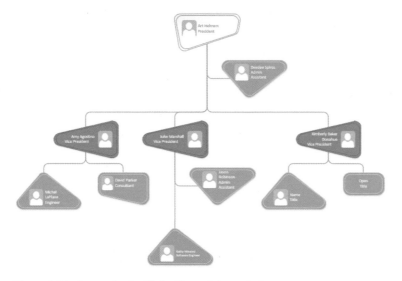

Figure 5-27 *An org chart with the Stone style applied*

As noted at the beginning of this topic, and as shown in Figure 5-26 and Figure 5-27, when you change to a different org chart style, Visio often changes the layout of the shapes. If this isn't what you want, perhaps because you have already spent time arranging the layout to your liking, you can instruct Visio to swap the shapes but leave the layout alone.

The names keep changing!

In the Organization Chart Shapes stencil, each of the six primary shape names includes the name of the currently active org chart style. Consequently, the shapes might have different names than the last time you worked on an org chart.

The name of the default style is Belt; consequently, when you begin a new org chart, the upper portion of the stencil looks like Figure 5-28. The word *Belt* appears both in the stencil name bar and in each shape name.

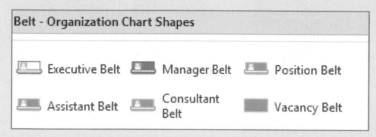

Figure 5-28 *The Organization Chart Shapes stencil showing the Belt style*

When you click a different style icon in the Shapes group, the names of the stencil and the shapes change, as shown in Figure 5-29.

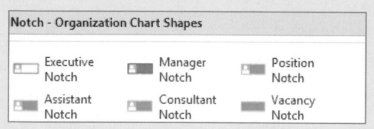

Figure 5-29 *The Organization Chart Shapes stencil showing the Notch style*

The Shapes group also provides buttons to change the height and width of org chart shapes, either to accomodate the display of more data on a shape or to reduce unneeded space. Figure 5-30 shows the results of reducing both the width and height of three org chart shapes.

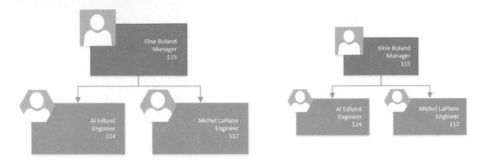

Figure 5-30 *Original and reduced size versions of the same three org chart shapes*

> **TIP** You can change the width and height of all org chart shapes on all pages from the Option tab in the Options dialog box. Click the Shapes dialog box launcher on the Org Chart tab to open the Options dialog box.

Finally, you can use the Change Position Type button to convert a shape from one organizational role to another, as described in "Understand organization charts" earlier in this chapter.

To change the style of an org chart

1. On the **Org Chart** tab, in the **Shapes** group, click one of the 10 style icons.

Or

1. If the style you want is not visible, click the **More** button at the lower-right corner of the style section to display a gallery on the **Styles** menu.

2. Click one of the 10 style icons.

To change the style but not the layout of an org chart

1. Click a style button to change both style and layout, and then click the **Undo** button or press **Ctrl+Z**. (This works because Visio makes the changes in two separate blocks. Undoing once reverts the layout; undoing again reverts the style change.)

Or

1. At the bottom of the **Styles** menu, clear the **Apply Automatic Layouts to Shape Styles** check box.

2. Click one of the 10 style icons.

Or

1. In the **Layout** group, click the **Layout** button, and then clear the **Apply Automatic Layouts to Shape Styles** check box.

2. Click one of the 10 style icons.

To change the height or width of one or more shapes

1. Select one or more shapes.

2. In the **Shapes** group, click the **Increase the Height** or **Increase the Width** (+) button, or the **Decrease the Height** or **Decrease the Width** (-) button.

> **TIP** If you don't select any shapes prior to clicking the height or width buttons, Visio will adjust all shapes on the page.

Work with pictures

You can add photos to an org chart when you create it, as you will discover in "Import photographs as you create organization charts" later in this chapter. You can also add either one or multiple photos to an existing organization chart by using the Insert button in the Picture group, shown in Figure 5-31.

> **SEE ALSO** For more information about the types of images you can use in an org chart, see "Import photographs as you create organization charts" later in this chapter.

Figure 5-31 *The Picture group on the Org Chart tab*

The Change and Delete buttons in the Picture group provide a means to replace or remove photographs.

The Show/Hide button makes either photographs or the picture placeholders appear or disappear. The Hide function is very convenient if you don't have photos because the default display for all 10 org chart styles is to include a picture placeholder. One click of the Show/Hide button turns the image on the left in Figure 5-32 into the cleaner-looking image on the right.

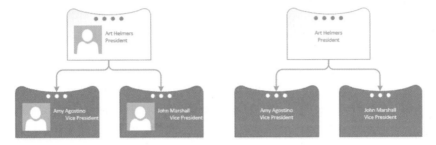

Figure 5-32 *Org chart shapes with and without picture placeholders*

To add photographs to an existing org chart

1. Select one or more org chart shapes.

2. On the **Org Chart** tab, in the **Picture** group, click the **Insert** button, and then click either **Picture** to insert a single image, or click **Multiple Pictures** to insert more than one.

> **TIP** Clicking Multiple Pictures attempts to match images to org chart shapes based on file names and people's names.

To replace a photo in an org chart shape

1. Select one shape.

2. In the **Picture** group, click the **Change** button.

3. Select an image file, and then click **Open**.

To delete photos or photo placeholders

1. Select one or more shapes.

2. On the **Org Chart** tab, in the **Picture** group, click the **Delete** button.

 IMPORTANT Clicking a Delete button on any other tab or pressing the Delete key deletes the entire shape, not just the photo.

To show or hide photos or photo placeholders

1. Select one or more shapes, and then click the **Show/Hide** button.

Apply themes

Besides modifying org charts by using buttons on the Org Chart tab, you can also use Visio 2016 themes, which are located on the Design tab. You can use themes to apply a wide array of colors, effects, and embellishments to create the look you want.

The three examples in Figure 5-33 use, from top to bottom, the Bound style with the Whisp theme; the Pip style with the Sequence theme; and the Coin style with the Organic theme.

Figure 5-33 *Three combinations of themes and styles applied to the same org chart shapes*

Import photographs as you create organization charts

Visio 2013 was the first Visio version in which you could import multiple photographs at once. That feature is carried forward to Visio 2016. In previous versions, you were restricted to importing one picture at a time.

If you build an org chart by using data in Excel or a database, you can import photos from a folder on your computer or a server. If you create your org chart by using data in Microsoft Exchange Server, you can import the same photos that people use in their Microsoft Outlook profiles.

The key to automatically adding photos as you generate an org chart is on one page in the Organization Chart Wizard. When you select Locate The Folder That Contains Your Organization Pictures on the wizard page shown in Figure 5-34, you can then browse to select the folder that contains your photos.

 TIP You can import photographs in a variety of common image formats, including .jpeg, .png, .gif, and .tif.

You also need to tell the wizard which data field to use to match image files with org chart shapes. Either accept the default of *Name* or select a different field in the Match Pictures Based On list.

IMPORTANT The file names of the pictures you want to import are critical. They must be in the specific format shown in the note in the lower half of the wizard page shown in Figure 5-34. When you use Name as the match field, the file name can include spaces; both "FirstnameLastname" and "Firstname Lastname" are acceptable.

Figure 5-34 *You can indicate on this page that pictures should be imported*

Including pictures when the wizard builds your organization chart doesn't change the likelihood that you might want to rearrange the chart. Figure 5-35 is the top portion of an automatically generated org chart with photos. In Figure 5-36, the chart has been styled (Panel), themed (Ion), and laid out for distribution to the organization's employees.

Figure 5-35 *An automatically generated org chart with photographs*

5

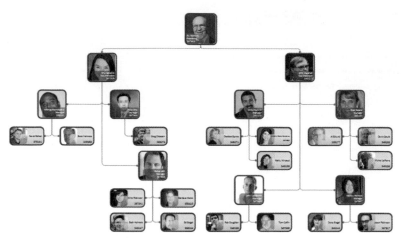

Figure 5-36 *An org chart with photos, a style, and a theme*

When you import photographs into an org chart, Visio crops and positions each image in a way it considers to be the best fit for the picture frame in the org chart shape. In most cases, the positioning done by Visio should be suitable. However, you might find that you want to reposition, resize, or otherwise edit a photo.

You can do so by selecting the photo and then using the tools on the Picture Tools Format tool tab. As an example, Figure 5-37 shows how to crop a photo. A preview of the entire image is displayed, and the portions that are outside the photo frame have a gray overlay. You can drag the picture to position it the way you want it.

Figure 5-37 *Pictures in org chart shapes can be cropped and edited*

SEE ALSO For information about adding pictures to an existing organization chart, see "Work with pictures" in "Alter layout and appearance," earlier in this chapter.

To include photos when you generate an org chart by using the wizard

1. Prepare the folder of photographs by giving each file a name that matches one of the fields in your data.

2. Start the **Organization Chart Wizard**.

3. On the pictures page of the wizard, click **Locate the folder that contains your organization pictures**, and then browse to the folder that contains the pictures.

4. Either leave **Name** selected in the **Match pictures based on** list, or select a different match field from the list.

5. Finish the wizard.

To crop or edit a photo in an org chart

1. Click the shape containing the photo, and then click the photo.

2. On the **Picture Tools Format** tab, select the appropriate tool, and then edit the photo.

3. Click anywhere outside the image to exit edit mode.

Skills review

In this chapter, you learned how to:

- Understand organization charts

- Build organization charts manually

- Use existing data to create an organization chart

- Use the Organization Chart Wizard with new data

- Alter layout and appearance

- Import photographs as you create organization charts

Practice tasks

The practice files for these tasks are located in the Visio2016SBS\Ch05 folder. You can save the results of the tasks in the same folder.

Understand organization charts

There are no practice tasks for this topic.

Build organization charts manually

Start Visio, and then perform the following tasks:

1. Start a new diagram by using the **Organization Chart** template. (Do not use the Organization Chart Wizard template.)

2. Drag an executive, at least one manager, and a combination of position, consultant, vacancy, and assistant shapes onto the page.

3. Drag at least one **Three positions** shape onto the page.

4. Drag at least one **Multiple shapes** shape onto the page.

5. Change the type of one of the position shapes to **Manager**.

6. Add names and titles to several shapes.

Use existing data to create an organization chart

Start Visio, and then perform the following tasks:

1. Start the **Organization Chart Wizard**.

2. Select Excel as the data source type, and then browse to the **OrgChartData** worksheet in the Visio2016SBS\Ch05 folder.

3. Add **Extension** to the **Displayed fields** section.

4. Add **Extension** and **Employee Number** to the **Shape Data fields** section.

5. Do not include pictures in your org chart.

6. Finish the wizard to create an org chart that uses the data in Excel.

7. Save the file as **MyOrgChart** for use in the "Alter layout and appearance" task.

Use the Organization Chart Wizard with new data

Start Visio, and then perform the following tasks:

1. Start the **Organization Chart Wizard**.

2. Indicate that you want the wizard to create an Excel workbook for you, and then provide a path and file name.

3. Enter data in the Excel workbook, and then close Excel.

4. Finish the wizard to create an org chart.

Alter layout and appearance

Use the file you created in the "Use existing data to create an organization chart" task, or open the AlterLayout diagram in Visio, and then perform the following tasks:

1. Change the style of the org chart shapes several times to observe the effects on the diagram.

2. Clear the **Apply Automatic Layouts to Shape Styles** setting, and then change the style several times again. Notice that the layout does not change.

3. Change the layout of the entire organization chart so more of it is visible on your monitor.

4. Change the layout of the subordinates of one manager on the chart, but leave the rest of the org chart as is.

5. Randomly move shapes or groups of shapes around on the page, and then lay out the diagram again.

6. Fit the diagram to the page.

7. Adjust the vertical spacing between shapes in the chart, and move shapes or groups of shapes.

8. Hide the subordinates of at least one manager.

9. Adjust the height and width of one or more shapes.

10. Add one or several photos to the page by using the images in the **Photos** subfolder in the Visio2016SBS\Ch05 folder.

11. Delete or hide the photos or photo placeholders on several shapes.

Import photographs as you create organization charts

Start Visio, and then perform the following tasks:

1. Start the **Organization Chart Wizard**.

2. Select Excel as the data source type, and then browse to the **OrgChartData** worksheet.

3. Select fields to add to the **Displayed fields** and to the **Shape Data fields** sections.

4. Include pictures in your org chart by using the images in the **Photos** folder.

5. Finish the wizard to create an org chart that uses the data in Excel.

6. Crop one photograph, and then adjust the brightness or contrast of another photo.

Add style, color, and themes

6

Some Visio diagrams are simple and straightforward; they exist solely to convey a mechanical or functional illustration. However, the purpose of many diagrams is to communicate information and, perhaps, to tell a story.

Regardless which description applies to your diagram, you can use many techniques to enhance its appearance and deliver information more effectively. A common way to start is by adding color to the interiors of shapes and to the lines in a diagram. However, choosing a striking, yet complementary, set of colors isn't easy, which is why Visio themes and Quick Styles were created. They offer professionally designed color palettes, and include variations on the main theme for those occasions when you need something just a little bit different. Whether you decide to use Visio themes or design your own palette, you can always apply specific colors, gradients, and patterns to individual shapes.

This chapter guides you through procedures related to aligning and spacing shapes; applying predefined themes and variants to pages or entire diagrams; using effects and Quick Styles; applying solid, gradient, and pattern fills; applying colors and patterns to specific shapes; and using the Format Painter.

In this chapter

- Align and space shapes
- Understand theme concepts
- Apply themes and variants
- Use effects and Quick Styles
- Apply solid, gradient, and pattern fills
- Apply line colors and patterns
- Use the Format Painter

Practice files

For this chapter, use the practice files from the Visio2016SBS\Ch06 folder. For practice file download instructions, see the introduction.

Align and space shapes

Part of creating a good Visio diagram is making it easy for the reader to understand and learn from the content of the diagram. You can provide significant assistance to your reader by removing distractions like lines that cross unnecessarily and shapes that are almost, but not quite, aligned.

You know from some of the preceding chapters that the Dynamic Grid, AutoConnect, rulers, and guides can help you build a neat diagram. You also know that you can nudge and move shapes manually to arrange them more precisely.

In this topic, you will explore a variety of features that you can use to position and align multiple shapes with just a click. Most of the features are located in the Arrange group on the Home tab; many are also accessible on the mini toolbar.

Align shapes

You can use the Visio align functions to move multiple shapes into position at the same time. Whether you need to arrange two shapes or dozens of shapes, you can accomplish the task with a single click.

Figure 6-1 shows four shapes that will serve as examples for the align functions.

> **TIP** The two orange dots in Figure 6-1 through Figure 6-4 are included to provide visual reference points. They are positioned at the center and middle of the orange rectangle and remain in fixed positions on the page while the other shapes are moved.

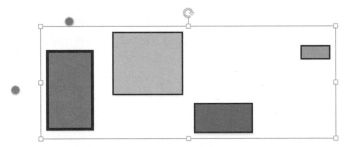

Figure 6-1 *Visio shapes in need of alignment*

Figure 6-3 *Four rectangles that are aligned at the middle*

To align shapes to the left, center, or right of

1. On the **Home** tab, in the **Arrange** group,
    either **Align Left**, **Align Center**, or **Align**

To align shapes to the top, middle, or bottom

1. Click the **Align** button, and then click eith
    Bottom.

Space and orient shapes

Adjusting the space between shapes is another e
presentable. Although you can use rulers, guide
in many cases, you can accomplish everything y

For example, the distribute functions ensure tha
for a set of shapes, on either the horizontal or t
shown in Figure 6-3, and then click Distribute H
will see the result shown in Figure 6-4.

 TIP You can adjust the amount of space that
by clicking the Position button and then click

What's in front?

Although Visio is a two-dimensional drawing tool, understanding that there is a third dimension at work in every drawing is critical to using the tools described in this topic.

When you drop shapes onto a Visio drawing page, their horizontal and vertical positions on the X-axis and Y-axis, respectively, are obvious. Less obvious is that each shape is also positioned on the Z-axis. Think of a shape's Z-axis position as its distance out from the back of the page.

You see evidence of a shape's relative position on the Z-axis, known as the shape's Z-order, when shapes on a page overlap each other: some shapes appear to be "in front of" or "behind" other shapes.

Even when shapes are not on top of each other, however, Visio keeps track of each shape's position on the Z-axis. By default, the first shape you drop on a page is at the back, and every subsequent shape you add is one step in front of the previous one.

If you're in doubt, try the following experiment:

1. Drop three shapes in separate parts of the drawing page so no shapes are touching.

2. Drag the second shape you dropped so it partially overlaps the third. Notice that it appears behind the third shape.

3. Drag the first shape so it overlaps part of the second and part of the third. The first shape maintains its Z-order and appears behind the other two.

You can alter the Z-order of any shape or set of shapes by using the Bring To Front or Send To Back button.

TIP The buttons on both the Home tab and the mini toolbar move shapes the full distance in one direction. However, the buttons also have menus that include Bring Forward and Send Backward commands to move shapes one step at a time.

6

> **IMPORTANT** The orange rectang[le]
> the shape Visio uses as the anchor
> suggests, the anchor shape stays in place—

The role of the anchor shape is apparent i[n]
center, and right of the orange rectangle. S[imilarly,]
shows that the yellow, blue, and green sh[apes]
rectangle.

Prior to aligning shapes, it's important to [know]
results can vary greatly with different anc[hor]
chooses the anchor and how to change th[e]

Visio usually selects the anchor based on Z[-order]
shapes, the anchor is usually the shape tha[t]
using Ctrl+A, the anchor shape is usually t[he]
permanently change which shape is the an[chor]
Backward or Send Forward command to a[pply]

You can also override the Z-order tempor[arily]
selecting the shape you want to be the an[chor]

If you select all four rectangles, the left,[center, and right]
the results shown in Figure 6-2.

Figure 6-2 *Visio shapes that are aligned left, ce[nter, and right]*

Similarly, the Align Top, Align Middle, a[nd Align Bottom]
moving them vertically. Figure 6-3 sho[ws]

> **TIP** The Live Preview feature is ext[remely helpful because it]
> shows the results of an alignment c[hange]

Among its properties, each theme consists of a color palette that includes base colors and accent colors. You will explore the color palette, along with a set of standard Visio colors, in "Apply solid, gradient, and pattern fills" later in this chapter.

Hundreds of Visio masters have been redesigned to take advantage of the Visio 2016 theming concepts. Many of the redesigned masters consist of multiple subshapes that take on different accent colors within a theme. When you apply themes that are primarily monochromatic, such shapes have a uniform appearance. But when you select themes that employ varied accent colors, you can create diagrams with interesting visual highlights.

The Themes gallery on the Design tab presents 26 themes plus a No Theme button. Themes are organized into four categories: Professional, Modern, Trendy, and Hand Drawn, as shown in Figure 6-8. In addition, the bottom row of the gallery shows thumbnails of themes that are active in the current drawing.

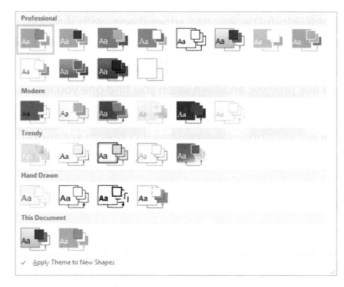

Figure 6-8 *Use the Themes gallery to apply predefined combinations of colors, styles, fonts, and effects to a diagram*

> **TIP** The Apply Theme To New Shapes option at the bottom of the Themes gallery causes the active theme to be applied to all new shapes that you drop on the page. Apply Theme To New Shapes is selected by default when you install Visio, but you can click it to change this setting for the current drawing and all future drawings.

Hand-drawn themes

Have you ever wanted to show a diagram to an audience to get their feedback, and you didn't want the diagram to look too polished or complete? Visio 2016 offers an intriguing set of themes you can use so your audience immediately understands that the drawing is a work in progress.

Compare the flowcharts in the pair of images in Figure 6-9. The image on the left uses the Whisp theme and appears to be a well-thought-out depiction of a company's workflow. In contrast, the one on the right begs viewers to help sketch out and refine the process, largely because it employs the Marker theme from the Hand Drawn section of the Themes gallery.

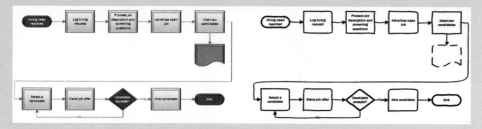

Figure 6-9 *The same flowchart with a finished look and a work-in-progress look*

Similarly, contrast the professional, finished-looking diagram on the left in Figure 6-10 with the "help me finish the network layout" diagram on the right.

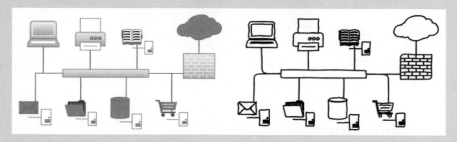

Figure 6-10 *A network diagram showing the effects of two themes*

Apply themes and variants

The figures in the following sections feature office furniture shapes that are among many redesigned shapes for Visio 2016. The furniture shapes feature significant visual variety even without themes, as illustrated in Figure 6-11.

> **TIP** Some of the redesigned furniture shapes contain intelligent behavior in addition to enhanced appearance. All of the conference tables that include chairs, for example, automatically add and remove chairs as you resize the tables.

The following sections provide you with examples of how changing the theme or variant can affect the look of your diagrams.

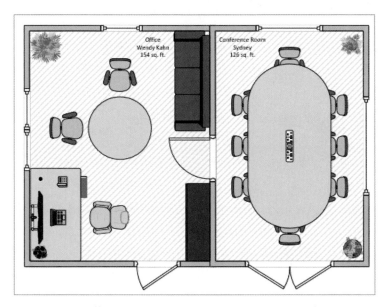

Figure 6-11 *An office layout created by using shapes redesigned for Visio 2016*

Choose themes and variants

In the upper-left image in Figure 6-12, the Shade theme is applied, which provides a monochromatic look. Compare it to the Whisp theme in the upper right, which features more prominent accent colors on many shapes.

> ✓ **TIP** At the time of this writing, a known issue causes the Sofa shape from the Office Furniture stencil to remain brown, no matter what theme or variant is applied. This problem will most likely be fixed in a future update.

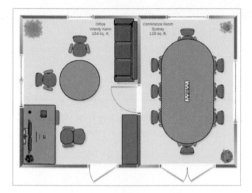
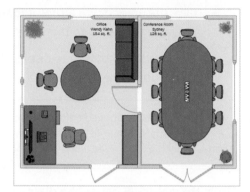
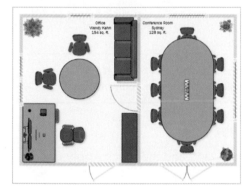
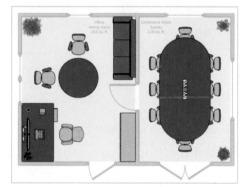

Figure 6-12 *The effects of themes and variants on office furniture and office plan shapes*

Introducing variants adds more visual differentiation. Compare the two office plan images on the left in Figure 6-12. Both use the Shade theme, but Variant 2 has been applied in the lower image. The chairs retain a similar color but the walls, door, tables, and plants all display contrasting colors. Similarly, the images on the right share a common theme, but Variant 4 in the lower right uses a completely different color palette.

To apply a theme

1. On the **Design** tab, in the **Themes** group, do any of the following:

   - Click the thumbnail for the theme you want.

   - Click the up or down arrow at the right end of the gallery to scroll through available themes, and then click the theme you want.

   - Click the **More** button to display the Themes gallery, and then click the theme you want.

 TIP Themes are applied only to the active page by default, which means that you can assign different themes to different pages. However, you can apply the same theme to all pages at once, as described in the next procedure.

To apply themes to all pages in a diagram

1. Right-click the thumbnail of the theme you want, and then click **Apply to All Pages**.

   ⚠ **IMPORTANT** From this moment forward, every time you select a different theme, it will be applied to all pages unless you reset the apply themes option.

To revert to applying themes to the current page

1. Right-click the thumbnail of the theme you want, and then click **Apply to Current Page**.

   ⚠ **IMPORTANT** From this moment forward, every time you select a different theme, it will be applied to only the current page unless you change the apply themes option.

To apply a variant

1. On the **Design** tab, in the **Variants** group, click the variant you want.

To remove the theme from the current page

1. Click the **More** button to display the Themes gallery, and then at the end of the **Professional** section, click the **No Theme** thumbnail.

To remove themes from selected shapes

1. On the **Home** tab, in the **Shape Styles** group, click the **More** button, and then clear the **Allow Themes** check mark.

To disallow the use of themes for all future shapes

1. Click the **More** button to display the Themes gallery, and then clear the **Apply Theme to New Shapes** check mark.

Customize themes and variants

Your exploration of themes doesn't have to end simply because you applied one to your diagram. You can customize any theme/variant combination to create your own color and design scheme, as follows:

- **Colors** You can choose a predefined color set, or design your own palette by clicking Create New Theme Colors at the bottom of the Colors gallery.

  If you choose to create your own set of colors, Visio presents a dialog box, shown in Figure 6-13, in which you select accent colors, colors for text on light and dark fills, and an overall background color.

 TIP Creating a custom color set disables variants, and they will appear dimmed (unavailable) in the Variants gallery.

Figure 6-13 *You can customize individual theme colors by using the New Theme Colors dialog box*

When you create custom theme colors, Visio adds your color set to the Custom section of the Colors gallery, a portion of which is shown in Figure 6-14. The same figure also shows examples of predesigned color sets that you can select.

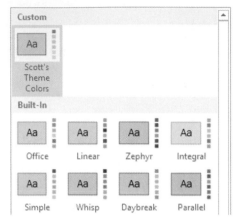

Figure 6-14 *You can select an alternate color scheme for any theme*

> ✓ **TIP** You cannot delete the built-in colors, effects, or themes. However, you can delete custom colors sets. To do so, display the Colors gallery for themes, right-click the custom color set, and then click Delete.

- **Effects** You can select one of 26 built-in theme effects.

> ⚠ **IMPORTANT** Customizing the colors and effects of a variant is not the same as setting custom colors or effects on a shape. You will explore the latter in "Use effects and Quick Styles" and "Apply solid, gradient, and pattern fills" later in this chapter.

- **Connectors** You can apply one of 26 styles to a dynamic connector.

> ✓ **TIP** The style you apply to dynamic connectors is also applied to other 1-D lines on the page. However, the style is not applied to the lines that comprise shape borders.

- **Embellishment** You can change the embellishment level. Note that not all shapes use embellishments, so you might not see a difference after modifying the embellishment setting.

> **TIP** If you want to copy a customized theme from one Visio drawing to another, copy a shape containing the theme from the first drawing and paste it into the second one. You can then delete the shape; the theme will remain behind. Your copied theme will not appear in the Themes gallery but any custom color sets will appear under the Custom section in the Colors gallery.

> **SEE ALSO** For detailed information about themes from a developer's perspective, see the theme-related posts in Visio MVP John Goldsmith's blog at *visualsignals.typepad.co.uk /vislog/archive.html*.

To customize variant colors

1. On the **Design** tab, in the **Variants** group, click the **More** button to display the Variants gallery, and then point to **Colors**.

2. Click the color set you want.

   Or

   Click **Create New Theme Colors**, select the colors you want in the **New Theme Colors** dialog box, enter a color set name, and then click **OK**.

To customize effects

1. Display the **Variants** gallery, point to **Effects**, and then click the effect you want.

To change the connector style

1. Display the **Variants** gallery, point to **Connectors**, and then click the connector style you want.

To change the embellishment level

1. Display the **Variants** gallery, point to **Embellishment**, and then click the embellishment level you want.

Use effects and Quick Styles

After you've used themes and variants to give your diagram the overall look that you want, you can use effects and Quick Styles to add sophistication or provide emphasis to one or more selected shapes within your drawing.

Highlight shapes by using effects

Visio includes six types of effects: shadows, reflections, glows, soft edges, bevels, and 3-D rotation. If you have used effects in Microsoft PowerPoint, you might recognize this list because Visio and PowerPoint share the same set of effects. In all six cases, you can choose from predefined effects, or you can customize specific features of each effect.

The flowchart example shown in several preceding chapters is enhanced in Figure 6-15 with three effects:

- The flowchart shapes—but not the dynamic connectors—have a reflection.

> **TIP** Selecting flowchart shapes, but not connectors, is easy because flowchart shapes are automatically placed on a special layer. For a refresher on selecting shapes by using layers, refer to "Understand and use layers" in Chapter 3, "Manage text, shapes, and pages." To review other techniques for selecting multiple shapes, see "Select shapes" in Chapter 2, "Create diagrams."

- The flowchart shapes have a bevel.
- The shape on the left end of the bottom row has a yellow glow.

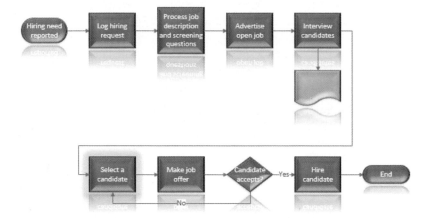

Figure 6-15 *Multiple effects applied to a flowchart*

You can apply effects in two ways, but there is an important difference between the two techniques. Clicking the Effects button in the Shape Styles group on the Home tab displays a menu that only gives you access to predefined effects, whereas the Format Shape task pane gives you precise control over the properties of each effect. As an example, the image on the left of Figure 6-16 shows the glow options available from the Glow submenu of the Effects menu, and on the right are the equivalent options from the Format Shape task pane.

> **IMPORTANT** The Bevel option on the Effects menu has a different name in the Format Shape task pane, where it is called 3-D Format.

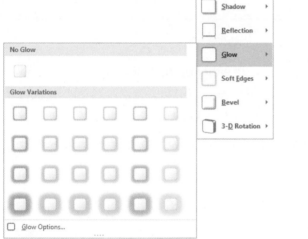

Figure 6-16 *You can apply a glow from the gallery or the Format Shape task pane*

> **SEE ALSO** For an example that uses multiple effects to create replicas of Olympic medals, see the article by Visio MVP David Parker at *blog.orbussoftware.com /data-graphics-text-calllouts-visio-2013/.*

> **TIP** Each section of the Format Shape task pane includes a Presets button that displays the same galleries as the Effects button. However, there is one important difference: accessing the galleries from the Format Shape task pane does not provide a live preview.

To display the Effects page of the Format Shape task pane

1. Select one or more shapes, and then do any of the following:

   - On the **Home** tab, in the **Shape Styles** group, click the dialog box launcher to display the **Format Shape** task pane. At the top of the task pane, click the **Effects** button.

   - On the **Home** tab, in the **Shape Styles** group, click the **Effects** button, point to any of the six types of effects, and then click the **Options** button at the bottom of the menu.

> **TIP** To see an example, refer to the Glow Options button shown on the left in Figure 6-16.

To apply an effect

1. Select one or more shapes, and then do either of the following:

   - In the **Shape Styles** group, click the **Effects** button, point to any of the six types of effects, and then click the effect you want.

   - On the **Effects** page of the **Format Shape** task pane, click the name of the effect you want, and then set the values you want.

Or

1. Right-click the shape you want to enhance.

   Or

   Select multiple shapes, and then right-click any of the selected shapes.

2. On the mini toolbar, click the **Styles** button, point to the **Effects** button, point to any of the six types of effects, and then click the effect you want.

To change an effect on a shape

1. On the **Effects** page of the **Format Shape** task pane, click the name of the effect you want to change, and then make the changes you want.

To remove an effect from a shape

1. In the **Shape Styles** group, click the **Effects** button, point to any of the six types of effects, and then click the **No** *<effect name>* button, where *<effect name>* is the name of the effect you want to remove.

TIP To see an example, refer to the No Glow button shown on the left in Figure 6-16.

Embellish shapes by using Quick Styles

Similar to the way that themes provide a coordinated set of design options for an entire page, Quick Styles offer predesigned collections of visual effects for a set of shapes that you have selected.

⚠ **IMPORTANT** There is one important difference between themes and Quick Styles: you can remove a theme by clicking the No Theme thumbnail in the Themes gallery. There is no equivalent way to remove all of the changes made by a Quick Style.

Visio provides two versions of the Quick Styles gallery, and you can use either of them to achieve the same result. The image on the left in Figure 6-17 on the following page shows the gallery when displayed from the Shape Styles group on the Home tab. The image on the right shows the gallery that appears when you use the mini toolbar. The gallery on the right appears in a shorter pane that includes a scroll bar; it's easy to miss the scroll bar and not realize that all of the same choices are available.

The Quick Styles gallery includes two sections that present the following options:

- Four variant styles

- A six-by-seven matrix of theme styles that provide theme-appropriate color and style alternatives. From top to bottom, the rows of the matrix offer style changes that range from subtle to intense; the columns offer variations numbered from one to seven.

The gallery that appears when you use the mini toolbar also presents Fill, Line, Font Color, and Effects buttons. These are also available on the Home tab.

✓ **TIP** Although the color differences across the columns in the Theme Styles section of the gallery in Figure 6-17 are readily identifiable, realize that each row incorporates differences in gradients, bevels, and other effects that are less visible in the thumbnails.

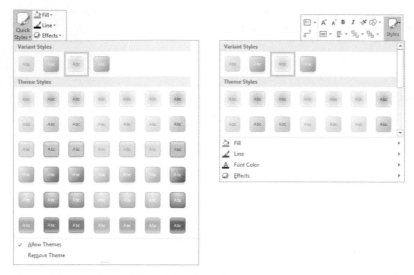

Figure 6-17 *Two views of the Quick Styles gallery*

> **TIP** Based on choices made by the shape designer, you will find that some shapes do not change when you attempt to apply a Quick Style.

To apply a Quick Style to one or more shapes

1. Do either of the following:

   - On the **Home** tab, in the **Shape Styles** group, click the **More** button, and then click a thumbnail in either the **Variant Styles** or the **Theme Styles** section of the **Quick Styles** gallery.

   - Right-click the selected shape or shapes. On the mini toolbar, click the **Styles** button, and then click a thumbnail in either the **Variant Styles** or the **Theme Styles** section of the gallery.

   > **TIP** Remember to use the scroll bar to reveal additional rows of theme styles.

To change a Quick Style

1. Display the **Quick Styles** gallery, and then click a different thumbnail.

Apply solid, gradient, and pattern fills

Despite the incredible range of design options provided by themes, variants, and effects, sometimes you just need the basics, such as applying a color or pattern to a shape.

In Visio, you accomplish these tasks in familiar ways by choosing from the color picker, shown in Figure 6-18. Even here, however, themes and variants are part of your color selection decision because individual color choices are grouped into four sections: Theme Colors, Variant Colors, Standard Colors, and Recent Colors.

When you choose from the Theme Colors or Variant Colors section, the fill in your shape will change color each time you apply a different theme. However, if you pick from the Standard Colors or Recent Colors section, or click More Colors, you have locked the color of your shape; it will no longer be affected by themes.

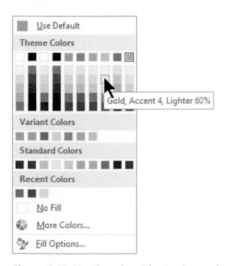

Figure 6-18 *Use the color picker to view and select colors and tints*

If you choose to work with the colors in the Theme Colors section, it's helpful to understand the structure behind this section of the color picker.

- **Columns** From left to right, the columns in the Theme Colors section are White, Black, Light, Dark, and then six accent colors named Accent 1 to Accent 6. (Light and Dark are used for light-colored text on a dark background, and dark-colored text on a light background, respectively.)

- **Rows** The top row represents the base color for each column. The next five rows display three lighter tints and two darker tints of each color.

227

A ScreenTip appears when you point to any color selection, as shown in Figure 6-18.

Clicking More Colors below the color picker opens the Colors dialog box, which you can use when the color you want is not available in the color picker. The Standard tab of the Colors dialog box includes dozens of color choices, or you can use the color selector and tint slider on the Custom tab to create virtually any color. For a third alternative, also on the Custom tab, you can type specific values in order to create colors that use the Red-Green-Blue (RGB) or Hue-Saturation-Lightness (HSL) color scheme. Regardless of the technique you use, selecting a color from the Colors dialog box adds it to the Recent Colors section of the color picker.

In addition to solid color fills, you can apply fill patterns, transparency, and gradient fills. The easiest way to work with pattern and gradient fills is to use the Format Shape task pane. Figure 6-19 shows the details of the Format Shape task pane for a gradient fill on the left, and a pattern fill on the right.

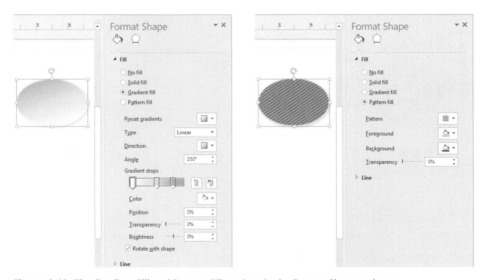

Figure 6-19 *The Gradient Fill and Pattern Fill settings in the Format Shape task pane*

> **TIP** You can fine-tune multiple options for each of the fill types shown in Figure 6-19. It's worth spending some time exploring the choices so you'll be aware of the many alternatives.

To display the color picker

1. Do either of the following:

   - On the **Home** tab, in the **Shape Styles** group, click the **Fill** button.

   - Right-click a shape. On the mini toolbar, click the **Styles** button, and then point to **Fill**.

To display the Format Shape pane

1. Do either of the following:

   - Display the color picker, and then click **Fill Options**.

   - Right-click a shape, and then click **Format Shape**.

To open the Colors dialog box

1. Display the color picker, and then click **More Colors**.

To apply a solid fill color

1. Do any of the following:

   - Display the color picker, and then click a color button in the **Theme Colors**, **Variant Colors**, **Standard Colors**, or **Recent Colors** section.

   - Open the **Colors** dialog box, click the **Standard** tab, and then click the color you want.

   - Open the **Colors** dialog box, click the **Custom** tab, and then in the **Colors** pane, slide the tint slider to the color you want.

   - Open the **Colors** dialog box, click the **Custom** tab, click **RGB** or **HSL** in the **Color model** list, and then enter values to specify the color you want.

   - In the **Format Shape** task pane, click **Solid fill**, click the **Fill Color** button, and then use any of the preceding techniques.

2. (*Optional*) Set a **Transparency** value.

To apply a gradient fill

1. In the **Format Shape** task pane, click **Gradient fill**, click the **Preset gradients** button, and then click the gradient you want.

2. (*Optional*) Set **Type**, **Direction**, **Angle**, or **Gradient stops** values.

6

To apply a pattern fill

1. In the **Format Shape** task pane, click **Pattern fill**, click the **Pattern** button, and then click a pattern.

2. (*Optional*) Set **Foreground**, **Background**, or **Transparency** values.

To remove a shape fill

1. Do either of the following:

   - In the color picker, click **No Fill**.

   - In the **Format Shape** task pane, click **No fill**.

Apply line colors and patterns

Many theme and variant combinations include styles and colors for lines. In addition, just as you can apply specific colors and patterns to two-dimensional shapes, you can also customize lines and dynamic connectors.

With few exceptions, most changes you make to lines affect both the lines you draw between shapes and the border lines around two-dimensional shapes. (One exception was noted in the "Customize themes and variants" section earlier in this chapter.) The techniques you use to change the appearance of lines are very similar to those described for fills in the preceding topic.

The color picker for lines includes additional options that are not on the menu for fills: you can set Weight, Dashes, and Arrows, as shown in Figure 6-20.

> **TIP** Visio MVP John Marshall suggests that "Line Patterns" would be a better name than "Dashes" because many line patterns have nothing to do with dots and dashes. In addition, you can create custom line patterns; for examples, refer to an article from an earlier version of Visio when line patterns actually were called *line patterns*: *msdn.microsoft.com /en-us/library/aa200997(v=office.10).asp*.
>
> In a more recent view of the subject, Visio MVP John Goldsmith wrote a two-part series beginning with this article at *visualsignals.typepad.co.uk/vislog/2008/03/creating-random.html*.

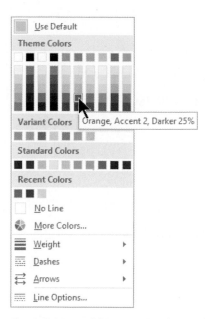

Figure 6-20 *In addition to color choices, the color picker for lines includes several line style options*

The Line Options entry at the end of the color picker menu opens the Line section of the Format Shape task pane, which includes even more options for fine-tuning the appearance of both solid and gradient lines. In addition to customizing the lines themselves, you can tailor properties like the caps (line ends), corners, and arrows.

Figure 6-21 illustrates the variety of line types that you can configure by using the Format Shape task pane.

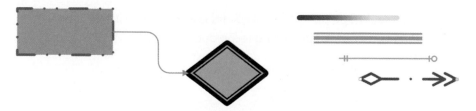

Figure 6-21 *Examples of highly varied line types you can create*

To open the color picker for lines

1. Do either of the following:

   - On the **Home** tab, in the **Shape Styles** group, click the **Line** button.

   - Right-click a shape. On the mini toolbar, click the **Styles** button, and then point to **Line**.

To open the Format Shape pane to the Line section

1. Do either of the following:

   - Open the color picker, click **Line Options**, and then click **Line**.

   - Right-click a shape; click **Format Shape**, and then click **Line.**

To apply a solid line color

1. Do any of the following:

   - Open the color picker, and then click a color button in the **Theme Colors**, **Variant Colors**, **Standard Colors**, or **Recent Colors** section.

   - Open the **Colors** dialog box, click the **Standard** tab, and then click the color you want.

   - Open the **Colors** dialog box, click the **Custom** tab, and then in the **Colors** pane, use the tint slider to create the color you want.

   - Open the **Colors** dialog box, click the **Custom** tab, click **RGB** or **HSL** in the **Color model** list, and then enter values to specify the color you want.

   - In the **Format Shape** task pane, click **Solid line**, click the **Fill Color** button, and then use any of the preceding techniques.

2. (*Optional*) Set additional line values.

To change line appearance

1. Open the color picker, and then do any of the following:

   - Point to **Weight**, and then click a line weight.

   - Point to **Dashes**, and then click a line pattern.

   - Point to **Arrows**, and then click an arrow type.

Or

1. Open the **Format Shape** task pane to the **Line** section, and then use the available options to change line attributes.

To apply a gradient line

1. In the **Format Shape** task pane, click **Gradient line**, click the **Preset gradients** button, and then click the gradient you want.

2. (*Optional*) Set **Type**, **Direction**, **Angle**, **Gradient stops**, and any additional line options you want.

Use the Format Painter

The Visio Format Painter operates very similarly to the way it does in other applications in the Microsoft Office suite. You can use it to copy simple formatting or more sophisticated themes, variants, effects, and Quick Styles.

To copy formatting to one shape

1. Select the shape from which to copy formatting, and then on the **Home** tab, in the **Clipboard** group, click the **Format Painter** button.

   Or

   Right-click a shape. On the mini toolbar, click the **Format Painter** button.

2. Click the shape to which you want to transfer the formatting.

To copy formatting to multiple shapes

1. Select the shape from which to copy formatting, and then on the **Home** tab, in the **Clipboard** group, double-click the **Format Painter** button.

   Or

   Right-click a shape. On the mini toolbar, double-click the **Format Painter** button.

2. Click the shapes to which you want to transfer the formatting.

3. On the **Home** tab, in the **Tools** group, click the **Pointer Tool** button.

   Or

   Press **Ctrl+1**.

6

Skills review

In this chapter, you learned how to:

- Align and space shapes
- Understand theme concepts
- Apply themes and variants
- Use effects and Quick Styles
- Apply solid, gradient, and pattern fills
- Apply line colors and patterns
- Use the Format Painter

Practice tasks

The practice files for these tasks are located in the Visio2016SBS\Ch06 folder. You can save the results of the tasks in the same folder.

Align and space shapes

Open the AlignSpaceShapes diagram in Visio, and then perform the following tasks:

1. Use a bounding box to select at least three shapes of different sizes, and then align them on their left edges, centers, and right edges.

2. Use the Live Preview feature to see how the shapes would look if you aligned them at the top and bottom.

3. Choose an anchor shape, and then align the selected shapes at the middle.

4. Undo the alignment from the previous step, click a shape that was NOT previously the anchor shape, and then align the shapes to its middle, noting the difference in placement.

5. Using the same shapes, distribute them either horizontally or vertically so that the spacing between all pairs of shapes is equal.

6. Click the orange triangle, and then experiment with rotating and flipping it.

7. Drag any shape to the edge of the page so that Visio expands the page.

8. Use the **Position** button to move the shape off the page break.

9. On **Page-2** of the diagram, experiment with the **Auto Align**, **Auto Space**, and **Auto Align & Space** functions.

Understand theme concepts

There are no practice tasks for this topic.

Apply themes and variants

Start Visio, choose any template you want to use, add shapes of various types to several pages, and then perform the following tasks:

1. Apply various themes, including at least one hand-drawn theme, to a page.

2. Choose a theme and apply it to all pages in the diagram.

3. Revert to applying themes to a single page.

4. Experiment with variants of one or two themes.

5. Customize variant colors.

6. Apply your choice of effects to the page.

7. Customize connector styles.

8. Set a different embellishment level for several shapes.

9. Remove the theme from one page.

10. Save the drawing as **ThemesVariantsEffects** for use with the next tasks.

Use effects and Quick Styles

Open the ThemesVariantsEffects diagram that you created in the previous practice task, and then perform the following tasks:

1. Apply a glow, reflection, and bevel to one or more shapes.

2. Change one glow to be larger or smaller, or to be a different color, and then alter one of the bevels you previously applied.

3. Select two shapes, and then remove all effects from those shapes.

4. Select several shapes, and then apply a Quick Style.

5. Select one of the shapes with a Quick Style applied, and then apply a different one.

Apply solid, gradient, and pattern fills

Continue using the diagram from the previous task, or create a new diagram, and then perform the following tasks:

1. Add 10 to 12 shapes to the page, select one or more shapes, and then apply a new solid fill color.

2. Apply a gradient fill to several shapes.

3. Experiment with changing the gradient fill settings for **Type** and **Direction**.

4. Adjust the **Gradient stop** settings.

5. Apply a fill pattern to one or more shapes.

6. Remove the fill from one shape.

Apply line colors and patterns

Continue using the diagram from the previous tasks, or create a new diagram, and then perform the following tasks:

1. Add several lines and dynamic connectors to the page. If there aren't any 2-D shapes on the page, add several.

2. Apply a solid color to one line, one dynamic connector, and one 2-D shape.

3. Change the line weight, line pattern, and several other characteristics.

4. Apply a gradient to one line, one dynamic connector, and one 2-D shape.

5. Adjust various aspects of the line gradient.

6. Save the drawing as **ColorsPatterns** for use with the next tasks.

Use the Format Painter

Open the ColorsPatterns diagram that you created in the previous practice task, and then perform the following tasks:

1. Copy the formatting from one line to another.

2. Copy the formatting from one 2-D shape to another.

3. Copy the formatting from one shape to three other shapes.

Create network and datacenter diagrams

7

Creating network diagrams is among the most common uses for Visio. Whether your goal is to create simple, stylized representations of network connectivity or create photo-realistic rack diagrams that show real-time equipment status, you can accomplish your goal with Visio.

The Standard edition of Visio 2016 includes two main templates: Basic Network Diagram and Basic Network Diagram – 3D. The former incorporates modern-looking, two-dimensional (2-D) shapes that are compatible with Visio 2016 themes. The latter includes three-dimensional (3-D) shapes that are identical to the shapes used in Visio 2010 and earlier.

The Professional edition includes both Standard-edition templates plus a more sophisticated version of each, called Detailed Network Diagram and Detailed Network Diagram – 3D. Visio Professional also includes Rack Diagram, Active Directory, and LDAP Directory templates.

> ✓ **TIP** Both the Basic Network Diagram and Detailed Network Diagram templates feature starter diagrams. See Chapter 1, "Get started with Visio 2016," for information about starter diagrams.

This chapter guides you through procedures related to building basic and detailed network diagrams, using 2-D or 3-D equipment shapes, creating rack diagrams, changing the drawing scale, and running computer and network reports.

In this chapter

- Build basic network diagrams
- Build detailed network diagrams
- Use 3-D equipment shapes
- Create rack diagrams
- Change the drawing scale
- Run computer and network reports

Practice files

For this chapter, use the practice files from the Visio2016SBS\Ch07 folder. For practice file download instructions, see the introduction.

Build basic network diagrams

A key component of many networks is an Ethernet network. The Visio Ethernet shape is a smart shape whose appearance belies its sophistication. When you drag an Ethernet shape onto the drawing page, it looks as shown on the left side of Figure 7-1.

Based on the five lines with dots at the ends, you might assume you can connect only five network devices to one Ethernet segment. However, you can actually connect up to 64 devices to one segment.

Figure 7-1 *An Ethernet shape offers 64 movable connection points*

The secret lies in the yellow control handles that appear when you select the shape (see the image on the right side of Figure 7-1). In addition to the control handles at the ends of the five lines, what appears to be a pair of control handles in the middle of the shape is actually two stacks of control handles. As you drag one of the control handles out of the middle, another appears until you reach the total of 64. Figure 7-2 shows seven connected devices and eight available connection points, and there are still two control handles in the middle of the Ethernet segment.

> **IMPORTANT** If you drag a connection point before selecting the Ethernet shape, you will drag the entire shape and not just the connector. Be sure to select the Ethernet shape first.

The two-dimensional computer and network shapes accept all of the themes and effects you learned about in Chapter 6, "Add style, color, and themes." For example, Figure 7-3 uses Variant 4 of the Zephyr theme. In addition, the Art Deco bevel effect is applied to the computer shapes, and the Dark Red, 8 pt, Accent Color 6 glow effect is added to the two network segments.

Most of the shapes in the Basic Network Diagram stencils are computers and network components that are used inside buildings. Most of the wide area network components are in stencils that are part of the Detailed Network Diagram template described in the following topic.

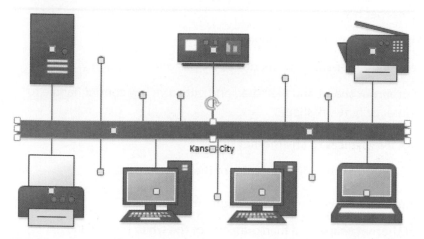

Figure 7-2 *An Ethernet shape can be lengthened by dragging the resize handles, and you can add text to the shape*

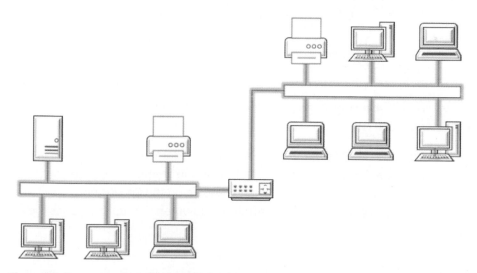

Figure 7-3 *You can create stylish network diagrams by using themes and effects*

> ✅ **TIP** If you end up with unneeded control handles outside the Ethernet segment shape, don't try to delete them—you'll end up deleting the entire Ethernet segment. Instead, you can hide unused connections by dragging those control handles back into the interior of the Ethernet shape where they will only be visible if you select the network segment.

> ✅ **TIP** Don't forget that you can use the Dynamic Grid to align the new shapes with each other and with the Ethernet segment.

To diagram an Ethernet network

1. Drag an **Ethernet** shape onto the page.

2. Drag various computer and network device shapes onto the page.

3. Select the **Ethernet** shape, and then drag and glue a yellow control handle to each computer or network shape.

To add more than five devices to an Ethernet shape

1. Drag a yellow control out from the center of the **Ethernet** shape.

To adjust the length or width of an Ethernet segment

1. Select the **Ethernet** shape, and then drag one of the white resize handles.

Build detailed network diagrams

 IMPORTANT The information in this topic applies only to the Professional edition of Visio 2016.

Visio Professional 2016 includes an advanced network diagram template that offers additional stencils you can use to create diagrams that are more sophisticated.

The primary differences between the Basic Network Diagram and Detailed Network Diagram templates are visible in the two versions of the Shapes window shown in Figure 7-4. The Basic Network Diagram template (shown on the left) includes only two stencils. The Detailed Network Diagram template (shown on the right) includes the same two, plus five additional stencils.

 IMPORTANT If a scroll bar appears when you move the pointer into the upper part of the Shapes window when you are using the Detailed Network Diagram template, drag the separator between the title bar section and the shapes section down to reveal all of the stencil titles.

The Servers stencil contains 17 shapes that you can use to represent specific server types to create a realistic depiction of your network. The Rack Mounted Servers stencil contains a corresponding set of 17 rack-mounted server shapes. The remaining stencils provide dozens of symbols for network equipment and locations. Figure 7-5 shows an example of the type of enterprise diagram you can create by incorporating shapes from multiple stencils.

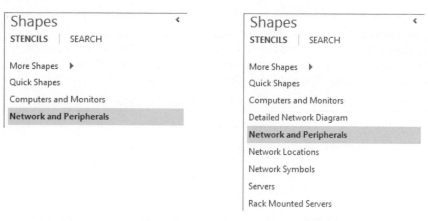

Figure 7-4 *Additional network stencils are available in Visio Professional*

 TIP For network and computer shapes with a light-hearted, work-in-progress look, see the Crayon Network Shapes on the Visio Guy blog at *www.visguy.com/2011/08/16/ crayon-visio-network-shapes-revisited/.*

TIP The local area network (LAN) shapes on the left and right sides of Figure 7-5 are enclosed in containers. You will explore the use of containers in Chapter 13, "Add structure to your diagrams."

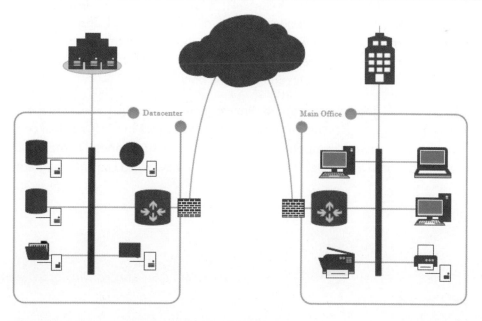

Figure 7-5 *A representation of an enterprise network*

> ✅ **TIP** Early versions of Visio—Visio 2000 and before—included a network discovery and auto-mapping capability. In essence, you could point those early versions of Visio at a network and it would discover what was on the network and then build a map for you. Although that capability no longer exists in Visio, several vendors provide Visio add-ins that have this capability.

> 🔍 **SEE ALSO** For information about storing and using data in network shapes, see Chapter 8, "Work with shape data," and "Run computer and network reports" later in this chapter.

To diagram an enterprise network

1. Drag local and wide area network shapes and computer shapes onto the page.

2. Connect device shapes to local area network shapes as described in the preceding topic.

3. Connect wide area network device shapes by using dynamic connectors or the **Comm-link** shape in the **Network and Peripherals** stencil.

Use 3-D equipment shapes

The preceding topics featured the modern, two-dimensional network and computer shapes that were introduced with Visio 2013. Remember, however, that the traditional three-dimensional shapes are still available in the Basic Network Shapes - 3D and Detailed Network Shapes - 3D (Professional edition only) stencils.

Figure 7-6 provides a good comparison of the two shape styles. The network in the upper half of the diagram uses the 2-D shapes, and the network in the lower half consists of the identical network components represented with 3-D shapes. Neither style is right or wrong—both are available so you can choose how you'd like your diagram to look.

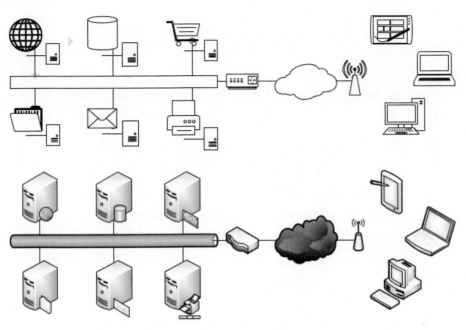

Figure 7-6 *Modern, two-dimensional network shapes contrast sharply with traditional, three-dimensional shapes*

When you select the appropriate style for your diagrams, two additional considerations might affect your decision:

- Many of the stencils and shapes provided by equipment vendors are drawn in the 3-D style. (See the "Where can I find more network shapes?" sidebar later in this chapter.)

- The 2-D network shapes were designed specifically for Visio 2016 themes. Although these shapes look more basic than the 3-D shapes when no theme is applied, as shown in Figure 7-6, they are much more attractive than the older shapes when you use themes.

Where can I find more network shapes?

The network shapes that are included with Visio might look something like your servers, routers, and other equipment, but they can't match exactly because they are generic shapes.

If you want to create diagrams that are more realistic, thousands of downloadable Visio stencils and shapes are available from three main sources:

- Network and computer equipment vendors often provide shapes, usually photo-realistic shapes, for their equipment. For vendor-specific shapes, browse or search a vendor's website.

- Some companies design and sell both product-specific and generic Visio shapes.

- Individuals have created network and computer equipment shapes. Many provide them for free; some charge for their artwork.

For Microsoft-specific shapes, try the following:

- The "Microsoft Azure, Cloud and Enterprise Symbol / Icon Set" download includes Visio stencils and .png images. Details and the download are available at *www.microsoft.com/en-us/download/details.aspx?id=41937.*

- Microsoft created a collection of server and network shapes for use in wall posters that depict product deployment scenarios. You might not need to create posters, but the free, downloadable stencils offer an alternative to traditional Visio shapes. You can download the shapes from *www.microsoft.com/en-us/download/details.aspx?id=21480.*

If you want to customize the 3-D server shapes that are delivered with Visio, the Visio Guy blog includes an article and a tool at *www.visguy.com/2009/09/11/visio-server-shape-icon-customization-tool/.*

For large collections of links to various stencil sources (most are free), go to the following sites:

- *www.visiocafe.com*

- *visio.mvps.org/3rdParty/default.html*

You can also try these commercial stencil vendors:

- *www.visiostencils.com*

- *www.shapesource.com*

Create rack diagrams

 IMPORTANT The information in this topic applies only to the Professional edition of Visio 2016.

The diagrams in the preceding topics all contain equipment that is generally located outside the wiring closet or datacenter. To create diagrams of equipment in those backroom areas, you use some of the shapes from the computer and network stencils. However, you also need additional stencils that are provided with Visio Professional. This topic explores the special behavior of a key backroom component—the shapes you use to build rack diagrams.

Figure 7-7 on the following page shows three of the equipment room and rack-related stencils.

 IMPORTANT A rack diagram is an example of a scaled drawing, one in which the size of the shapes on the page is dependent on the size and scale of the page itself.

The pages in the Rack Diagram template are preset with a scale factor; however, you can add scaled drawing pages to any diagram. For more information about scaled drawings, see the sidebar "What is a scaled drawing?" and the topic "Change the drawing scale," both later in this chapter.

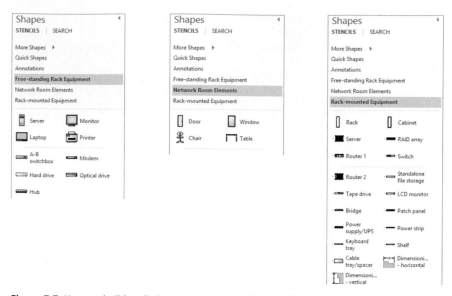

Figure 7-7 *You can build realistic representations of wiring closets and datacenters by using rack shapes*

When you drag a rack shape onto the drawing page, it appears like the one shown in Figure 7-8, with a measurement of "42 U" displayed above the rack. U is the abbreviation for one rack unit, which is 1.75 inches or 44.45 mm.

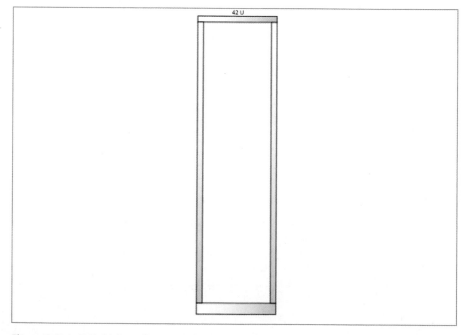

Figure 7-8 *A 42 U–high equipment rack*

> ✅ **TIP** The rack shape was designed to be included in a scaled drawing. Consequently, if you drop a rack shape onto a page with no drawing scale, it behaves very differently—the entire rack will be only 1 U high.

In addition to the rack shape displaying its height, each piece of equipment you drag into a rack displays its height in rack units, as shown in several subsequent figures.

Figure 7-9 shows a 2 U Power Supply/UPS shape being placed into a rack. Based on what you learned about connection points in Chapter 2, "Create diagrams," three items in the figure would lead you to think that the rack and the equipment shape have active connection points despite the lack of obvious one-dimensional (1-D) shapes:

- There are green squares at the lower corners of the Power Supply/UPS shape.
- The words *Glue to Connection Point* appear in a ScreenTip.
- There are gray squares along the edges of the rack that appear only when you move a rack-mounted shape near the rack.

What you are observing in this figure is a unique feature of rack equipment shapes and a few other Visio shapes: they look like 2-D shapes, yet they behave like lines, dynamic connectors, and other one-dimensional shapes. The result of the 2-D/1-D combination for rack diagrams is a set of shapes that look like the physical equipment they represent, but can be glued to precise locations on the edges of a rack.

Figure 7-9 *Dragging equipment into a rack activates glue at connection points that are spaced at 1 U intervals*

> ✅ **TIP** The gray squares representing connection points on both edges of the rack are located precisely at 1 U intervals, allowing U-sized shapes to be positioned in exactly the same way as their real-world counterparts.

Many rack shapes, like the Server shape shown in both parts of Figure 7-10, are adjustable. When you drag a server into a rack, its default height is 8 U, as shown on the left side of the figure. However, because the server exhibits two-dimensional properties and resize handles, you can change its height, as shown on the right. The intent of the shape's design is to let your network diagram mimic the real world as closely as possible.

> **TIP** While you drag the resize handle on a server shape like the one in Figure 7-10, the appearance of the shape changes. At 7 U, 6 U, and 5 U, the lower half of the shape remains unchanged and the upper half of the shape gets smaller. However, at 4 U and below, the lower part of the shape begins to adjust too. Even a seemingly simple Visio shape can have reasonably sophisticated behavior.

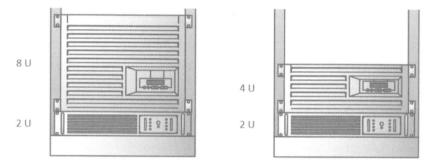

Figure 7-10 *A rack-mounted server shape changes appearance as you adjust its height*

Figure 7-11 shows what a completed rack might look like. On the left side of the figure, the U dimensions of all shapes are visible. On the right, display of the dimensions has been disabled.

> **TIP** The Show U Size and Hide U Size commands affect all shapes on the page.

Each rack in Figure 7-11 contains five servers and a router, which is the same equipment configuration in the datacenter portion of the stylized network diagram in Figure 7-5. Many network administrators include both views in their network maps. They also include a hyperlink on each server in the high-level view that leads to that server's location in the rack diagram, making it easy for map users to view any level of detail they want. You will explore using hyperlinks to add "drill-down" capabilities like this to your Visio diagrams in Chapter 11, "Add and use hyperlinks."

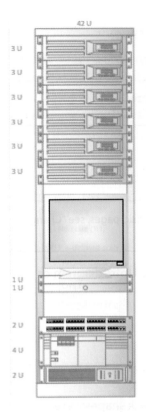

Figure 7-11 *The U height of rack components can be visible or hidden*

To create a rack diagram

1. Drag a **Rack** or **Cabinet** shape onto the page.

2. Drag shapes from the **Rack-mounted Equipment** and **Free-standing Rack Equipment** stencils onto the page, and then glue them to the rack.

To show or hide the U height for racks and rack-mounted equipment shapes

1. Right-click the rack or a shape in a rack, and then do either of the following:

   - Click **Show U sizes**.

   - Click **Hide U sizes**.

Notice that the lower-left corner of the Drawing Scale tab shows the size of the drawing page expressed in measurement units at the current page scale. In Figure 7-13, the custom scale, when used on 11-by-8.5-inch printer paper (refer to the dimensions under the thumbnail image on the right side of the dialog box), represents a real-world space that is 8' 9.6" by 6' 9.6".

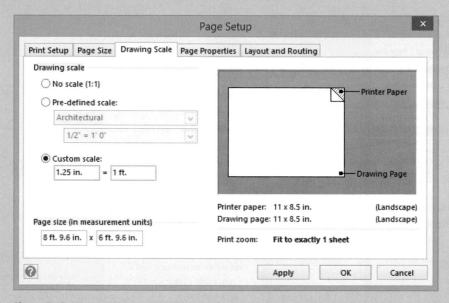

Figure 7-13 *You can create a Custom Scale for your diagram*

TIP Unscaled drawings use the No Scale (1:1) option at the top of the dialog box shown in Figure 7-13.

Change the drawing scale

A real-world scenario: You've created a rack diagram that includes three racks, and you need to add several more. However, there isn't room to fit another rack onto the drawing page. Are you forced to start over with a new diagram? The answer is no, because scaled drawings easily accommodate this type of change. You simply adjust the scaling factor, and Visio does the rest.

For example, if you have the drawing shown in Figure 7-14 and you want to add three more racks, it's clear that you need more space on the page. The Drawing Scale tab in the Page Setup dialog box indicates that the scale in this metric drawing is currently 1:10.

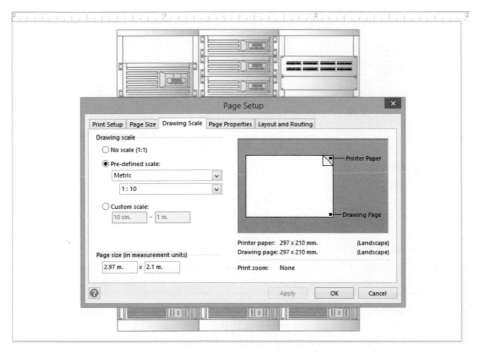

Figure 7-14 *Three full-height racks fit comfortably on an A4-sized page when the Metric scale is set to 1:10*

Doubling the scale to 1:20 produces the result shown in Figure 7-15. Clearly, you have more space to work with but it might be more than you need. In addition, at this scale, each rack is rather small.

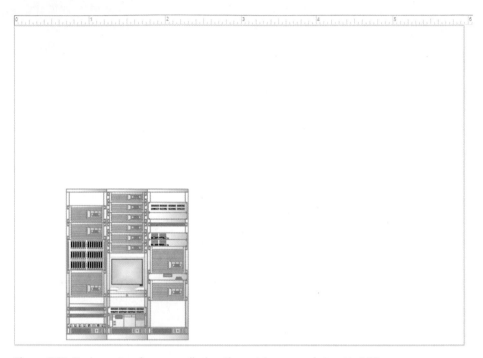

Figure 7-15 *Equipment racks are small when the metric page scale is set to 1:20*

The list of predefined scales does not include an entry between 1:10 and 1:20, but you can create a custom scale of 1:15 that results in what's shown in Figure 7-16.

> ✓ **TIP** The screen shots in Figure 7-14 through Figure 7-16 include the ruler at the top of the drawing page. You can confirm that changing the scale from 1:10 to 1:20 doubled the available space by noticing that the amount of wall space represented by each diagram changed from 3 meters to 6 meters. Similarly, 1:15 yields a wall measurement that is halfway in between.

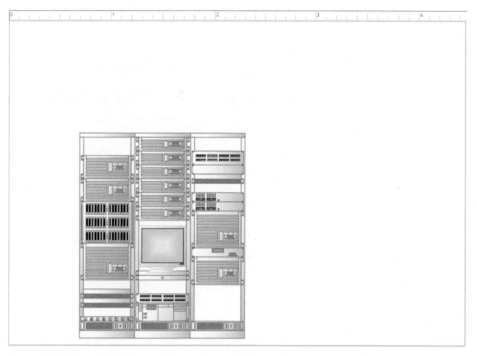

Figure 7-16 *The scale factor for this page is suitable for the three existing equipment racks and provides additional room for more*

> ⚠ **IMPORTANT** Although this topic describes how to adjust the scale factors for a rack diagram, you can use the steps in these procedures to adjust the scale in any scaled drawing.

To display the Drawing Scale tab of the Page Setup dialog box

1. Right-click a page name tab, and then click **Drawing Scale**.

To change the drawing scale for an Architectural diagram

1. Display the **Drawing Scale** tab.

2. Click **Pre-defined scale**, click the arrow, and then click **Architectural**.

3. Click the scale factor arrow, and then click a factor from **3/32" = 1′ 0″** to **1′ = 1′ 0″**.

   Or

   Click **Custom Scale**, and then enter numbers, with or without unit abbreviations, into the boxes on either side of the equal (=) sign.

To change the drawing scale for a Civil Engineering diagram

1. Display the **Drawing Scale** tab.

2. Click **Pre-defined scale**, click the arrow, and then click **Civil Engineering**.

3. Click the scale factor arrow, and then click a factor from **1" = 1"** to **1" = 100' 0"**.

   Or

   Click **Custom Scale**, and then enter numbers, with or without unit abbreviations, into the boxes on either side of the equal (=) sign.

To change the drawing scale for a Metric diagram

1. Display the **Drawing Scale** tab.

2. Click **Pre-defined scale**, click the arrow, and then click **Metric**.

3. Click the scale factor arrow, and then click a factor from **1:1000** to **50:1**.

   Or

   Click **Custom Scale**, and then enter numbers, with or without unit abbreviations, into the boxes on either side of the equal (=) sign.

To change the drawing scale for a Mechanical Engineering diagram

1. Display the **Drawing Scale** tab.

2. Click **Pre-defined scale**, click the arrow, and then click **Mechanical Engineering**.

3. Click the scale factor arrow, and then click a factor from **1/32:1** to **10:1**.

   Or

   Click **Custom Scale**, and then enter numbers, with or without unit abbreviations, into the boxes on either side of the equal (=) sign.

To change the drawing to unscaled

1. Display the **Drawing Scale** tab, and then click **No scale (1:1)**.

Enhance your network diagrams

What can you do to further enhance a network drawing or rack diagram like those you've explored throughout this chapter? Consider these ideas:

- Use data linking (Chapter 10, "Link to external data") to link the equipment in your diagram to a worksheet or database containing asset IDs, serial numbers, and other inventory information.

- Link your equipment to a real-time or near-real-time data source and employ data graphics (Chapter 9, "Visualize your data") so the equipment shows live status information.

- Add a patch panel and network cabling. Consider putting the cabling on a separate layer (Chapter 3, "Manage text, shapes, and pages") so you can easily show or hide it.

- Add data to each rack shape so their locations and other key data are part of your network inventory reports.

- Add hyperlinks (Chapter 11, "Add and use hyperlinks") to a rack and/or the equipment in a rack and link to photographs of the actual wiring closet or equipment.

- Publish your diagrams to the web (Chapter 12, "Print, reuse, and share diagrams") or to Microsoft SharePoint (Chapter 15, "Collaborate and publish diagrams") so users without Visio can view and even collaborate with you on the diagrams.

7

Run computer and network reports

You will explore the many uses of shape data in the next chapter, including the capability to run reports that summarize key data attributes of the shapes on a drawing page.

As a preview, this topic displays three of the predefined reports that are included with Visio 2016 network diagrams. For example, Figure 7-17 shows data about network devices.

	A	B	C	D	E	F	G	H	I
1				Network Device					
2	Displayed Text	Network Name	IP Address	Subnet Mask	MAC Address	Network Description			
3	Branch Office 1	Branch_1				Branch Office 1 :LAN			
4	Branch Office 2	Branch_2				Branch Office 2 :LAN			
5		Branch_2	10.0.12.11			Ethernet LAN			
6		Branch_2	10.0.12.12			Ethernet LAN			
7		Branch_2	10.0.12.13			Ethernet LAN			
8		Branch_2	10.0.12.14			Ethernet LAN			
9		Branch_2	10.0.12.15			Ethernet LAN			
10		Branch_2	10.0.12.16			Ethernet LAN			
11		Corporate	10.0.5.1			WAN			
12		Branch_1	10.0.5.101			Ethernet LAN			
13		Branch_1	10.0.5.102			Ethernet LAN			
14		Branch_1	10.0.5.103			Ethernet LAN			
15		Branch_1	10.0.5.104			Ethernet LAN			
16		Branch_1	10.0.5.105			Ethernet LAN			

Figure 7-17 *The Network Device report is included with the network templates*

If you need additional data about the equipment in your network, the report in Figure 7-18 should provide what you need.

 TIP Only part of the Network Equipment report is shown in Figure 7-18; additional fields exist to the right of the Product Description column.

	A	B	C	D	E	F	G	H
1							Network Equipment	
2	Building	Room	Displayed Text	Network Name	Network Description	IP Address	Manufacturer	Product Description
3				Corporate	WAN	10.0.5.1	A. Datum Corporation	Router
4	Coolidge	476		Branch_2	Ethernet LAN	10.0.12.15	A. Datum Corporation	Laptop
5	Coolidge	478		Branch_2	Ethernet LAN	10.0.12.14	Contoso, Ltd	Laptop
6	Coolidge	544		Branch_2	Ethernet LAN	10.0.12.16	Contoso, Ltd	PC
7	East Atwater	216		Branch_1	Ethernet LAN	10.0.5.104	Contoso, Ltd	PC
8	East Atwater	311		Branch_1	Ethernet LAN	10.0.5.105	A. Datum Corporation	Laptop
9	Fillmore	111		Branch_2	Ethernet LAN	10.0.12.11	A. Datum Corporation	Printer
10	Fillmore	267		Branch_2	Ethernet LAN	10.0.12.13	Contoso, Ltd	Laptop
11	Fillmore	298		Branch_2	Ethernet LAN	10.0.12.12	A. Datum Corporation	PC
12	Fillmore	G40	Branch Office 2	Branch_2	Branch Office 2 :LAN			
13	West Atwater	103		Branch_1	Ethernet LAN	10.0.5.101	Contoso, Ltd	Server
14	West Atwater	103		Branch_1	Ethernet LAN	10.0.5.102	A. Datum Corporation	Printer
15	West Atwater	215		Branch_1	Ethernet LAN	10.0.5.103	Contoso, Ltd	PC
16	West Atwater	316	Branch Office 1	Branch_1	Branch Office 1 :LAN			

Figure 7-18 *The Network Equipment report provides extensive detail on network and computer equipment*

Visio provides the report shown in Figure 7-19 for those times when you need data about PCs rather than network equipment.

> ⚠️ **IMPORTANT** The PC Report shown in Figure 7-19 runs correctly with the network shapes in the Basic Network Diagram – 3D and Detailed Network Diagram – 3D templates. However, the new shapes in the Visio 2016 Basic Network Diagram and Detailed Network Diagram templates contain an error that prevents the PC Report from running. As a workaround, the author has posted a modified PC Report definition on his website at *www.visiostepbystep.com/downloads/2016/Visio_2016_Modified_PC_Report.vrd*.

	A	B	C	D	E	F	G	H	I
1				**PC Report**					
2	*Displayed Text*	*Network Name*	*Network Description*	*Operating System*	*Memory*	*CPU*	*Hard Drive Capacity*		
3		Branch_1	Ethernet LAN	Windows XP	2 GB		360 GB		
4		Branch_1	Ethernet LAN	Windows 7	3 GB		250 GB		
5		Branch_1	Ethernet LAN	Windows 7	2 GB		360 GB		
6		Branch_2	Ethernet LAN	Windows 7	4 GB		500 GB		
7		Branch_2	Ethernet LAN	Windows 7	6 GB		1 TB		
8		Branch_2	Ethernet LAN	Windows XP	2 GB		180 GB		
9		Branch_2	Ethernet LAN	Windows XP	3 GB		250 GB		
10		Branch_2	Ethernet LAN	Windows 7	2 GB		500 GB		

Figure 7-19 *The PC Report*

Skills review

In this chapter, you learned how to:

- Build basic network diagrams
- Build detailed network diagrams
- Use 3-D equipment shapes
- Create rack diagrams
- Change the drawing scale
- Run computer and network reports

Practice tasks

The practice files for these tasks are located in the Visio2016SBS\Ch07 folder. You can save the results of the tasks in the same folder.

Build basic network diagrams

Start Visio, click the Network template category thumbnail, double-click the Basic Network Diagram template, and then perform the following tasks:

1. Drag an **Ethernet** shape to the page, and then extend it so it occupies about two-thirds of the page width.

2. Drag six or eight shapes from the **Computers and Monitors** and **Network and Peripherals** stencils onto the page, and then glue them to the network.

3. Click the **Ethernet** shape and label it Branch Office Network.

Build detailed network diagrams

 IMPORTANT The tasks in this topic can be completed only by using the Professional edition of Visio 2016.

Start Visio, click the Network template category thumbnail, double-click the Detailed Network Diagram template, and then perform the following tasks:

1. Drag shapes from various network and computer stencils onto the page.

2. Link network shapes to each other to represent the connectivity of your network.

3. If you are using 2-D shapes, select a theme and variant.

Use 3-D equipment shapes

There are no practice tasks for this topic.

Create rack diagrams

 IMPORTANT The tasks in this topic can be completed only by using the Professional edition of Visio 2016.

Start Visio, click the Network template category thumbnail, double-click the Rack Diagram template, and then perform the following tasks:

1. Build a rack that contains server shapes and other rack-mounted equipment shapes.

2. Adjust the height of one or more server shapes.

3. Turn off the display of U height for the page.

 TIP You will work with a different diagram in the remaining steps of this task.

4. Open the **CreateRacks** diagram.

5. Add a rack diagram page to the existing network diagram and set a scale that is appropriate for this U.S. Units diagram.

6. On the new page, build a rack that represents the equipment in the **Data Center** network on the left side of the page.

Change the drawing scale

Open the ChangeDrawingScale diagram in Visio, and then perform the following tasks:

1. Change the drawing scale to **1:20** for this Metric diagram.

2. Experiment with other scale factors to see the effect on the diagram.

Run computer and network reports

There are no practice tasks for this topic.

Part 2

Add data to your diagrams

Work with shape data

8

You can use many diagramming apps to create useful and attractive drawings. The place where most apps fall short, however, is where Visio excels: in addition to putting shapes on a page, you can store data in the shapes. You can then use that data for many purposes, including affecting the behavior and appearance of almost any aspect of the diagram. A data-driven Visio diagram becomes a powerful tool for communicating ideas and facts by displaying and reacting to data values.

All three chapters in Part 2 of this book focus on data. This chapter covers the basics of viewing and working with data. Chapter 9, "Visualize your data," explores techniques for building dynamic dashboards by using icons and graphics to represent your data values. In Chapter 10, "Link to external data," you will discover how easy it is to connect a diagram to a database or other external data source.

This chapter guides you through procedures related to viewing and editing shape data; viewing, changing, and defining shape data fields and attributes; inserting fields; and creating, editing, and running reports.

In this chapter

- Understand shape data
- View shape data
- Edit shape data
- Modify shape data field attributes
- Define shape data fields
- Insert fields
- Run predefined reports
- Create or modify reports

Practice files

For this chapter, use the practice files from the Visio2016SBS\Ch08 folder. For practice file download instructions, see the introduction.

Understand shape data

The data fields that any Visio shape can contain are referred to collectively as shape data. Some shape data fields merely store data for subsequent reporting or display. The values in other data fields control the appearance or behavior of shapes and can serve many other purposes.

The following list describes what can be stored in each of the eight shape data field types in Visio 2016 and how users enter data values.

- **String** Free-form text; users enter any characters.

- **Number** Any numeric data; users enter numbers.

- **Fixed List** A list from which users must make a selection.

- **Variable List** A list from which users can make a selection; in addition, users can add values to the list by entering them in the data field.

- **Duration** A time value expressed in one of five time units supported by Visio: seconds (es.), minutes (em.), hours (eh.), days (ed.), weeks (ew.); users enter a number followed by one of these time unit abbreviations.

- **Date** Calendar date; users can either enter a date or select a date from a calendar.

- **Currency** Monetary value expressed in currency units that are based on the user's region and language settings in Windows; users enter numbers.

- **Boolean** *True* or *False*; users select a value from a list.

 TIP The data fields that are called *shape data* in Visio 2016 were called custom properties in Visio 2003 and earlier.

TIP Although this chapter focuses on data fields that are contained in shapes, it's useful to know that pages and even the Visio document itself can contain shape data fields. Although the average Visio user isn't likely to take advantage of this capability directly, developers of Visio add-ins frequently store data in some combination of shapes, pages, and the document.

View shape data

The primary means for viewing shape data is the Shape Data window. You can position the Shape Data window so it floats in any location over the drawing page, as is the case in Figure 8-1, and you can resize the window to show as many or as few fields as you need.

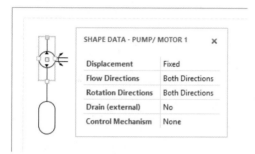

Figure 8-1 *Data from a representative shape, a Pump/Motor 1, floating over the drawing page*

> **TIP** The master for the Pump/Motor 1 shape is located in the Fluid Power – Equipment stencil that opens when you select the Fluid Power template in the Engineering template category. The Fluid Power template is included only with the Professional edition of Visio.

You can also dock the window in a fixed position by dragging it to any edge of the drawing window. When the window is docked, you can use the pushpin button in the window header to turn AutoHide on or off, as shown in Figure 8-2. If you turn Auto-Hide on, the window "rolls up" into the header when you're not using it.

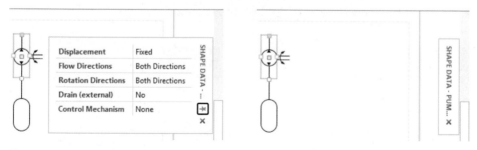

Figure 8-2 *A docked Shape Data window is open on the left and hidden on the right*

Data is so integral in Visio that the shapes in most stencils include predefined data fields. This is true for many of the shapes used in previous chapters. For example:

■ In Chapter 4, "Create business process diagrams," you worked with flowchart shapes in both flowcharts and swimlane diagrams. That chapter didn't discuss the data inside the shapes; however, all of the standard flowchart shapes include the set of predefined data fields shown in Figure 8-3.

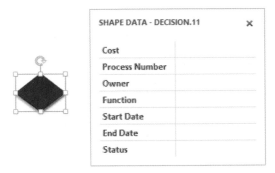

Figure 8-3 *Shape data fields in a decision diamond flowchart shape*

■ The org chart shapes that you worked with in Chapter 5, "Create organization charts," also contain a set of predefined data fields, as shown on the left in Figure 8-4. In addition, you can import custom fields when you run the Organization Chart Wizard. The results of a Wizard import are shown on the right. As you can see, the import accomplished three things:

• It replaced data in existing fields.

• It created new fields and added data to them.

• It generated new fields even though they contain no data.

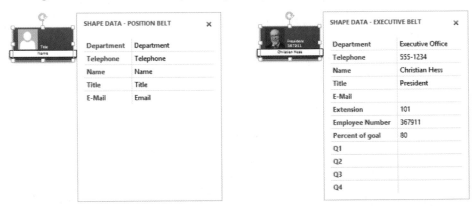

Figure 8-4 *Default and customized org chart shape data fields*

> ✅ **TIP** It might seem odd at first that the org chart shape data fields on the left in Figure 8-4 contain text values that match the field names. Those text values are present because the org chart shapes were designed to display the contents of certain data fields. By including the field names as text values, the designers of the org chart shapes convey to you at a glance what will appear on the shape when you enter real data.

- The network shapes in Chapter 7, "Create network and datacenter diagrams," also include shape data. The default data fields vary depending on what piece of equipment a shape represents. Figure 8-5 shows the fields for a router.

Figure 8-5 *Computer and network shape data fields*

- The Business Process Model and Notation (BPMN) shapes you explored in Chapter 4, "Create business process diagrams," include a variety of shape data fields, as shown in Figure 8-11 later in this chapter.

Another way to view shape data

Some Visio shapes, especially older shapes, provide an alternative method for viewing shape data. When you right-click some shapes, the shortcut menu displays a Properties option. For certain shapes, clicking Properties opens the same Shape Data window as the Data submenu technique. However, for other shapes, it opens the Shape Data dialog box instead. Although the dialog box and the window look a bit different, you can view and edit data in either.

TIP When it is present, the Properties entry is usually at the bottom of the shortcut menu.

For example, the Shape Data dialog box for the Fluid Power Pump/Motor 1 shape shown in Figure 8-6 was opened by clicking Properties on the shortcut menu; compare it with the corresponding Shape Data window in Figure 8-1.

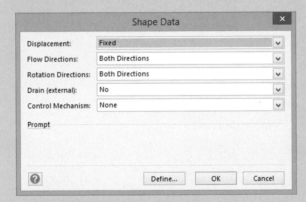

Figure 8-6 *The Shape Data dialog box*

IMPORTANT The Shape Data dialog box is limited to displaying 20 shape data fields. The Shape Data window does not have this limitation and will display scroll bars whenever there are fields that do not fit in the window at its current height.

To open the Shape Data window

1. Right-click a shape, point to **Data**, and then click **Shape Data**.

Or

1. (Professional edition only) On the **Data** tab, in the **Show/Hide** group, select the **Shape Data Window** check box.

To position the Shape Data window over the drawing page

1. Drag the header of the **Shape Data** window until the window is away from the edge of the drawing window.

To dock the Shape Data window

1. Do either of the following:

   - Drag the header of the **Shape Data** window until it is near an edge of the drawing window to dock it within the drawing window.

   - Drag the header of the **Shape Data** window past an edge of the drawing window to dock it as a separate window.

To close the Shape Data window

1. Do any of the following:

   - Click the **Close** button (**X**) in the corner of the **Shape Data** window.

   - Right-click anywhere inside the **Shape Data** window, and then click **Close**.

   - (Professional edition only) On the **Data** tab, in the **Show/Hide** group, clear the **Shape Data Window** check box.

8

To enter data in a text field

1. Do any of the following:

    - **String** Click in the field and enter any characters you want.

    - **Number** Click in the field and enter numbers only.

    - **Fixed List** Click the arrow at the right end of the field, and then select a value.

    - **Variable List** Do either of the following:

        - Click the arrow, and then select a value.

        - Enter a value.

    - **Duration** Enter a number followed by one of the five time unit abbreviations: es., em., eh., ed., ew.

    - **Date** Do either of the following:

        - Click in the field and enter a valid date according to regional date format rules.

        - Click the arrow, and then click the date you want from the calendar.

    - **Currency** Enter a number with or without a currency separator.

    - **Boolean** Click the arrow, and then click **True** or **False**.

To exit a field in the Shape Data window after entering data

1. Do one of the following:

    - Press **Tab**.

    - Press **Enter**.

    - Click anywhere outside the field.

Modify shape data field attributes

You can examine and change the attributes of existing shape data fields or create new shape data fields by using the Define Shape Data dialog box.

View shape data field attributes

The Define Shape Data dialog box shown on the left in Figure 8-12 appears for most Visio users. The one on the right appears if you are running Visio in developer mode, and offers several additional options.

 SEE ALSO For information about developer mode, refer to Appendix A, "Look behind the curtain."

8

Figure 8-12 *The options available in the Define Shape Data dialog box depend on how it's accessed*

In both variations of the dialog box, each data field has the following attributes:

- **Label** Field name
- **Type** One of the eight types described in "Understand shape data" earlier in the chapter
- **Format** Determines how data entered by the user is presented (different field types have different format options)

- **Value** The data value entered when a shape is defined or that is entered by the user

- **Prompt** A ScreenTip that appears when the user points to the shape's name in the Shape Data window

When you operate in developer mode, Visio displays the additional attributes described in the following list. Although some of them are primarily for use by programmers or Visio solution developers, one or two might be of value to power users.

- **Name** This is an internal name used by Visio developers; it can be the same as Label except that you cannot use spaces or most special characters in the Name field (underscore characters are acceptable).

- **Sort key** Visio uses the alphanumeric value in this field to determine the sequence in which fields will be presented in the Shape Data window.

> ⚠ **IMPORTANT** Visio treats the contents of the Sort Key field as text even if you enter a number, which means that it arranges fields based on alphabetic sequence rather than numeric sequence. For example, if field A has a sort key of 1, field B has a sort key of 2, and field C has a sort key of 10, Visio will place them in the Shape Data window in the sequence A, C, B, because the first character "1" in field C is less than the "2" in field B.

- **Add on drop** If selected, Visio opens the Shape Data dialog box whenever the user either drags a shape containing this field onto a page, or duplicates an existing shape containing this field.

- **Hidden** If selected, Visio hides this field; that is, the field does not appear in either the Shape Data window or the Shape Data dialog box. A Visio solution developer might set the value of the hidden attribute by using a formula based on other data values, thereby showing or hiding a field under different conditions.

> ✓ **TIP** As with the Shape Data window, you can create, edit, or delete shape data fields for more than one shape at a time. When you select multiple shapes before opening the Define Shape Data window, the changes you make are applied to *all* selected shapes. This feature also can be very powerful or very destructive.

To open the Define Shape Data dialog box

1. Do one of the following:

   - Right-click a shape, point to **Data**, and then click **Define Shape Data**.

   - Right-click in the **Shape Data** window, and then click **Define Shape Data**.

To view the attributes of a different shape data field

1. In the lower portion of the **Define Shape Data** dialog box, scroll up or down to the field you want, and then click the field name.

To close the Define Shape Data dialog box

1. Do any of the following:

   - Click **OK**.

   - Click **Cancel**.

   - Click the **Close** button in the upper-right corner of the dialog box.

8

Change shape data field attributes

To truly appreciate the power and flexibility of the data features in Visio, it's helpful to know how to change the attributes of existing data fields and how to create new data fields. You will explore the former in this section and the latter in the following topic.

You can change nearly any property of a field by using the Define Shape Data dialog box that was described in the preceding section. For example, for the Currency field shown in Figure 8-13, you can change the display format for the currency value by selecting an entry from the list. The available choices in the Format list depend on the country and region settings for your edition of Windows.

 TIP For Currency fields, it often makes sense to leave the format set to System Setting, the default, so Visio uses the currency format setting from Windows.

Entering characters in the Value box causes your entry to appear as the default value the next time you open the Shape Data window. You can always change the value by using the Shape Data window, but entering a value here sets the default.

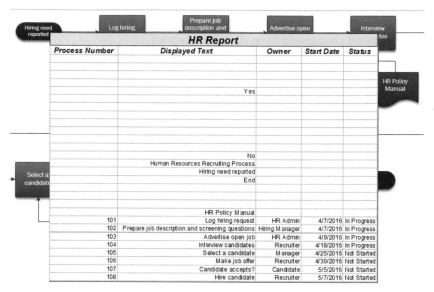

Process Number	Displayed Text	Owner	Start Date	Status
	Yes			
	No			
	Human Resources Recruiting Process			
	Hiring need reported			
	End			
	HR Policy Manual			
101	Log hiring request	HR Admin	4/7/2016	In Progress
102	Prepare job description and screening questions	Hiring Manager	4/7/2016	In Progress
103	Advertise open job	HR Admin	4/9/2016	In Progress
104	Interview candidates	Recruiter	4/18/2016	In Progress
105	Select a candidate	Manager	4/25/2016	Not Started
106	Make job offer	Recruiter	4/30/2016	Not Started
107	Candidate accepts?	Candidate	5/5/2016	Not Started
108	Hire candidate	Recruiter	5/7/2016	Not Started

Figure 8-25 *A report with multiple blank rows because of insufficient selection criteria*

Using the same process map as an example, the setting in the Advanced dialog box shown in Figure 8-26 causes shapes to be included only if the Process Number field exists and contains a value greater than zero.

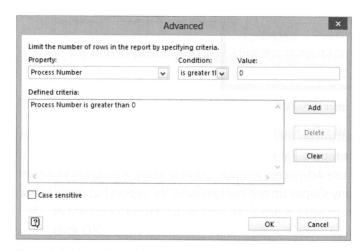

Figure 8-26 *The Advanced criteria selection dialog box*

The result of the additional selection criteria is shown in Figure 8-27.

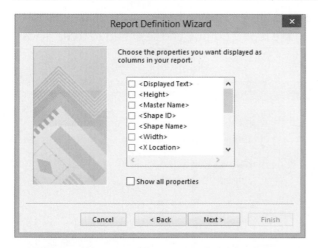

Process Number	Displayed Text	Owner	Start Date	Status
101	Log hiring request	HR Admin	4/7/2016	In Progress
102	Prepare job description and screening questions	Hiring Manager	4/7/2016	In Progress
103	Advertise open job	HR Admin	4/9/2016	In Progress
104	Interview candidates	Recruiter	4/18/2016	In Progress
105	Select a candidate	Manager	4/25/2016	Not Started
106	Make job offer	Recruiter	4/30/2016	Not Started
107	Candidate accepts?	Candidate	5/5/2016	Not Started
108	Hire candidate	Recruiter	5/7/2016	Not Started

Figure 8-27 *A more concise HR Report as a result of using advanced selection criteria*

You use the second page of the Report Definition Wizard to select specific properties for display in your report. The list of available properties includes shape data fields, in addition to many other shape properties. You can see a portion of the list of properties in Figure 8-28.

 TIP Each property you select is displayed in a separate column in the report.

8

Report Definition Wizard

Choose the properties you want displayed as columns in your report.

- [ ] <Displayed Text>
- [ ] <Height>
- [ ] <Master Name>
- [ ] <Shape ID>
- [ ] <Shape Name>
- [ ] <Width>
- [ ] <X Location>

[ ] Show all properties

Cancel | < Back | Next > | Finish

Figure 8-28 *The field selection page of the Report Definition Wizard*

If you are looking for less frequently used properties to include in your report, you can select the Show All Properties check box at the bottom of the page.

On the third page of the wizard, shown in Figure 8-29, you enter the title that will appear at the top of your report, and you can set options for totaling and grouping, sorting, and formatting.

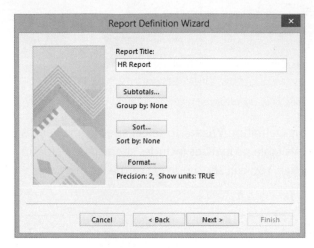

Figure 8-29 *The third page of the Report Definition Wizard*

For example, if you click Sort, you can use the Sort dialog box (shown in Figure 8-30) to change the sequence of columns in the report output, and select up to three fields on which to sort.

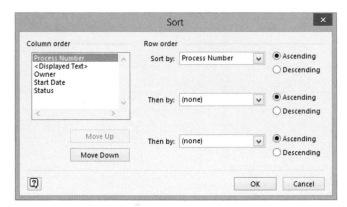

Figure 8-30 *Column sequence and sort selection dialog box*

On the final page of the wizard, shown in Figure 8-31, you enter a name for the report definition, optionally enter a description, and then indicate where you would like to store the report definition. You can save the report definition in the current Visio drawing, which is the default, or you can save it to an external file.

Figure 8-31 *The final page of the Report Definition Wizard*

> ✓ **TIP** Save the report definition to an external file if you think you'll want to use it with multiple drawings. If you do, you can retrieve the report definition by clicking the Browse button in the Reports dialog box shown in Figure 8-32.

8

When you finish defining your report, the name you assigned on the last wizard page appears the next time you open the Reports dialog box. Figure 8-32 shows an example.

Figure 8-32 *The Reports dialog box showing the Custom HR Report*

To create a report definition

1. On the **Review** tab, in the **Reports** group, click the **Shape Reports** button.

2. In the **Reports** dialog box, click the **New** button.

3. Provide the required information on the pages of the **Report Definition Wizard**.

To modify an existing report definition.

1. Open the **Reports** dialog box, click the name of the report you want to edit, and then click the **Modify** button.

2. Make the required changes on the pages of the **Report Definition Wizard**.

Skills review

In this chapter, you learned how to:

- Understand shape data

- View shape data

- Edit shape data

- Modify shape data field attributes

- Define shape data fields

- Insert fields

- Run predefined reports

- Create or modify reports

Practice tasks

The practice files for these tasks are located in the Visio2016SBS\Ch08 folder. You can save the results of the tasks in the same folder.

Understand shape data

There are no practice tasks for this topic.

View shape data

Start Visio, click the Network template category thumbnail, double-click the Basic Network Diagram template, and then perform the following tasks:

1. Drag a **Server** shape onto the drawing page.

2. Open the **Shape Data** window.

3. Drag a **Router** shape onto the page, and then compare its shape data fields with those of the server.

4. Create diagrams from several other templates, and then examine the shape data fields in various shapes.

Edit shape data

Open the EditShapeData diagram in Visio, and then perform the following tasks:

1. Open the **Shape Data** window and dock it on either side of the drawing window.

2. Select the **Log hiring request** shape.

3. Enter a number in both the **Cost** and **Process Number** fields.

4. Enter text in the **Start Date** field, and then exit the field. Notice the error message.

5. Click **OK** to clear the error message.

6. Enter a valid date in the **Start Date** field or use the calendar to select a date.

7. Change the **Status** from **In Progress** to **Deferred**.

Modify shape data field attributes

Open the ModifyDataAttributes diagram in Visio, and then perform the following tasks:

1. Select the **Advertise open job** and **Interview candidate** shapes, and then open the **Define Shape Data** dialog box.

2. Select the **Cost** field, and then choose a different display format.

3. Select the **Status** field, and then in the **Prompt** property box, enter Select a status for this task.

4. In the **Format** property box, add ;Waiting Approval at the very end of the text that is already in the box. (Be sure to include the semicolon.)

5. Click **OK** to close the **Define Shape Data** dialog box.

6. Open the **Shape Data** window to verify that the changes you've made have been applied to both of the selected shapes but not to any other shapes.

Define shape data fields

There are no practice tasks for this topic.

Insert fields

Open the InsertFields diagram in Visio, and then perform the following tasks:

1. Select both the server and printer shapes.

2. Insert the shape data field named **Network Name**. A network name should appear below both shapes.

3. Add a text box or rectangle to the page, and then insert the document author's name.

Run predefined reports

Open the RunReports diagram in Visio, and then perform the following tasks:

1. Run the **Inventory** report by using **Excel** output.

2. Run the **Space Report** by using **HTML** output.

3. Run the **Window Schedule** report by using **Visio shape** output.

4. Change the dimensions of several windows in the floor plan, and then rerun the report.

5. Browse to the **Vegetation Report** located in the Visio2016SBS\Ch08 folder, and run it using any output format you want.

6. Open any Visio diagram you previously recreated, and then run one or more of the built-in reports it contains.

Create or modify reports

Open the CreateModifyReports diagram in Visio, and then perform the following tasks:

1. Create a report that includes three columns, in this order:

   - **Product Description**

   - **Manufacturer**

   - **Asset Number**

2. Save the report definition in the drawing.

3. Run the new report.

4. Modify the report you just created to sort the output by Manufacturer.

5. Modify the built-in **Network Equipment** report to make two changes:

   - Delete the **Part Number** and **Serial Number** columns.

   - Sort the report by **Network Name**, and then **Product Description**.

6. Save the modified report in a file.

7. Run the modified report.

Visualize your data

In Chapter 8, "Work with shape data," you viewed and reported on data stored in Visio shapes. Although those techniques are useful in many circumstances, Visio provides an even more effective way to take advantage of data: you can create data graphics that enhance shapes by adding text callouts and icons based on the data contained in the shapes. Even better, data graphics are dynamic, so when the data in a shape changes, Visio refreshes the graphics automatically.

In the next chapter, you will take data graphics to another level by visualizing data stored in an external location. In this chapter, you will work with data graphics by using data that is stored in the diagram and discover the amazing ways you can visualize data by using Visio 2016.

 IMPORTANT The information in this chapter applies only to the Professional edition of Visio 2016.

This chapter guides you through procedures related to enhancing diagram effectiveness, creating and applying data graphics, editing data graphics, and creating data graphic legends.

In this chapter

- Enhance diagram effectiveness
- Create data graphics
- Apply data graphics
- Edit data graphics
- Create data graphic legends

Practice files

For this chapter, use the practice files from the Visio2016SBS\Ch09 folder. For practice file download instructions, see the introduction.

Enhance diagram effectiveness

A person using a Visio diagram that you created can learn a lot about the subject of the diagram based on your choice of shapes, their positions on the page, the way they are connected, and many additional visual cues. The five sections in this topic demonstrate the power of data visualization to tell even more of the story.

View network and datacenter performance

Chapter 7, "Create network and datacenter diagrams" contains several hints about the data available in computer, network, and rack diagram shapes. This section explores techniques you can use to capitalize on the data that is included in the Visio network shapes.

The diagrams in this section might be used in a scenario such as the following:

- You are a datacenter manager and have created rack diagrams for each rack in your computer room.

- You've populated your diagrams with data.

- Each rack-mounted server includes the data fields shown in Figure 9-1. (The values shown in this figure will be visualized in the next two figures.)

SHAPE DATA - SERVER		✕
Height in U's	2	
Height	3.5 in.	
Location	Row 1 Rack 2	
Manufacturer	Contoso, Ltd.	
Product Description	database server	
Network Name	sql-sales-01	
IP Address	10.0.1.51	
Operating System	Windows Server 2016	
CPU (MHz)	3	
Memory (MB)	2048	
Status	OK	
Administrator	Anna Misiec	

Figure 9-1 *Sample server data*

You can visualize data like that shown in Figure 9-1 by using Visio data graphics to turn an ordinary rack diagram into a powerful means to understand server attributes.

In Figure 9-2, several data graphics are applied to the servers in an equipment rack to highlight the following:

- Server name and type (left)

- Server status (center)

- CPU and memory configuration (right)

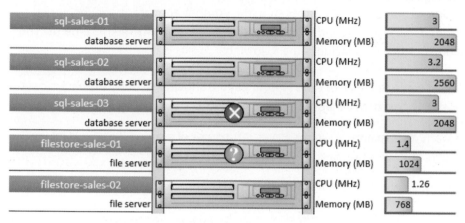

Figure 9-2 *A rack diagram showing server status and vital statistics*

Figure 9-3 shows the same equipment rack, but it uses different data graphics to highlight different information. In this version of the rack diagram, you find the following:

- Server name and IP address (left)

- Server status (center) shown by applying a fill color to the servers instead of attaching a status icon.

- Operating system name (right)

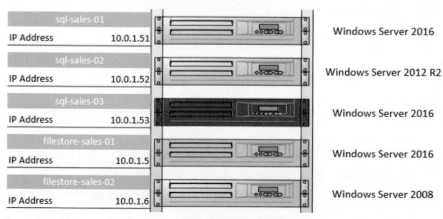

Figure 9-3 *Alternate visualizations provide different information*

Part of the appeal of data graphics is represented by these two examples—you can apply different graphics at different times depending on what you need to know.

Improve processes

In this example, data graphics are applied to process steps in a swimlane diagram for two reasons: to number each process step (the number appears above the upper-right corner of each shape), and to show several process quality measurements. The information in Figure 9-4 includes the following:

- The average duration of each step, in days, is shown in a progress bar across the bottom of each task shape.

- A warning icon appears in the lower-left corner of a shape if a step is taking 5 to 9 days or 10 or more days.

- The shape color indicates whether a step is improving or being investigated.

The symbolism used for each of these metrics is explained in the data graphic legend that appears in the upper-right corner of the page. You will learn more about legends in "Create data graphic legends" later in this chapter.

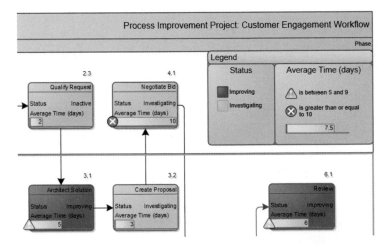

Figure 9-4 *A process diagram that displays data-driven graphics*

Manage casino operations

Figure 9-5 illustrates the types of near-real-time information that a casino manager might view in Visio, with a goal of monitoring critical operations. In all likelihood, your job doesn't involve managing a casino, but you can probably think of important operations that you do need to monitor.

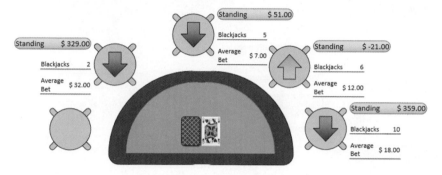

Figure 9-5 *A casino manager's view of a blackjack table*

In the graphic, text callouts highlight each bettor's recent history, including current dollar standing, average bet, and number of blackjacks. In addition, a red or green arrow represents how each player is trending.

> **TIP** The real-time nature of the graphics in this example are significantly enhanced when the diagram is linked to a live, external data source. You will explore this topic in Chapter 10, "Link to external data."

Manage employee performance

The organization chart in Figure 9-6 looks like those you explored in Chapter 5, "Create organization charts," with one notable exception: Trey Research has turned this org chart into more than just a picture of who reports to whom by including two key performance measures:

- Each employee's progress toward their annual training goal is depicted by an icon containing a combination of blue and gray squares.

- The three red manager shapes include a bar graph displaying quarterly performance numbers. Note that the bar graph is a single graphic item that contrasts data from four different shape data fields.

The legend in the upper-right corner of the page is automatically generated by Visio; however, you can customize the text and other aspects of the legend. In this example, the descriptions were customized and the font color was changed.

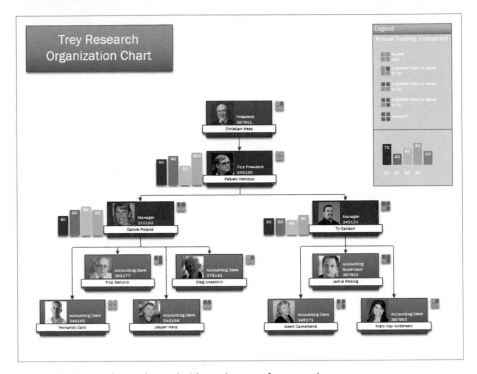

Figure 9-6 *An org chart enhanced with employee performance data*

> ✓ **TIP** You can apply only one data graphic to a shape at any given moment. However, as Figure 9-6 shows, one data graphic can contain multiple visual elements. In addition, you can apply different graphics to different shapes on the same page.

Assess risks

In the example shown in Figure 9-7, you are viewing part of a process map that was created by using a Visio add-in called TaskMap (*www.taskmap.com*).

This portion of the TaskMap shows three tasks in the middle of a sales proposal process, and data graphics depict the following two aspects of risk management:

- Yellow triangles and green diamonds identify risks and controls, respectively. The number in each risk triangle relates to an entry in a master list of risks. The number in each diamond identifies the control that the organization has put in place to mitigate the risk. (An organization might maintain the master list of risks and controls in something as simple as a worksheet, or they might employ a formal risk management system.)

  In a task like the one in the center, the organization has identified a risk but not a control, so the risk is more significant.

- The red arrows highlight tasks that exceed a defined time threshold—30 minutes in the case of this example.

Figure 9-7 also includes a third data graphic: two of the three tasks display a red diamond to indicate that they are decision points in the process.

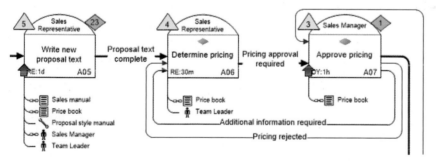

Figure 9-7 *A TaskMap process map used to convey risk and time threshold data*

> ✓ **TIP** If you would like to look at the full page from which Figure 9-7 was taken, open the RiskManagementTaskMap PDF in the Visio2016SBS\Ch09 folder. In addition, a web-published version of this TaskMap that includes hyperlinks to Microsoft Word and Excel documents is available at *www.visiostepbystep.com/downloads/2016 /RiskManagementTaskMap.htm*.

The examples in this section highlight the importance of the data behind a diagram and suggest a variety of creative ways you can add value to diagrams that contain data.

Create data graphics

In Chapter 10, "Link to external data," you will discover a simple technique for applying data graphics to shapes that are linked to data in an external file or database. However, linking to external data is not a requirement for using data graphics. Even if you've manually entered data into your shapes, you can still represent that data visually.

Each data graphic you create can contain one or more graphic items. Each graphic item is associated with a data field and presents data by using one of the following formats:

- **Callout** A formatted text box, sometimes accompanied by an icon, that is used to display text

> **TIP** In some places in the Visio user interface, the name of this category is shown as Text Callout or just Text.

- **Icon Set** A collection of up to five icons that are used to represent specific values or ranges of values

- **Data Bar** One of a set of progress bars, star ratings, pie charts, graphs, or other graphics used to represent numeric values

- **Color by Value** A technique for setting the color of a shape based on the value of a data field in the shape

You create and apply data graphics by using options on the Data tab. Portions of the Data tab—the Data Graphics gallery and several buttons—will be dimmed (unavailable) if you have not linked your diagram to external data; these portions are omitted from the images of the Data tab shown in Figure 9-8. However, the Advanced Data Graphics button on the right end of the tab is always available, and that's the button you use to create data graphics in an unlinked diagram.

Figure 9-8 *The Visio Professional Data tab*

Clicking the Advanced Data Graphics button opens the Data Graphics gallery, which includes a Create New Data Graphic button. The first step in creating a data graphic is to create a graphic item, and the first step in doing that is to select a data field.

The list of available data fields varies depending on which shapes are selected when you click the Create New Data Graphic button. If no shapes are selected, or if the selected shapes have one or more data fields in common, a list like the one shown in the upper half of Figure 9-9 is displayed. If a set of shapes with no common fields is selected, an abbreviated list such as the one shown in the lower half of Figure 9-9 is displayed.

In either case, you can use the More Fields entry shown in both parts of Figure 9-9 to create more sophisticated data graphics. For example, instead of creating a graphic based on a shape data field, you can create a graphic based on a document or page property, or based on a calculated result.

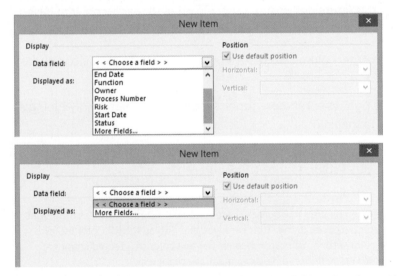

Figure 9-9 *New data graphics can be based on shape data fields or data that resides elsewhere in a diagram*

After selecting a data field, your next choice is which of the four graphic item types you want to use. The first three graphic types provide a list of choices, as shown from left to right in Figure 9-10 for the Text, Data Bar, and Icon Set lists.

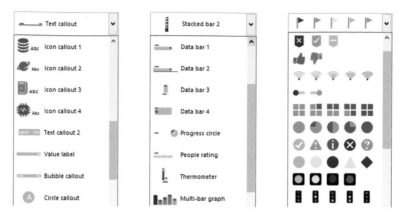

Figure 9-10 *Data graphics offer an impressive range of colorful choices for representing data*

Choosing an icon set requires you to specify which value, or range of values, applies to each icon. Figure 9-11 shows the settings for a data graphic you will apply in the following topic. Although this figure designates a specific value for each icon, you have considerable flexibility in defining the conditions for each flag. You can:

- Use the list in the center column to create a range of values for each icon and to set other conditions.

- Use the list on the right to enter more sophisticated values than simply typing a number or text into the field.

The fourth data graphic type, Color By Value, extracts data values from the selected field and matches each with a color, as shown in Figure 9-12.

> **TIP** The colors selected by Visio in Figure 9-12 are suitable for some purposes but might be too bold for other purposes. In the latter case, you can display the Fill Color list for any field and change the color setting. You can also leave the text color of affected shapes at the default setting (as shown in the figure) or you can manually change it.

> **IMPORTANT** Notice the Insert and Delete buttons to the right of the Color Assignments section in Figure 9-12. You can delete any combination of value and color, or you can add new ones, depending on what you want to highlight in the drawing. For example, if you don't want to apply a fill color when the selected field has a blank value, delete the row in which the value box is blank.

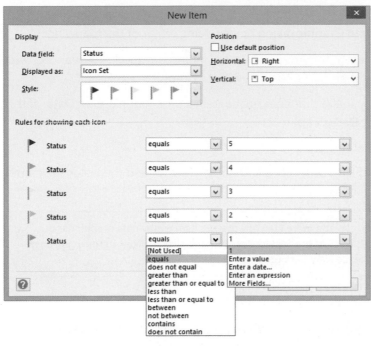

Figure 9-11 *The options for configuring icon set graphics are flexible*

9

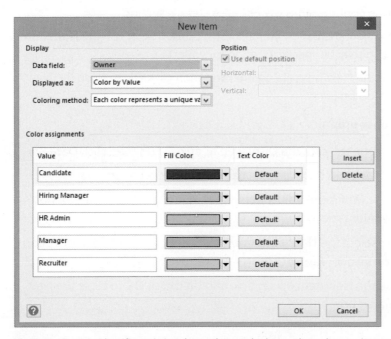

Figure 9-12 *Visio identifies existing data values and selects colors when you create a color-by-value data graphic*

To select a field to create a data graphic

1. Open the **New Data Graphic** dialog box by doing either of the following:

   - On the **Data** tab, in the **Advanced Data Linking** group, click **Advanced Data Graphics**, and then click **Create New Data Graphic**.

   - Right-click any shape that does not contain a data graphic, click **Data**, and then click **Edit Data Graphic**.

2. Click the **New Item** button.

3. In the **New Item** dialog box, click the **Data field** arrow, and then click the name of the field you want to visualize.

> ⚠ **IMPORTANT** You can add more than one graphic item to any data graphic as you create it. To do so in each of the next four procedures, click the New Item button again before clicking OK to close the New Data Graphic dialog box.

To create a Text data graphic

1. Select a field to visualize, click the **Displayed as** arrow, and then click **Text**.

2. Click the **Style** arrow, and then click the name of the text callout you want.

3. (*Optional*) Change configuration values in the **Details** section.

4. (*Optional*) Either select the **Use default position** check box, or use the **Horizontal** and **Vertical** lists to select a specific position for your data graphic.

5. Click **OK** to close the New Item dialog box, and then click **OK** to close the New Data Graphic dialog box.

To create a Data Bar data graphic

1. Select a field to visualize, click the **Displayed as** arrow, and then click **Data Bar**.

2. Click the **Style** arrow, and then click the name of the data bar you want.

3. (*Optional*) Change **Minimum Value**, **Maximum Value**, or other configuration values in the **Details** section.

4. (*Optional*) Either select the **Use default position** check box, or select an option from the **Horizontal** and **Vertical** lists to select a specific position.

5. Click **OK** to close the New Item dialog box, and then click **OK** to close the New Data Graphic dialog box.

To create an Icon Set data graphic

1. Select a field to visualize, click the **Displayed as** arrow, and then click **Icon Set**.

2. Click the **Style** arrow, and then click the icon set you want.

3. Click the appropriate condition from the list in the center column of the **Rules for showing each icon** section, and then enter values in the right column in the same section.

4. (*Optional*) Either select the **Use default position** check box, or select an option from the **Horizontal** and **Vertical** lists to select a specific position.

5. Click **OK** to close the New Item dialog box, and then click **OK** to close the New Data Graphic dialog box.

To create a Color By Value data graphic

1. Select a field to visualize, click the **Displayed as** arrow, and then click **Color by Value**.

2. (*Optional*) Click the **Coloring Method** arrow, and then click either **Each color represents a unique value** or **Each color represents a range of values**.

3. Either leave the entries in the **Value**, **Fill Color**, and **Text Color** fields in the **Color assignments** section as is, or make the changes you want.

4. Click **OK** to close the New Item dialog box, and then click **OK** to close the New Data Graphic dialog box.

Apply data graphics

You must select one or more shapes *before* opening the Data Graphics gallery because you can apply or remove data graphics only on preselected shapes. After selecting shapes, you can point to the options in the Available Data Graphics section of the gallery, shown in Figure 9-13, to provide a live preview so you can sample various graphics before choosing one.

9

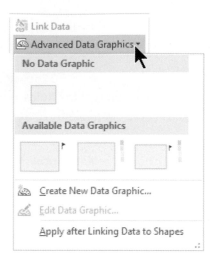

Figure 9-13 *Thumbnails of three data graphics appear in a data graphics gallery*

The examples shown in the next two figures use shape data fields called Risk and Owner. The Risk field was added to the shapes in this diagram, whereas Owner is a predefined field in all Visio flowchart shapes.

Figure 9-14 shows the result of assigning two different data graphics to the same set of process steps. The upper section of the figure uses an icon set to represent the level of risk associated with each step. The lower section employs a color-by-value graphic that is based on the Owner data field, essentially creating a map that is color-coded to show who does what within the process.

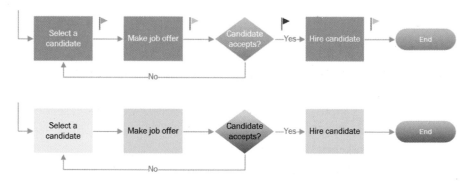

Figure 9-14 *The same set of flowchart shapes can impart dramatically different information by using different data graphics*

> **TIP** Visio data graphics are automatically assigned to a special layer in a diagram. (See "Understand and use layers" in Chapter 3, "Manage text, shapes, and pages.") If you want to hide data graphics without removing them, you can change the view properties for the data graphics layer.

You can assign only one data graphic at a time to any given shape. However, you can include multiple graphic items within one data graphic. The diagram in Figure 9-15 features a single data graphic that includes both of the graphic items that are shown separately in Figure 9-14.

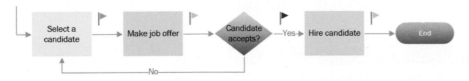

Figure 9-15 *You can create data graphics that have multiple graphic items*

> **TIP** Data graphics are applied to a single page at a time. If you want to apply the same data graphic to multiple pages, you must either apply it to each page separately, or write a Visio macro to do that for you.
>
> If you want to apply the same data graphic automatically to a shape regardless of the page on which the shape resides, you can apply the data graphic to the shape and save the shape as a master in a custom stencil. Then, whenever you drag the master onto the drawing page, it will automatically display the data graphic. You will learn about macros and creating custom stencils in Appendix A, "Look behind the curtain."

To apply a data graphic to one or more selected shapes

1. On the **Data** tab, in the **Advanced Data Linking** group, click the **Advanced Data Graphics** button to display a gallery of data graphic options and thumbnails.

2. In the **Advanced Data Graphics** gallery, click the thumbnail for the data graphic you want to apply.

To remove a data graphic from one or more selected shapes

1. Display the **Advanced Data Graphics** gallery, and then click the **None** thumbnail in the **No Data Graphic** section.

9

TIP In Chapter 10, "Link to external data," you will discover additional techniques for applying data graphics in diagrams that have been linked to external data sources.

Edit data graphics

The placement and appearance of data graphics are controlled by an editable set of parameters. Although you can't control every attribute of a data graphic without resorting to writing code, the Visio 2016 user interface provides tools to implement a surprising number of changes by using the Edit Data Graphic dialog box, shown in Figure 9-16.

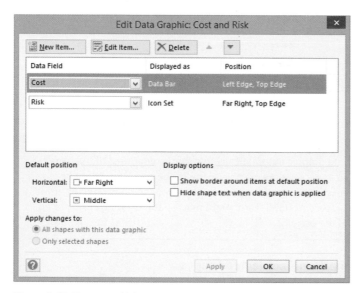

Figure 9-16 *Data graphics can contain multiple graphic items of different types*

The upper half of the Edit Data Graphic dialog box lists all of the graphic items that are part of the selected data graphic. You can add, edit, or delete each graphic item. In the lower half of the dialog box, you can modify the characteristics of the data graphic as a whole.

IMPORTANT You establish the default position for a data graphic by selecting from the Horizontal and Vertical lists in the Default Position of the Edit Data Graphic dialog box. (Both the horizontal and vertical positions are relative to the shape to which the graphic will be attached.) Data graphic items in the upper half of the dialog box whose Position is set to Default will appear at this location.

You use the Edit Item dialog box to change display properties. The specific properties in the dialog box vary based on the selected graphic item.

For the Thermometer graphic shown in Figure 9-17, you can specify the minimum and maximum values so Visio can properly scale the height of the red inside the thermometer. You can also adjust labels and other icon attributes.

> ⚠ **IMPORTANT** The Minimum Value and Maximum Value fields are critical for all Data Bar graphic items, not just the Thermometer icon. If these values are set incorrectly, the height or width, depending on the graphic item, will be incorrect.

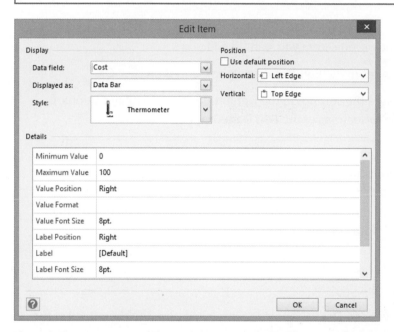

Figure 9-17 *You can accept default values in many situations but can customize data graphics as needed*

In the upper-right corner of the dialog box, you can select the check box to position a graphic item at the default position for the data graphic that contains it. You can also clear that check box and select from the options in the Horizontal and Vertical lists to set your own location relative to the underlying shape.

To edit a data graphic

1. Display the **Advanced Data Graphics** gallery, right-click the thumbnail of the data graphic you want to change, and then click **Edit**.

   Or

   Right-click any shape that contains the data graphic you want to change, click **Data**, and then click **Edit Data Graphic**.

2. In the **Edit Data Graphic** dialog box, click the graphic item you want to edit, and then click the **Edit Item** button.

   Or

   Double-click the graphic item you want to edit.

3. Make your changes in the **Edit Item** dialog box, and then click **OK**.

4. (*Optional*) Change the settings in the **Default position**, **Display options**, or **Apply changes to** sections of the **Edit Data Graphic** dialog box.

    TIP The next step is useful if you are still experimenting with how you want the data graphic to look on the page.

5. (*Optional*) Click the **Apply** button to see the changes in the diagram without closing the **Edit Data Graphic** dialog box.

6. Click **OK**.

To rename a data graphic

1. Display the **Advanced Data Graphics** gallery, right-click the thumbnail of the data graphic you want to rename, and then click **Rename**.

2. Enter a new name, and then click **OK**.

To duplicate a data graphic

1. Display the **Advanced Data Graphics** gallery, right-click the thumbnail of the data graphic you want to duplicate, and then click **Duplicate**.

To select all shapes that use a particular data graphic

1. Display the **Advanced Data Graphics** gallery, right-click the thumbnail of a data graphic, and then click **Select Shapes that use this Graphic**.

To delete a data graphic

1. Display the **Advanced Data Graphics** gallery, right-click the thumbnail of the data graphic you want to delete, and then click **Delete**.

 TIP In Chapter 10, "Link to external data," you will discover additional techniques for editing data graphics in diagrams that have been linked to external data sources.

Create data graphic legends

Data graphics like the one shown in Figure 9-15 earlier in this chapter are easier to use and understand with a key. With Visio 2016, a data graphic legend is just a click away. You can create either a vertical legend, or, as shown in Figure 9-18, a horizontal legend.

 TIP Visio always places the legend in the upper-right corner of the page.

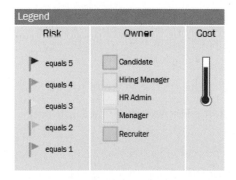 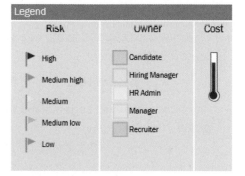

Figure 9-18 *Visio creates legends automatically, but you can customize them*

After Visio creates the legend, you can edit the elements within the legend. For example, the legend on the left in Figure 9-18 is the original version. In the legend on the right, the descriptions for the flag icons have been changed to be more meaningful for users of the diagram.

 IMPORTANT After placing a data graphic legend on the page, Visio never updates it. Consequently, if you add or delete a data graphic or change the attributes of a graphic in a way that affects the legend, you must delete the existing legend and insert a new one.

> **TIP** Visio constructs data graphic legends from a combination of containers and lists. For details about containers and lists, see Chapter 13, "Add structure to your diagrams."

To insert a data graphic legend

1. On the **Data** tab, in the **Display Data** group, click the **Insert Legend** button.

2. Click either **Horizontal** or **Vertical**.

To edit a data graphic legend

1. Click an entry inside the legend and enter new text.

2. Click an entry inside the legend and drag it to a new location.

To move a data graphic legend

1. Click the word **Legend** in the header of the data graphic legend, and then drag the legend to a new location.

To delete a data graphic legend

1. Do any of the following:

   • Click the word **Legend** in the header of the data graphic legend, and then press the **Delete** key.

   • Right-click the word **Legend**, and then click **Cut** on the shortcut menu.

   • Right-click the word **Legend**, and then on the **Home** tab, in the **Clipboard** group, click **Cut**.

Skills review

In this chapter, you learned how to:

■ Enhance diagram effectiveness

■ Create data graphics

■ Apply data graphics

■ Edit data graphics

■ Create data graphic legends

Practice tasks

The practice files for these tasks are located in the Visio2016SBS\Ch09 folder. You can save the results of the tasks in the same folder.

Enhance diagram effectiveness

There are no practice tasks for this topic.

Create data graphics

Open the CreateDataGraphics diagram in Visio, and then perform the following tasks:

1. Create a **Text** data graphic with the following characteristics:

Data field:	Owner
Style:	Heading 1
Horizontal:	Center
Vertical:	Top Edge
Horizontal Offset	None

2. Create a **Data Bar** graphic for the **Cost** field with the following characteristics:

   Located at the default position

Style:	Thermometer
Maximum Value	150

3. Create an **Icon Set** data graphic for the **Status** field and apply the settings shown in Figure 9-11.

4. Create a **Color by Value** data graphic for the **Owner** field, ensuring that there is not a color assigned to a blank value.

5. Save the diagram as **DataGraphicsFlowchart** for use in the next tasks.

Apply data graphics

Open the DataGraphicsFlowchart diagram in Visio, and then perform the following tasks:

1. Apply the **Text** data graphic to all process steps except **Start** and **End**.

2. Apply the **Data Bar** data graphic to all process steps except **Start** and **End**. Change the **Cost** value in several shapes and observe the results.

3. Apply the **Icon Set** data graphic to all process steps except **Start** and **End**. Change the **Status** value in several shapes and observe the results.

4. Apply the **Color by Value** data graphic to all process steps except **Start** and **End**. Change the **Owner** value in several shapes and observe the results.

5. Save your changes, and leave the diagram open if you'll be continuing to the next tasks.

Edit data graphics

Open the DataGraphicsFlowchart diagram in Visio, and then perform the following tasks:

1. Apply the **Data Bar** (**Thermometer**) data graphic to the process shapes in the top row, and then edit the data graphic by changing the **Vertical** position to **Top Edge**, and **Value Position** and **Label Position** to **Not Shown**.

2. Apply the **Icon Set** data graphic to any three-process steps, and then edit the data graphic by selecting a different set of icons.

3. Assign the **Color by Value** data graphic to the process steps in the lower row, and then edit the data graphic by assigning different fill colors and text colors to one or more data values.

4. Assign a more meaningful name to the data bar data graphic.

5. Create a duplicate copy of the **Icon Set** data graphic, and then change the visualization type to **Color by Value**.

6. Assign the duplicated data graphic to some of the process steps.

7. Select all shapes that currently use the **Data Bar** graphic and assign the duplicated data graphic to them.

8. Delete the duplicated data graphic.

9. Save your changes, and leave the diagram open if you'll be continuing to the next tasks.

Create data graphic legends

Open the DataGraphicsFlowchart diagram in Visio, and then perform the following tasks:

1. Apply the **Icon Set** data graphic to all process steps in the upper row.

2. Apply the **Data Bar** data graphic to all process steps in the lower row.

3. Add a **Vertical** legend to the page.

4. Move the legend to a new location.

5. Delete the legend, and then insert a **Horizontal** legend.

6. Change the text of one or more explanations in the **Status** column of the legend.

Link to external data

10

You explored shape data in Chapter 8, "Work with shape data," and in Chapter 9, "Visualize your data." In both chapters, you entered data manually into shape data fields. Although this works, you might prefer to populate your drawings automatically by linking them to data in a Microsoft Excel workbook, a database, or another external source.

You might also want to turn your Visio diagrams into dashboards by linking them to data and then visualizing key data attributes. Whether you need to display the status of the servers and printers in a network, show weekly attendance for all employees in an organization chart, or provide an up-to-the-minute office layout showing who is in or out today—you can do all this and more when you combine data linking and data graphics.

Visio 2016 introduces a feature called Quick Import that automates the process of linking to data in Excel and then applying data graphics. When Quick Import doesn't meet your needs, you can use the Custom Import wizard to link to virtually any data source.

 IMPORTANT The information in this chapter applies only to the Professional edition of Visio 2016.

This chapter guides you through procedures related to using Quick Import and Custom Import, managing linked data, using data graphic options for linked data, and refreshing linked data.

In this chapter

- Understand data linking
- Use Quick Import
- Use Custom Import
- Manage linked data
- Use data graphic options for linked data
- Refresh linked data

Practice files

For this chapter, use the practice files from the Visio2016SBS\Ch10 folder. For practice file download instructions, see the introduction.

Understand data linking

Linking a diagram to data and then visualizing that data requires four steps:

1. Link the diagram to a data source.

2. Link data records to individual shapes.

3. Create a suitable data graphic.

4. Apply the data graphic.

Quick Import, which you will explore in the following topic, does all four steps automatically. If you don't use Quick Import, you are required to perform each step yourself; however, Visio provides wizards to assist with the first two tasks.

Regardless of the technique you choose for creating a link to external data, you create a dynamic link. You can refresh the diagram, which in turn updates shape data fields and any applied data graphics. Consequently, your Visio diagram can become the primary window into your data.

Either method of data linking displays data in the External Data window, which is shown in Figure 10-1. Visio explicitly opens the External Data window when you use Custom Import, but does not always open it when you use Quick Import. However, you can open (and close) the window yourself by selecting or clearing the External Data Window check box located in the Show/Hide group on the Data tab.

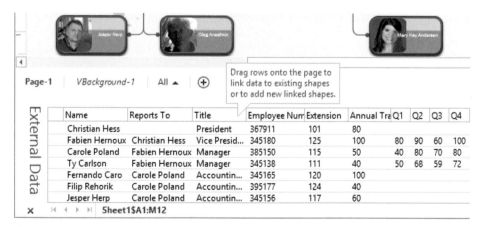

Figure 10-1 *The External Data window provides a view into a database or other data source*

Use Quick Import

If your data resides in Excel, Quick Import is the fastest way to link your shapes to external data.

To appreciate how easy it is to use the Quick Import wizard, see Figure 10-2, which contains part of an organization chart for Blue Yonder Airlines. The Shape Data window is open and displays the standard fields for a Visio organization chart. Four of the shape data fields contain default values, but the Name field identifies that the selected shape represents Carole Poland.

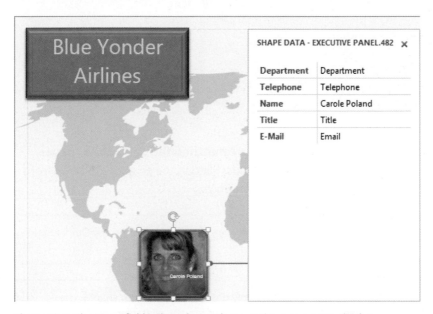

10

Figure 10-2 *The Name field is the only one that contains a user-entered value*

The data to which the diagram will be linked is shown in Figure 10-3.

	A	B	C	D	E	F	G	H	I	J
1	Name	Reports To	Title	Employee Number	Extension	Annual Training	Q1	Q2	Q3	Q4
2	Christian Hess		President	367911	101	80				
3	Fabien Hernoux	Christian Hess	Vice President	345180	125	100	80	90	60	100
4	Carole Poland	Fabien Hernoux	Manager	385150	115	50	40	80	70	80
5	Ty Carlson	Fabien Hernoux	Manager	345138	111	40	50	68	59	72
6	Fernando Caro	Carole Poland	Accounting Clerk	345165	120	100				
7	Filip Rehorik	Carole Poland	Accounting Clerk	395177	124	40				
8	Jesper Herp	Carole Poland	Accounting Supervisor	345156	117	60				

Figure 10-3 *An Excel workbook that will be linked to an organization chart*

When you start the Quick Import wizard and point it to your Excel data file, it does the rest, as shown in Figure 10-4.

 TIP You can link to an Excel workbook that is stored on your computer, on a network server, or in Excel Services in Microsoft SharePoint.

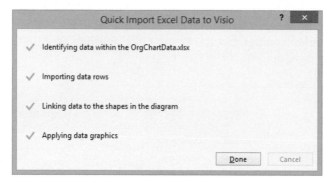

Figure 10-4 *All four Quick Import steps were successful*

The result is shown in Figure 10-5. Quick Import matched the data to the shapes based on employee name, added new data fields, filled in the shape data fields from the linked Excel workbook, and applied data graphics.

 IMPORTANT A single undo command will reverse all actions performed by Quick Import.

IMPORTANT If Quick Import does not apply data graphics to your shapes, it is probably for one of two reasons: either your shapes already contained data graphics (Quick Import will not replace them), or the Apply After Linking Data To Shapes option is not selected. This setting is located at the bottom of both the Data Graphics gallery and the Advanced Data Graphics gallery.

It's important to understand that Quick Import is choosing and applying data graphics based on its analysis of the shape data fields. It might choose appropriate fields and relevant data graphics, or it might not. If you want to know how to change the applied graphics, see "Use data graphic options for linked data" later in this chapter.

To understand how the diagram and its data graphics can be refreshed when the Excel data changes, see "Refresh linked data" later in this chapter.

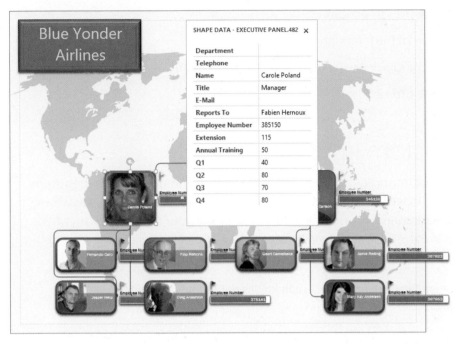

Figure 10-5 *All org chart shapes, including the Carole Poland shape, contain imported data*

Although it isn't shown in Figure 10-5, Visio opens the Data Graphic Fields task pane each time you use Quick Import. This task pane will be explained in "Use data graphic options for linked data" later in this chapter.

10

To use Quick Import

1. Do either of the following:

   - On the **Data** tab, in the **External Data** group, click **Quick Import**.

   - If the **External Data** window is open and there are no linked data sources, click **Quick Link Data to Shapes**.

2. In the **Data Selector** dialog box, click the **Browse** button to select an Excel workbook, and then click **Done**.

3. In the **Quick Import Excel Data to Visio** dialog box, click **Done**.

To undo Quick Import actions

1. Do either of the following:

    - On the Quick Access Toolbar, click the **Undo** button.

    - Press **Ctrl+Z**.

Use Custom Import

Whereas Quick Import performs all four data linking and data visualization steps described in "Understand data linking" earlier in this chapter, sometimes you will want to link to a data source yourself. One obvious case is if your data resides anywhere other than in Excel. However, even if your data is in Excel, you might want to link manually to have more control over the linking and visualization.

When you use Custom Import, you can link to data in any of the following repositories:

- Microsoft Excel workbook

- Microsoft Access database

- Microsoft SharePoint Foundation list

- Microsoft SQL Server database

- A repository that can be accessed via OLE DB or ODBC

Link your diagram to data

After telling the Data Selector wizard where your data is located, you have the option to refine your selection of data from that source.

Figure 10-6 shows the first of several selection pages for data in Excel. You can select from the What Worksheet Or Range Do You Want To Use? list to narrow the source to a specific worksheet or named range. Clicking the Select Custom Range button opens your workbook in Excel so you can choose the range you want. You can use the wizard page following the one shown in Figure 10-6 to exclude specific columns and rows.

Figure 10-6 *Data source options for an Excel workbook*

Figure 10-7 shows the first selection page for data in a SharePoint list.

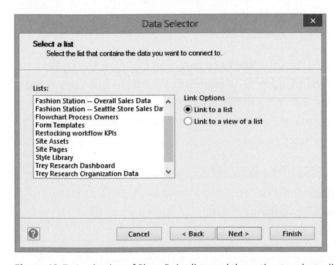

Figure 10-7 *A selection of SharePoint lists and the option to select a list by name or select a view of a list*

Other data source types provide similar filtering and selection options.

As a final step for some data source types, you can identify which field, or combination of fields, uniquely identifies each data record. Establishing a unique identifier in your data is valuable if you later want your diagram to reflect subsequent changes to data in the data repository.

Figure 10-8 shows that Visio analyzes your data and selects what appears to be a unique identifier. The software generally makes a good choice, but you can change its recommended option by selecting or clearing the check boxes shown in the figure.

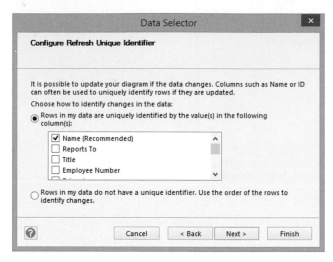

Figure 10-8 *Name is the unique identifier recommended by Visio*

If your data does not contain a unique value for each row, you can click the option at the bottom of wizard page shown in Figure 10-8, enabling Visio to use the sequence of the rows to identify them. Although this choice works for reasonably stable data sets, be aware that using this option has potentially serious consequences if you later reorder, add, or delete rows in the source data.

When the linking operation completes, the linked data appears in the External Data window. Figure 10-1, in the "Understand data linking" topic earlier in this chapter, shows the External Data window after linking an organization chart to data in Excel.

> **TIP** You can link a single diagram to more than one data source, even if the data sources are of different types. If you do link to more than one source, multiple name tabs will appear at the bottom of the External Data window.

To link a diagram to data by using Custom Import

1. Do either of the following:

   - On the **Data** tab, in the **External Data** group, click **Custom Import**.

   - Right-click anywhere inside the **External Data** window, click **Data Source**, and then click **Add**.

2. On the first page of the **Data Selector** wizard, click the type of data source to which you want to connect, and then click **Next**.

3. Complete the remaining pages of the **Data Selector** wizard (the specific pages will vary based on the data source type). When the wizard finishes, the External Data window will open if it wasn't open already, and a data tab will display the newly linked data.

Link data to your shapes

You can select any combination of three methods to connect data rows in the External Data window with shapes on the drawing page. You can:

- Drag data to an existing shape.

- Automatically link data to shapes.

- Use data to create a shape.

Whichever technique you use, the result is usually a one-to-one relationship between data rows and shapes. However, it's possible to create one-to-many relationships. For example, you can connect:

- One shape to multiple data sources. You might link some fields to values in a SharePoint list, and connect other fields in the same shape to data in a SQL database.

- One data row to multiple shapes. Fields from the same data row can be linked to multiple shapes on the same or different pages.

10

The External Data window, shown in Figure 10-1, presents data fields in the sequence it found them in the data source. In addition, each field has a name and a data type derived from the data source.

> ✓ **TIP** The default behavior for all three linking methods is to analyze your data fields during the linking operation, and then apply one or more data graphics. Sometimes the attempts to visualize your data are good; other times, such as the example in Figure 10-5 where the orange progress bar represents Employee Number, they are not very useful.
>
> If you do not like the automatically applied data graphics, you can remove them or change them. You can also prevent Visio from automatically applying data graphics in the first place. To do so, before you run the Automatic Link wizard, clear the Apply After Linking Data To Shapes check box at the bottom of either the Data Graphics gallery or the Advanced Data Graphics gallery.

> ✓ **TIP** You can change the sequence of fields, the field names, the data type of each field, and which fields appear in the window. Making these changes before using any of the linking techniques described in the following sections ensures that the data in your shapes meets your needs.

Drag data to an existing shape

Dragging a row of data onto an existing shape:

- Populates identically named fields in the shape with data.
- Adds unmatched field names to the shape.

When you drag a data row, notice that the pointer appears to be dragging a translucent version of a shape across the page, as shown on the left in Figure 10-9. The pointer is accompanied by a plus sign (+), which is how Visio informs you that you will be creating a copy of the translucent shape if you place it on an unused part of the page (see "Use data to create a shape" later in this topic).

When you've dragged the pointer far enough that it is located on top of an existing shape, the pointer is accompanied by a link symbol. In addition, the shape displays a thicker border, indicating that if you place the data row there, it will be assigned to the shape. (See the image on the right in Figure 10-9.)

Figure 10-9 *Adding external data to an existing shape*

> ✓ **TIP** If you are dragging a data row onto a shape that is already on the page, it doesn't matter whether the shape under the pointer matches the target shape. Visio adds the data to the existing shape.

To link data to an existing shape

1. In the **External Data** window, click a data row, and then drag it to a shape.

Automatically link data to shapes

When your rows of data and your existing shapes contain a matching data value, the Link Data wizard matches data to your shapes automatically.

Figure 10-10 shows a diagram before automatic linking. The shape data window contains the standard fields for a Visio organization chart. Four of the fields contain their default values, but the Name field identifies that this shape represents Fabien Hernoux.

In the External Data window, the highlighted row includes a field that contains the value Fabien Hernoux and several additional fields. (As you will discover in Figure 10-12, additional data fields are located to the right of the Employee Number field.)

The remaining shapes in this organization chart also contain a value for Name and have matching data rows in the External Data window.

10

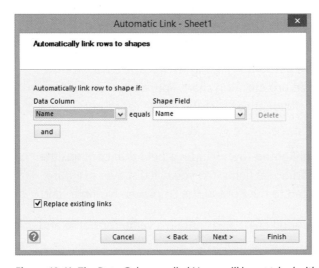

Figure 10-10 *An organization chart has been linked to external data and is ready for data to be linked to shapes*

You use the Automatic Link wizard page shown in Figure 10-11 to tell Visio which External Data column and which Shape Data field contain matching data values. In this example, the field names happen to be the same but that is not required—only the data values they contain need to match.

Figure 10-11 *The Data Column called Name will be matched with the Shape Data field called Name*

Figure 10-12 shows the same diagram after automatic linking. Notice several changes:

- In the Shape Data window, the Department, Telephone, Title, and E-Mail fields have new values (three of the four are now blank).

- Eight new fields appear after E-Mail; Visio created these fields for you because they existed in the external data but not in the shape data.

- Each row in the External Data window is preceded by a linking symbol.

> **TIP** To determine which rows are linked to which shapes, and vice versa, see "Manage linked data" later in this chapter.

- Two data graphics were automatically applied to every shape: an icon set pennant is located at the upper-right corner, and a data bar labeled Employee Number is below the pennant.

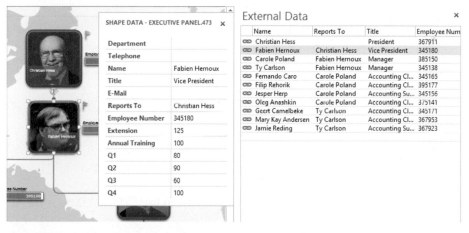

Figure 10-12 *An organization chart after automatic linking of data to shapes*

> **TIP** The Automatic Link wizard can link data to shapes only one page at a time.

To link data to shapes automatically

1. On the **Data** tab, in the **Advanced Data Linking** group, click **Link Data**.

2. On the first page of the **Automatic Link** wizard, click **Selected shapes** or **All shapes on this page**, and then click **Next**.

3. Click a column name from the list in the **Data Column** section, click a field name in the **Shape Field** section, and then click **Next**.

4. Click **Finish**.

Use data to create a shape

You can drag a data row onto an open section of the drawing page to create a new shape and populate it with data. When you use this method, be sure to select the master you want Visio to use to create the new shape before dragging the data row.

For example, the left side of Figure 10-13 shows the result of selecting the Executive Belt master in the Organization Chart Shapes stencil before dragging a data row onto the page. The right side of the figure shows the resulting shape after it has been dropped and automatically populated with data.

> **SEE ALSO** For more information about organization chart shapes and styles, see Chapter 5, "Create organization charts."

Figure 10-13 *An org chart shape created by dragging a data row onto the page*

After dropping the shape shown in Figure 10-13, one row in the External Data window displays a link symbol, as shown in Figure 10-14.

	Name	Reports To	Title	Employee Number
🔗	Christian Hess		President	367911
	Fabien Hernoux	Christian Hess	Vice Presid...	345180
	Carole Poland	Fabien Hernoux	Manager	385150
	Ty Carlson	Fabien Hernoux	Manager	345138
	Fernando Caro	Carole Poland	Accountin...	345165
	Filip Rehorik	Carole Poland	Accountin...	395177
	Jesper Herp	Carole Poland	Accountin...	345156

External Data

|◀ ◀ ▶ ▶| Sheet1

Figure 10-14 *Data for Christian Hess is linked to a shape*

To create a shape from data

1. If it is not already selected, click the master in the **Shape Data** window from which you want to create a new shape.

2. Click a data row in the **External Data** window, and then drag it to an open area of the drawing page.

> **TIP** You can create multiple shapes at one time by dragging multiple rows from the External Data window.

Manage linked data

Whether you use Quick Import or Custom Import, there are several maintenance and management functions that you should know about.

Identify links

After shapes are linked to external data, sometimes you need to find out which rows and shapes are linked to each other.

To identify the shapes to which a data row is linked

1. Right-click the row in the **External Data** window, and then click **Linked Shapes**.

To identify the rows to which a shape is linked

1. Right-click the shape, click **Data**, and then click **Show Linked Row**.

Change column settings

For other than the simplest of data imports, you might find that you want to change the way that data is linked to shapes:

- Your data source might contain more columns than you need to have available in your diagram.

- The sequence of columns in the data source might be different than the sequence of shape data fields you want in your diagram.

- The imported data might not be the correct type—a date field that is imported as text, for example.

Visio provides techniques for all of these circumstances.

IMPORTANT You must change column settings *before* linking data to shapes.

To change column settings before linking

1. Right-click in the **External Data** window, and then click **Column Settings**.

2. Use the **Column Settings** dialog box to change column sequence, rename columns, add and remove fields from view, or change the data type for a column, and then click **OK**.

Unlink data from shapes and diagrams

You might need to unlink shapes from data, or even unlink a diagram from a data source.

To unlink a shape from data

1. Right-click a shape, click **Data**, and then click **Unlink from Row**.

 TIP You can unlink multiple shapes at once by selecting multiple shapes before using this procedure.

To unlink a data row from shapes

1. Right-click a row in the **External Data** window, and then click **Unlink**.

 TIP You can unlink multiple rows at once by selecting multiple rows before using this procedure.

To unlink a diagram from a data source

1. Do either of the following:

   - Right-click the tab in the **External Data** window that contains the data you want to unlink, and then click **Remove**.

   - Right-click anywhere inside the **External Data** window, click **Data Source**, and then click **Remove**.

Use data graphic options for linked data

In Chapter 9, "Visualize your data," you used text callouts, icons, and colors to visualize data that resided inside shapes on the drawing page. In this chapter you've learned how to make your diagrams more dynamic by linking them to external data sources. The combination of the two is so powerful that Visio 2016 includes additional visualization features specifically for linked data.

The extra features are visible in the Data Graphics group of the Data tab. Compare the link-enabled version shown in Figure 10-15 with the non-linked version shown in Figure 9-8 in Chapter 9, "Visualize your data."

Figure 10-15 *Linking to external data enables the Data Graphics gallery, the Position button, and the Configuration button*

The Data Graphic Fields task pane, shown in Figure 10-16, is new in Visio 2016. It becomes active as soon as you link one data row to a shape, whether you've done it manually or via the Quick Import feature.

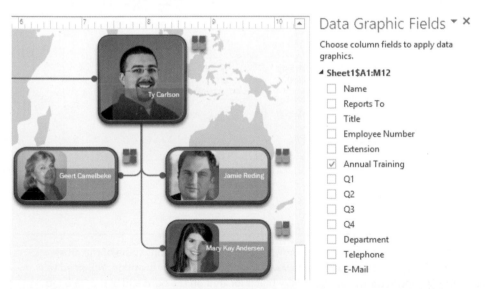

Figure 10-16 *Organization chart shapes display a data graphic for the percentage of Annual Training completed*

You can use the Data Graphic Fields task pane to apply one or more data graphics. If you don't select any shapes on the drawing page when you click a field name in the Data Graphic Fields task pane, Visio will apply a data graphic to all shapes on the page. If you select shapes, Visio will apply the graphic only to those shapes. In either case, Visio chooses a data graphic based on its analysis of your data.

You can use the Position and Configuration buttons and the Data Graphics gallery to change the automatically applied data graphic.

- If you like the graphic that Visio has applied but want to adjust it, use the Position and Configuration buttons to fine tune its appearance.

- If you would prefer to use an entirely different data graphic, use the Data Graphics gallery, shown in Figure 10-17, to select a new graphic.

> **TIP** The Data Graphics gallery and the Position and Configuration buttons are enabled only when at least one field name is selected in the Data Graphic Fields task pane.

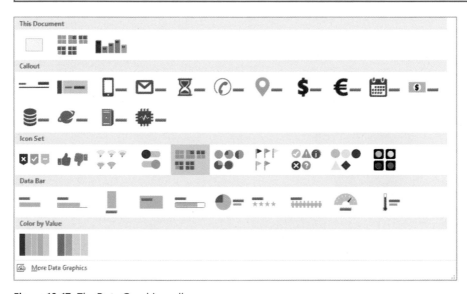

Figure 10-17 *The Data Graphics gallery*

> **TIP** The Data Graphics gallery shown in Figure 10-17 contains some of the most frequently used data graphics; however, it does not offer every option. You need to display the Advanced Data Graphics gallery that is located on the right end of the Data tab to see every data graphic. You also need the Advanced Data Graphics gallery to create and edit data graphics that contain multiple graphic items.

To show or hide the Data Graphic Fields task pane

1. Do any of the following:

    - On the **Data** tab, in the **Show/Hide** group, select the **Data Graphic Fields** check box.

    - Right-click any shape, click **Data**, and then click **Data Graphic Fields.**

    - Right-click anywhere in the **External Data** window, and then click **Data Graphic Fields**.

To remove a data graphic by using the Data Graphic Fields task pane

1. Click a field name that is currently selected.

To apply a data graphic by using the Data Graphic Fields task pane

1. Click a field name that is not currently selected.

To change to a different data graphic

1. In the **Data Graphic Fields** task pane, click a field name that is selected, and then in the **Data Graphics** gallery, click the thumbnail of the data graphic you want to apply.

To change the position of an existing data graphic

1. In the **Data Graphic Fields** task pane, click a field name.

2. On the **Data** tab, in the **Data Graphics** group, click **Position**.

3. Do either of the following:

    - Click one of the predefined positions on the menu.

    - Click either **Horizontal** or **Vertical**, and then click the position you want.

To edit an existing data graphic

1. In the **Data Graphic Fields** task pane, click a field name.

2. On the **Data** tab, in the **Data Graphics** group, do either of the following:

    - Click **Configuration**.

    - Display the **Data Graphics** gallery, and then click **More Data Graphics**.

3. Make the required change in the **Edit Item** dialog box, and then click **OK**.

10

TIP For more information about the Edit Item dialog box, see "Edit data graphics" in Chapter 9, "Visualize your data."

Refresh linked data

After you've linked a diagram to data and added data graphics, your diagram becomes a window into your data. Best of all, both the link to the data and the data graphics are dynamic; when the data changes, the graphics in the diagram change.

You can refresh diagram data manually, on a time schedule, or via code. The programming option is outside the scope of this book, but the first two options are described here:

- **Manual refresh** If your diagram is linked to more than one data source, you can choose whether to refresh a specific source or all sources when you click the Refresh All button.

- **Automatic refresh** You use the settings in the Configure Refresh dialog box, shown in Figure 10-18, to set up automatic refresh. After doing so, whenever your diagram is open, Visio refreshes the data from the specified data source at the time interval that you specify.

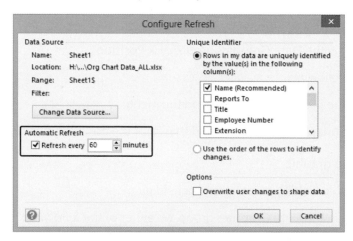

Figure 10-18 *The data in your diagram can be automatically refreshed as frequently as once per minute*

> **SEE ALSO** For information about writing code to refresh data graphics, see *Visualizing Information with Microsoft Office Visio 2007: Smart Diagrams for Business Users*, by David Parker (McGraw-Hill Osborne Media, 2007), or wait for David's new book, *Mastering Data Visualization with Microsoft Visio Professional 2016* (Packt Publishing), in the middle of 2016.

To refresh data manually for all linked sources

1. On the **Data** tab, in the **External Data** group, click the **Refresh All** button.

2. In the **Refresh Data** dialog box, click **Close**.

To refresh data manually for one linked source

1. On the **Data** tab, in the **External Data** group, click the **Refresh All** arrow, and then click **Refresh Data**.

2. In the **Refresh Data** dialog box, click the source you want to refresh, click **Refresh**, and then click **Close**.

Or

1. In the **External Data** window, click the tab for the source you want to refresh.

2. Right-click anywhere in the **External Data** window, and then click **Refresh Data**.

3. In the **Refresh Data** dialog box, click **Close**.

To refresh data automatically for one linked source

1. In the **External Data** window, click the tab for the source you want to refresh.

2. Right-click anywhere in the **External Data** window, and then click **Configure Refresh**.

3. In the **Configure Refresh** dialog box, select the **Refresh every** check box, enter a number in the **minutes** box, and then click **OK**.

10

Skills review

In this chapter, you learned how to:

- Understand data linking
- Use Quick Import
- Use Custom Import
- Manage linked data
- Use data graphic options for linked data
- Refresh linked data

Practice tasks

The practice files for these tasks are located in the Visio2016SBS\Ch10 folder. You can save the results of the tasks in the same folder.

Understand data linking

There are no practice tasks for this topic.

Use Quick Import

Open the UseQuickImport diagram in Visio, and then perform the following tasks:

1. Display the **Data Selector** dialog box by using **Quick Import**.

2. On the **Data Selector** page, browse to the **OrgChartData** workbook located in the Visio2016SBS\Ch10 folder, and then complete the **Quick Import** wizard.

3. (*Optional*) Undo the **Quick Import** actions.

Use Custom Import

Open the UseCustomImport diagram in Visio, and then perform the following tasks:

1. Display the **Data Selector** wizard by using **Custom Import**.

2. Browse to the **OrgChartData** workbook located in the Visio2016SBS\Ch10 folder, and then complete the **Custom Import** wizard.

3. Repeat tasks 1 and 2 but link to the **OrgChartData_Supplement1** workbook.

> **TIP** Notice that the tab names in the External Data window are the same as the tab names of the Excel workbooks to which the diagram was linked.

4. Click the **Sheet1** tab, and then drag each row of data onto the corresponding shape. Notice that one row has no corresponding shape. Notice, also, that none of the shapes includes a department name or telephone number.

5. Click the **Telephone List** tab, and then use the **Link Data** wizard to automatically link all rows with matching shapes. Again, notice that there is one unlinked data row. Also notice that all shapes now have department names and telephone numbers.

6. Click the **Position Stone** master in the **Stone - Organization Chart Shapes** stencil, and then drag the **Oleg Anashkin** row to a blank place on the page.

7. Drag the **Oleg Anashkin** shape on top of the **Carole Poland** shape. (The Organization Chart add-in will place the shape with **Carole Poland**'s other employees.)

> **SEE ALSO** For information about the Organization Chart add-in, see Chapter 5, "Create organization charts."

8. Click the **Sheet1** tab, and then drag the **Oleg Anashkin** row to the **Oleg Anashkin** shape.

9. Bonus points: Add a photograph to the **Oleg Anashkin** shape from the **Photos** folder located in the Visio2016SBS\Ch10 folder.

10. Save your diagram as **LinkedOrgChart**.

Manage linked data

Open the LinkedOrgChart diagram you created in the "Use Custom Import" practice task, and then perform the following tasks:

1. Determine which row of data the **Jamie Reding** shape is linked to.

2. Determine which shape the **Fernando Caro** row is linked to.

> **TIP** The result of the first two tasks is obvious in this diagram. These tasks are more useful when the key that links rows and shapes is less obvious than a name.

3. Click the **Sheet1** tab, and then change the name of the **Department** column by entering **Department Name**.

4. Hide the **Reports To** column.

5. Unlink the **Ty Carlson** shape from its data rows.

6. Unlink the **Jesper Herp** data row from its shape.

7. Remove the **Telephone List** data source from the diagram.

8. Close the file but do not save changes.

Use data graphic options for linked data

Open the LinkedOrgChart diagram you created in the "Use Custom Import" practice task, and then perform the following tasks:

1. Open the **Data Graphic Fields** task pane if it is not already open.

2. Remove data graphics from all shapes.

3. Apply a data graphic for the **Annual Training** field.

4. Change the **Annual Training** field data graphic to the **Boxes** graphic that is available in the **Icon Set** section of the **Data Graphics** gallery.

5. Change the position of the **Annual Training** data graphic to **Left** (**Horizontal**) and **Middle** (**Vertical**).

6. Change the configuration of the **Annual Training** data graphic so the box with four squares appears only when the data value equals 100, and the box with three squares appears when the data value is between 60 and 100.

7. Save the diagram as LinkedDataGraphic.

Refresh linked data

Open the LinkedDataGraphic diagram you created in the "Use data graphic options for linked data" practice task, and then perform the following tasks:

1. Zoom to **Carole Poland** and her direct reports.

2. Open the **OrgChartData** workbook, located in the Visio2016SBS\Ch10 folder, in Excel, and change the percentage values in the **Annual Training** field for **Fernando Caro**, **Carole Poland**, and **Filip Rehorik**.

 TIP Change the values by at least 20 points so the differences will be more obvious in the subsequent tasks.

3. Refresh data manually and notice the changes to the **Annual Training** data graphic.

4. Configure data refresh by setting a two-minute timer.

5. Change the **Annual Training** value for **Carole Poland**, and then wait two minutes to observe the change in the diagram.

Part 3

Enhance and share diagrams

Add and use hyperlinks

Linking from shapes in a Visio drawing to external resources is one of the most meaningful ways to enhance the value of a Visio diagram. As you create or edit a drawing, try to anticipate what resources your readers will require. Then use those ideas to build in the links that will enhance the viewer's experience with your diagram.

A simple form of hyperlink might lead to a website or to another page in the same Visio drawing. A more sophisticated hyperlink might take the viewer to a Microsoft Excel workbook—and not just to the workbook, but to a specific set of cells on a particular worksheet. A similar link might lead the reader to a particular phrase in a Microsoft Word document that provides supporting information about a section of the diagram.

The documents that are the targets of your hyperlinks can be on a shared network drive, in Microsoft SharePoint, or in Microsoft OneDrive or another cloud storage service. In short, you can link to virtually any electronic object, regardless of where it resides.

This chapter guides you through procedures related to using existing hyperlinks; adding, editing, and deleting hyperlinks; and setting the hyperlink base.

In this chapter

- Follow hyperlinks
- Enhance diagrams by adding hyperlinks
- Understand relative and absolute hyperlinks
- Set the hyperlink base

Practice files

For this chapter, use the practice files from the Visio2016SBS\Ch11 folder. For practice file download instructions, see the introduction.

Follow hyperlinks

Before you explore how to create hyperlinks, it's worth knowing how to find and take advantage of them in a Visio diagram.

If you point to a shape that has a hyperlink, two things occur, both of which are shown in the image on the left in Figure 11-1:

- A hyperlink symbol appears in the lower-right corner of the pointer.

- A ScreenTip appears that contains a description of the hyperlink and instructions for following the link.

If you right-click a shape containing a hyperlink, the shortcut menu, shown on the right in Figure 11-1, includes an entry you can use to follow the link.

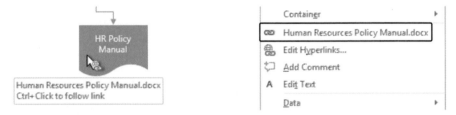

Figure 11-1 *Hyperlinks are visible when pointing to a shape and on the shape's shortcut menu*

> ✓ **TIP** One challenge for getting readers of your Visio diagrams to use embedded hyperlinks is that the hyperlinks are not normally visible. There is no way to know that a hyperlink exists unless you point to a shape containing one.

To follow a hyperlink

1. Do either of the following:

   - Hold down the **Ctrl** key, and then click a shape containing a hyperlink.

   - Right-click a shape containing a hyperlink, and then click the description of the hyperlink on the shortcut menu.

Enhance diagrams by adding hyperlinks

Any Visio diagram can be enhanced by adding hyperlinks. For example:

- A process box in a flowchart can be linked to a policy manual or other documentation about that step, or to an online form or IT system used to complete the task represented by the process box.

- Each person in an organization chart can be hyperlinked to detailed contact information on the company intranet.

- Each piece of equipment in a data center map can be connected to purchase records, warranty information, or service manuals.

- Each cubicle in an office floor plan can be linked to an equipment inventory worksheet or a computer configuration worksheet for an employee.

Open the Hyperlinks dialog box

Adding hyperlinks in Visio begins with the Hyperlinks dialog box, shown in Figure 11-2. You use the fields in the upper portion of the dialog box to specify the hyperlink target. The lower portion of the dialog box lists the existing hyperlinks, if any, on a shape.

> **SEE ALSO** For information about including more than one hyperlink on a shape, see "Add multiple hyperlinks" later in this topic.

11

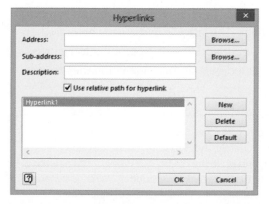

Figure 11-2 *You use the Hyperlinks dialog box to enter hyperlinks of all types*

> ⚠️ **IMPORTANT** You can add the same hyperlink to multiple shapes at once as easily as you can add the link to a single shape—just select more than one shape before opening the Hyperlinks dialog box. However, because it's so easy to do, be careful that you don't apply a link to multiple shapes by mistake.

To open the Hyperlinks dialog box

1. Do any of the following:

   - On the **Insert** tab, in the **Links** group, click the **Hyperlink** button.

   - Right-click a shape, and then click **Hyperlink**.

   - Press **Ctrl+K**.

Link to another Visio page

A hyperlink that leads from a shape on one drawing page to another page can be useful for several reasons. You might add hyperlinks to:

- Simplify navigation from page to page within a diagram.

- Enable navigation among pages in several related diagrams.

- Implement a drilldown capability to enable the reader to click a shape in a higher-level view and be taken to the next lower-level view. (You can continue this practice for as many levels as required.)

The page-to-page hyperlinks you create can move the reader to a page, or you can hyperlink to a specific shape on the target page. The latter is particularly helpful when you include a zoom-level setting as part of your hyperlink; the combination allows you to focus the reader's attention on a selected part of the page when they follow the hyperlink.

> ⚠️ **IMPORTANT** Linking to a specific shape on another page requires that you know the internal name of the target shape. Unfortunately, the Hyperlink dialog box does not provide any means to determine the internal name while the dialog box is open. You need to find the target shape's name before you create the hyperlink. The sidebar, "What is a shape name? Where do I find it?" later in this chapter contains several techniques for determining the name of a shape.

To link to a page in the current Visio diagram

1. Open the **Hyperlinks** dialog box.

> ⚠ **IMPORTANT** To link to another page in the Visio drawing you are currently editing, you *must* leave the Address field blank. If you do not leave this field blank and later decide to publish this map as a webpage, your hyperlink might not work.

2. Click the **Sub-address** field, and then enter the target page name.

   Or

   Do all of the following:

   - Click the **Browse** button to the right of the **Sub-address** field.

   - In the **Hyperlink** dialog box, in the **Page** list, select the name of the target page, and then click **OK**.

3. (*Optional*) Enter text in the **Description** field.

> ✓ **TIP** If you enter text in the Description field, your text will appear in a ScreenTip when a user points to the hyperlinked object. If you leave the Description field blank, the ScreenTip will display the page name for links to the current document, or it will display the file name for links to a different Visio document.

4. Click **OK**.

To link to a page in a different Visio diagram

1. In the **Hyperlinks** dialog box, click the **Browse** button to the right of the **Address** field, and then click **Local File**.

> **TIP** "Local File" is misleading terminology. You can link to a file in any local or networked location.

2. Select the Visio diagram to which you want to link, and then click **Open**.

3. Follow the instructions in the previous procedure for linking to a page in a Visio diagram.

11

What is a shape name? Where do I find it?

Every shape in a Visio drawing is referred to internally as a sheet, and Visio ensures that every shape has a unique identifier. Consequently, every Visio shape has an internal name in the form *Sheet* or *Sheet.n*, where *n* is a number representing the internal ID of the shape.

Shapes can have additional names related to the name of the master from which they were created. For example, you will come across shapes with names like *Process* or *Process.12*.

One way to determine the name of a shape is to run Visio in developer mode. Follow these steps to determine a shape's name:

1. Turn on developer mode, and then select the target shape.

   SEE ALSO For information about how to turn on developer mode, see Appendix A, "Look behind the curtain."

2. On the **Developer** tab, in the **Shape Design** group, click the **Shape Name** button to open the **Shape Name** dialog box, shown in Figure 11-3.

Figure 11-3 *Shape properties are displayed in the Shape Name dialog box*

3. Make note of, or copy, the text to the right of the **Name** box, and then close the **Shape Name** dialog box.

TIP You can also refer to the shape called Process.24 in Figure 11-3 as Sheet.24.

The Shape Data window, which is described in the "View shape data" topic in Chapter 8, "Work with shape data," provides another method for determining the name of a shape. You can see the shape name, Process.24, in the title bar of the Shape Data window shown in Figure 11-4.

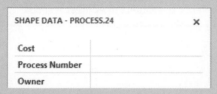

Figure 11-4 *The title bar of the Shape Data window displays the shape name*

To link to a specific shape on a page

1. In the **Hyperlinks** dialog box, either leave the **Address** field blank to link to the current diagram or select a different Visio diagram.

2. Click the **Browse** button to the right of the **Sub-address** field.

3. In the **Hyperlink** dialog box, in the **Page** list, select the name of the target page.

4. Enter the target shape name in the **Shape** field.

 SEE ALSO For information about finding and using Visio shape names, see the sidebar titled "What is a shape name? Where do I find it?" earlier in this chapter.

5. (*Optional*) In the **Zoom** list, select the zoom level you want, and then click **OK**.

   TIP The Zoom setting ensures that whenever someone follows your hyperlink, the target page will always appear with the same zoom setting. Select Page to show a full-page view, Width to show the full width of the page regardless of its height, and a percentage value to zoom in to that level of detail. If you don't select a zoom level, the target page will always be displayed at its most recent zoom level.

6. (*Optional*) Enter text in the **Description** field.

7. Click **OK**.

11

Link to a website

You can link from a Visio shape to a page on your organization's intranet or to a page on the public World Wide Web.

 TIP If your target webpage contains HTML bookmarks, you can include a bookmark in the address for the page. Clicking this type of hyperlink will take the user directly to the place on the page where the bookmark is located.

In addition to creating links to websites, you can also create hyperlinks to email addresses by prefixing the email address with *mailto:* when you enter or paste it in the Address text box.

To link to a webpage

1. Open the **Hyperlinks** dialog box.

2. Enter or paste the URL of the webpage you want.

   Or

   Do all of the following:

   - Click the **Browse** button to the right of the **Address** field, and then click **Internet Address**. Visio opens your web browser.

   - Browse to the webpage you want, and then switch the focus back to Visio. The address of the webpage will now be in the Address field and the website title will be in the Description field, as shown in Figure 11-5.

Figure 11-5 *The address and title for a hyperlink to a website*

3. (*Optional*) Enter text or edit existing text in the **Description** field.

4. Click **OK**.

Link to a document

If a picture is worth a thousand words, yours can be worth a lot more than that when you link it to the documents—Word, Excel, Portable Document Format (PDF), and more—that are important in the context of the diagram.

To say that another way, regardless what you are diagramming in Visio, adding hyperlinks can turn your diagram into the visual starting point that people use to find everything they need to do their work.

To link to a document

1. Open the **Hyperlinks** dialog box.

2. Click the **Browse** button to the right of the **Address** field, and then click **Local File**.

> **TIP** "Local File" is misleading terminology. You can link to a file in any local or networked location.

> ⚠ **IMPORTANT** When you open the Link To File dialog box, Visio displays the names of Visio files only. Consequently, you must change the file type filter or you won't see the files you want.

3. Click the file type arrow in the lower-right corner of the **Link to File** dialog box to display the list of file types, as shown in Figure 11-6.

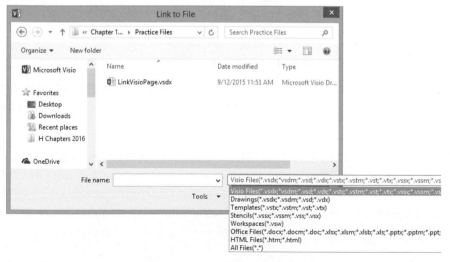

Figure 11-6 *Visio always assumes you want to link to a Visio document, so you need to select a different file type in all other cases*

11

TIP Use the All Files entry in file type list to link to PDF documents and other non-Office documents.

4. Click **Office Files** or another file type.

5. Select the file you want to link to, and then click **Open**. The Hyperlinks dialog box now contains the path to the target document and uses the file name as the default description, as shown in Figure 11-7.

Figure 11-7 *The relative path to a Word document in a subfolder*

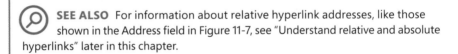 **SEE ALSO** For information about relative hyperlink addresses, like those shown in the Address field in Figure 11-7, see "Understand relative and absolute hyperlinks" later in this chapter.

6. (*Optional*) The **Description** field generally contains the name of the selected file, but you can enter different text if you want to.

7. Click **OK**.

Link to a specific location in a document

If you think that linking to a document is a powerful capability, you might be surprised to know that it gets better: You can create a hyperlink to a specific location inside a document.

Imagine a process map that refers to the same budget workbook at 13 different steps in the process. Imagine also that the budget workbook contains five worksheets, each with different data. If each of the 13 hyperlinks opens the workbook by using a generic hyperlink to the document, the reader will be left to guess where the data relevant to that step in the process resides.

Now imagine that instead of just opening the workbook, each of the 13 hyperlinks presents the reader with a specific cell or set of cells!

The secret to accomplishing scenarios like this is knowing that you can create links to named locations in Excel worksheets, Word documents, and PowerPoint presentations.

- In Excel, you can assign names to individual cells or to cell ranges. In either case, a hyperlink to a named cell or range will open the appropriate worksheet and highlight the target cell or cells.

- In Word, you can create named bookmarks in two ways:

    - You can assign a name to the location of the insertion point.

    - You can assign a name to a range of text—anything from one character to multiple paragraphs.

    If you create a bookmark by using the first method, your Visio hyperlink will jump to the part of the page containing the bookmark; if you create the second type of bookmark, your hyperlink will jump to and highlight the selected text.

- In PowerPoint, you can't assign names to specific locations, but you can refer to slides either by number or slide title.

To link to a specific location in an Office document

1. Open the **Hyperlinks** dialog box.

2. Click the **Browse** button to the right of the **Address** field, and then click **Local File**.

> **TIP** "Local File" is misleading terminology. You can link to a file in any local or networked location.

3. In the **Link to File** dialog box, click the file type arrow in the lower-right corner to display the list of file types, as shown in Figure 11-6.

4. Click **Office Files,** select the file you want to link to, and then click **Open**.

11

5. In the **Sub-address** box, enter the following information pertaining to the Office document you selected:

   - **Excel** The name of a cell or cell range
   - **Word** The name of a bookmark
   - **PowerPoint** A slide number or a unique slide title

6. (*Optional*) Although the **Description** field generally contains the name of the selected file, you can enter different text if you want to.

7. Click **OK**.

Edit and delete existing hyperlinks

You can both edit and delete existing hyperlinks.

To open the Hyperlinks dialog box when a shape already contains a hyperlink

1. Do any of the following:

   - On the **Insert** tab, in the **Links** group, click the **Hyperlink** button.
   - Right-click a shape, and then click **Edit Hyperlinks**.
   - Press **Ctrl+K**.

To edit a hyperlink

1. Open the **Hyperlinks** dialog box.

2. Select the hyperlink you want to change if it is not already selected. After it's selected, the hyperlink's details will appear in the appropriate boxes at the top of the Hyperlinks dialog box.

3. Change the **Address, Sub-address,** or **Description** information by using the techniques described in any of the sections earlier in this topic, and then click **OK**.

To delete a hyperlink

1. Open the **Hyperlinks** dialog box.

2. Select the hyperlink you want to delete if it is not already selected.

3. Click **Delete**, and then click **OK**.

Add multiple hyperlinks

You can provide the readers of your diagrams with a choice of destinations by adding multiple hyperlinks to a Visio shape. The set of hyperlinks on a shape can include any combination of documents, websites, Visio pages, or other link types.

Visio signals the presence of multiple hyperlinks in three ways, two of which are shown in Figure 11-8.

- Pointing to a shape generates a ScreenTip that displays the text *Multiple Hyperlinks*.

- The right-click shortcut menu lists all available links.

- The lower section of the Hyperlinks dialog box, which is visible in Figure 11-2, displays the descriptions of all existing links.

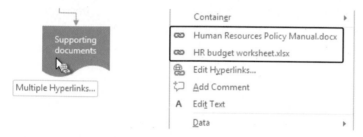

Figure 11-8 *The presence of multiple hyperlinks appears in two ways*

To add additional hyperlinks

1. Open the **Hyperlinks** dialog box, and then click the **New** button.

2. Use any of the techniques described earlier in this topic to add a hyperlink, and then click **OK**.

Understand relative and absolute hyperlinks

You have probably noticed a Use Relative Path For Hyperlink check box in the Hyperlinks dialog box. If you're *very* observant, you might also have noticed that this check box is unavailable if you haven't yet saved your drawing, but is available and selected by default if your current drawing has been saved. What's this all about?

With Visio, you can build two types of links:

- **Relative link** This type of link provides a path to a target by assuming a known starting location.

  As an analogy in the physical world, let's say you need to attend a meeting in Room 216 at Lucerne Publishing. If you're standing at the reception desk in the lobby of the company's office and ask where the meeting is located, the receptionist might say, "Go up to the second floor. It's the second door on the right." Based on the known starting location you share with the receptionist— the lobby—that information is sufficient to get you to the intended location.

  Relative links in a Visio drawing work in a similar way. The folder containing the Visio drawing serves as *the lobby*, and hyperlink targets on the same disk drive are located relative to that starting point.

  For Visio drawings, relative links work nicely when the relationship between the starting point and the hyperlink targets remains fixed. Problems can arise, however, if you need to move the Visio drawing file to another computer or even to another location on the same computer. In this case, you must preserve the relative relationships from the new location of the Visio file to the target folders and files. One way you can accomplish this is by copying the entire directory structure containing the Visio drawing and its hyperlink targets.

- **Absolute link** This type of link contains all of the information required to locate a linked resource, regardless of the starting point.

  Returning to our meeting analogy, if you're at home and need directions to the conference room at Lucerne Publishing, you need a lot more information to arrive at your destination. An absolute address for the meeting room would look more like the following:

  Lucerne Publishing, 3456 Elm St., Room 216, San Francisco, CA 94117 USA

  Armed with an absolute address, you can get to the meeting from your home, or for that matter, from any starting location in the world.

  For Visio hyperlinks, absolute links work regardless of where your Visio drawing is located. You can move the drawing to a different computer and the links will continue to function without requiring any other changes.

 TIP Relative and absolute hyperlinks are not mutually exclusive within a single drawing.

What does all of this have to do with the check box in the Visio Hyperlinks dialog box?

For a saved drawing, Visio assumes that the path to the target of a hyperlink begins in the same folder that contains the Visio diagram. Thus, the default behavior in Visio is to create a relative hyperlink by using the location of your Visio drawing as the starting point for the path. When someone clicks your hyperlink, Windows figures out where the target object is by navigating from the location of the Visio drawing.

Just knowing this much explains why the Use Relative Path For Hyperlink check box is unavailable if you haven't yet saved your drawing—Visio can't create a relative link yet because there is no known starting point for the Visio drawing. Consequently, the only option in this situation is to use an absolute path that contains all of the information Windows will need to track down the target object.

Although there are no firm guidelines on when to use relative links rather than absolute links, it's a good idea to think about your environment and the nature of your document collection before creating very many links in Visio. If all of your target documents are in their final resting place—on a network server or in a SharePoint repository, for example—then absolute links probably make the most sense. However, if your environment is more volatile, or you know in advance that you'll be moving your Visio drawing and its hyperlink targets to another computer or to a CD or DVD, then carefully constructed relative links are a good choice.

The following examples should help to make the alternatives clearer. In the examples, assume that the *HR Process Maps* Visio diagram is saved in C:\Human Resources \Process Maps\ and that the hyperlink target is one of the Word documents shown in the directory listing in Figure 11-9. The file name of each Word document includes a parenthetical note to indicate its relative position compared to *HR Process Maps*. Consequently, the file names of the Word documents include notations like (*above*), (*below*), and (*same*).

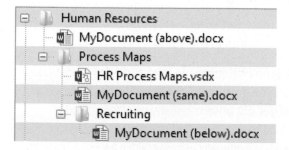

Figure 11-9 *The directory structure for the hyperlink examples that follow*

11

Based on the file structure shown in Figure 11-9, each of the following examples describes the action Visio takes in response to the user selecting a target document. In each case, Visio fills in the Address field and sets the Use Relative Path For Hyperlink check box based on the locations of the Visio drawing and the target document.

- When the target document is in the same folder as *HR Process Maps.vsdx*, Visio creates a relative hyperlink with the Address field result shown in Figure 11-10.

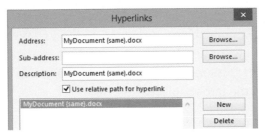

Figure 11-10 *A relative address to a Word document located in the same directory as the Visio document containing the hyperlink*

If you now clear the Use Relative Path For Hyperlink check box, the link becomes an absolute link that begins at the root of drive C. The Address field displays the full path to the document:

C:\Human Resources\Process Maps\MyDocument (same).docx

The first part of the absolute path is visible in the Address field in Figure 11-11.

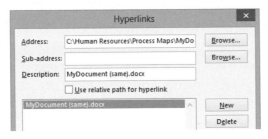

Figure 11-11 *An absolute address to a Word document located on drive C*

- When you link to a document located in C:\Human Resources\Process Maps \Recruiting\, which is a subfolder of the one containing the Visio drawing, Visio creates a relative hyperlink and the Address field contains the text shown in Figure 11-12, indicating that the target document is in a subfolder called *Recruiting*.

Figure 11-12 *A relative address to a Word document located in a subdirectory of the folder containing the Visio document that includes the hyperlink*

- When the target document is located in C:\Human Resources\, which is a parent folder of the one containing the Visio document, Visio creates a relative hyperlink. The Address text is shown in Figure 11-13.

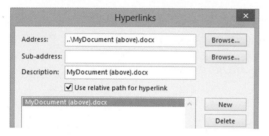

Figure 11-13 *A relative address to a Word document located in a directory above the folder containing the Visio document that includes the hyperlink*

 TIP "..\" is syntax that predates Windows. It means "go up one directory level."

- When the target document is located on any drive other than the one containing the Visio document, for example, drive D, drive K, or a network share such as \\MyServer\Human Resources\FY2016\, Visio always creates an absolute link and the Address field contains something like one of the following entries:

K:\HR Folder\MyDocument.docx

or

\\MyServer\Human Resources\FY2016\MyDocument.docx

The Address field in Figure 11-14 shows the first part of the path to a target document on drive N.

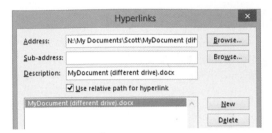

Figure 11-14 *An absolute address to a Word document located on a different drive than the one containing the Visio document that includes the hyperlink*

One final note: Visio always creates an absolute link if you begin your address with a server name, drive letter, or web protocol. All of the following will create absolute links regardless of the location of the Visio drawing:

- *C:\SomeFolder\MyWorkbook.xlsx*

- *\\MyServer\Presentations\MySlideShow.pptx*

- *http://www.contoso.com/Somepage.html*

Set the hyperlink base

Visio includes a document-level property called the hyperlink base, which you can use to shift all relative hyperlinks in a document from one location to another. If you enter a value in the hyperlink base field, Visio will prepend all relative links with that value.

For example, if you create a hyperlink base of http://OurIntranet/Finance/ and create a relative hyperlink of AuditInfo.html, Visio will combine the two to create a link that consists of the following string of characters:

http://OurIntranet/Finance/AuditInfo.html

> ⚠️ **IMPORTANT** There is only one hyperlink base per Visio document. If you create a directory path hyperlink base or a web-based hyperlink base, Visio will use it for *all* relative links in your document. You must be extremely careful when establishing a hyperlink base in a diagram.
>
> As a rule, you should create a hyperlink base only if all relative links in the diagram are of the same type; that is, all relative links consist of URLs to web locations or all lead to files on a disk.

To edit the hyperlink base

1. In the Backstage view, display the **Info** page, and then click the **Properties** button that is located on the right side of the screen. The button is easy to overlook; you can see the pointer resting on top of it in Figure 11-15.

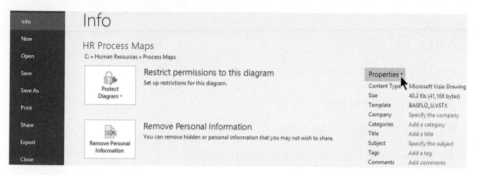

Figure 11-15 *The Properties button might not be obvious unless the pointer is on top of it*

2. On the menu that appears, click **Advanced Properties**.

3. In the **Properties** dialog box, enter text in the **Hyperlink base** field. Figure 11-16 shows two examples: a disk-based example on the left and a web-based example on the right.

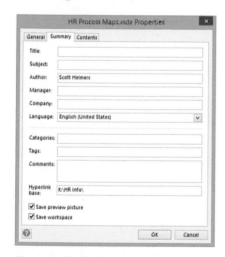

Figure 11-16 *The Properties dialog box with two Hyperlink Base examples*

4. Click **OK**.

To remove the hyperlink base

1. Open the **Properties** dialog box.

2. Delete the text from the **Hyperlink base** field, and then click **OK**.

Skills review

In this chapter, you learned how to:

- Follow hyperlinks
- Enhance diagrams by adding hyperlinks
- Understand relative and absolute hyperlinks
- Set the hyperlink base

Practice tasks

The practice files for these tasks are located in the Visio2016SBS\Ch11 folder. You can save the results of the tasks in the same folder.

Follow hyperlinks

Open the FollowHyperlinks diagram in Visio, and then perform the following tasks:

1. Follow the hyperlink on the **HR Policy Manual** shape. Notice that the Word document opens to the Interviewing page.

2. Follow the hyperlink on the **Advertise open job** shape.

Enhance diagrams by adding hyperlinks

Open the EnhanceDiagrams diagram in Visio, and then perform the following tasks:

 IMPORTANT After each of the tasks listed below, follow the hyperlink you've created to ensure that it works.

1. Link the shape on **Page-1** to **Page-3**.

2. Link the first triangle on **Page-3** to the second triangle on **Page-2**, and set the **Zoom** level to **200%**.

3. Link the second triangle on **Page-3** to **Page-1** of **FollowHyperlinks.vsdx** in the Visio2016SBS\Ch11 folder.

4. Link the third triangle on **Page-3** to any website you want.

5. Link the first star on **Page-4** to **Human Resources Policy Manual.docx** in the Visio2016SBS\Ch11 folder. Close the Word document after following the hyperlink.

6. Link the second star on **Page-4** to an Excel workbook.

7. Link the third star on **Page-4** to a PDF document.

8. Edit the hyperlink on the first star on **Page-4** so it links to a bookmark in the same document by entering **Recruiting** in the **Sub-address** box.

9. Delete the bookmark from the second star on **Page-4**.

10. Add a second hyperlink of any type to the third star on **Page-4**.

11. Bonus points: Add a mailto URL to the fourth star on **Page-4** so it sends email to Scott@VisioStepByStep.com.

12. Save the diagram to use it in the next tasks.

Understand relative and absolute hyperlinks

There are no practice tasks for this topic.

Set the hyperlink base

Open the EnhanceDiagrams diagram that you edited in the previous practice task, and then perform the following tasks:

1. Test the Word document hyperlink on the first star on **Page-4** to ensure that the target Word document opens.

2. Close Word.

3. Set the hyperlink base in the Visio diagram to X:\Another folder\.

4. Test the Word document hyperlink on the first star on **Page-4** again and notice the path Visio tried to follow that is displayed in the error message.

5. Remove the hyperlink base from the document.

Print, reuse, and share diagrams

When you create a Visio diagram, chances are good that you will want to share it with other people. If you want to share a paper copy, Visio offers flexible printing options.

In many cases, however, you will want to share all or part of your diagram in electronic form, often with people who don't have Visio. When that need arises, you can turn your diagram into a Visio template, save it as a PDF document, or create multiple types of images. You can even save your diagram as a fully functional website that is tailored to the needs of your audience.

> 🔍 **SEE ALSO** For other ways to share a diagram, see "The Share page" section in Chapter 1, "Get started with Visio 2016."

Because Visio diagrams can contain private information, it's important to understand the Visio features that are available to remove private content before sharing a file. You can also use the Microsoft Office Information Rights Management (IRM) capabilities to help protect your document.

This chapter guides you through procedures related to previewing and printing drawings, removing personal information from Visio diagrams, creating graphics, saving diagrams in other file formats, creating templates, sharing diagrams by using the Visio Viewer, and publishing diagrams to the web.

In this chapter

- Preview and print drawings
- Remove personal information
- Create graphics
- Save drawings in other file formats
- Create templates
- Share diagrams by using the Visio Viewer
- Publish diagrams to the web

Practice files

For this chapter, use the practice files from the Visio2016SBS\Ch12 folder. For practice file download instructions, see the introduction.

Preview and print drawings

The Visio 2016 print preview pane displays page images so you can easily determine how your diagram will print. Figure 12-1 shows a network diagram that will require four sheets of paper to print based on the diagram size and the current printer and drawing page size settings.

> **TIP** The diagram in Figure 12-1 is one of the starter diagrams included with the Detailed Network Diagram template in Visio Professional 2016. For information about starter diagrams, see Chapter 1, "Get started with Visio 2016."

The preview pane on the Print page always opens to the active page in your diagram. If your diagram contains more than one page, you can use the page selector in the lower center of the Print page to preview other diagram pages (look for 1 Of 2 with a pair of arrows in the lower center of Figure 12-1). You can also zoom in and out on the preview image by using the slider in the lower-right corner.

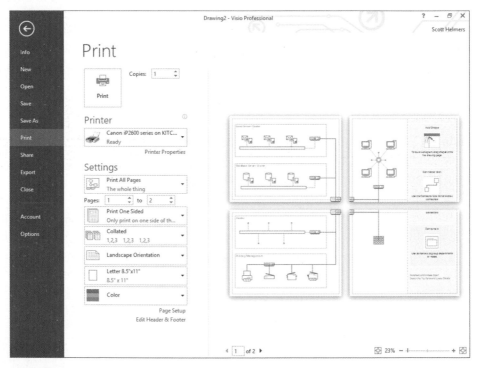

Figure 12-1 *In addition to the visible controls, you can drag to pan the print preview image*

TIP Print preview images are displayed in either grayscale or color depending on your printer capabilities and settings.

Notice that a portion of the router shape in the center of the diagram in Figure 12-1 will print on each of the four printer pages. You can use the Move Off Page Breaks feature, which is new in Visio 2016, to have Visio assist in shifting shapes so the diagram will print more effectively. Figure 12-2 shows the result for the center portion of the print preview. You might still want to nudge the router farther to the right to eliminate the last bit of shape residue.

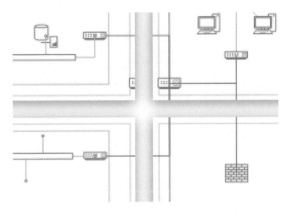

Figure 12-2 *A close-up of the center of the preview pane*

 TIP When you move the cursor into the preview pane on the Print page, the pointer changes to a hand. You can click anywhere on the preview image and drag to reposition the preview.

The network diagram in the preceding two figures was created in US units and both the drawing pages and printer paper are set to 8.5-by-11 inches. Because there are network shapes beyond the 11-inch width and 8.5-inch height, Visio expanded the drawing page, which is why four printer pages are required to accommodate the large diagram.

If you change the printer paper dimensions to a size that contains all four drawing pages, the print preview reflects the change, as shown in Figure 12-3.

12

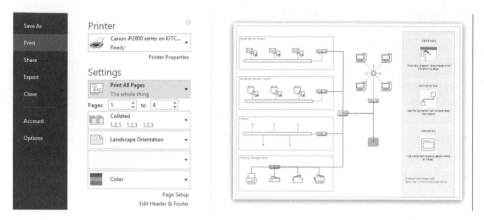

Figure 12-3 *A large printer-paper size can contain the entire network diagram on one sheet*

> 🔍 **SEE ALSO** For information about setting drawing page and printer paper sizes, see "Manage pages" in Chapter 3, "Manage text, shapes, and pages."

The left pane of the Print page contains the Printer menu and the Settings menus that are common to all Microsoft Office applications.

You use the first menu in the Settings section, shaded in blue in Figure 12-3, to select the range of pages or parts of the current page to be printed, just as you do for other Office applications. However, two additional print options are available at the bottom of the menu for this button in Visio:

- **No Background** Switches between inclusion and exclusion of the page background from the print preview and printed output.

- **High Quality** Switches between inclusion and exclusion of certain effects, such as reflections, from the print preview and printed output.

At the end of the Settings section is an Edit Header & Footer link. In Visio, headers and footers print information on the top and bottom of each printer page and are independent of the drawing page. Consequently, you might use headers and footers for Visio diagrams in which the drawing page is spread across multiple printer pages.

However, the majority of Visio documents are configured to print each drawing page on a single sheet of paper. If you have text or graphics that you want to appear on every printed page, it's better practice to put that content on a background page.

 SEE ALSO For information about background pages, see the section "Work with background pages and borders" in Chapter 3, "Manage text, shapes, and pages."

To display a print preview

1. Do any of the following:

   - In the left pane of the Backstage view, click **Print**.

   - Press **Ctrl+P**.

   - Press **Alt+F, P**.

   - Press **Alt+F, V** (to maintain compatibility with Visio 2007 and earlier).

To print a diagram

1. On the **Print** page of the Backstage view, click **Print**.

To add or edit the header and footer

1. On the **Print** page of the Backstage view, click **Edit Header & Footer**, make the required change, and then click **OK**.

To move shapes off page breaks

1. On the **Home** tab, in the **Arrange** group, click the **Move off Page Breaks** button.

12

Remove personal information

Every Visio document contains a collection of metadata about the document itself. The contents of some of the data fields are supplied by Visio, including the name of the document author; some are prefilled based on the template from which you create a document; some are blank unless you enter values.

You can view and change metadata fields in the Properties section on the right side of the Info page in the Backstage view, as shown in Figure 12-4.

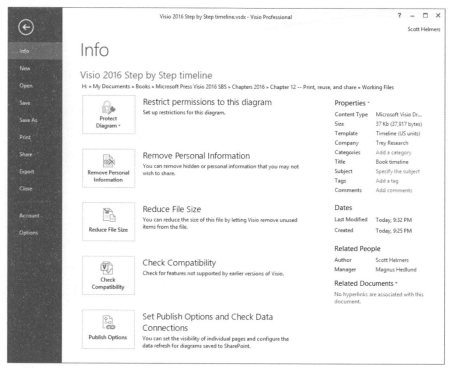

Figure 12-4 *The Info page includes document properties and a button to remove personal information*

You can also view or update metadata in the document's Properties dialog box, as shown in Figure 12-5.

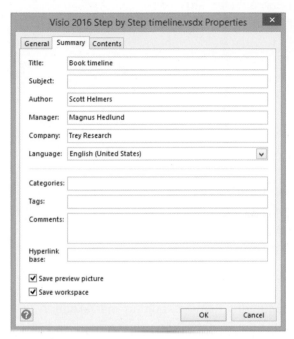

Figure 12-5 *The Properties dialog box displays the author's name, manager's name, and company name*

If you plan to post your diagram in a public place or simply want to ensure that personal information, reviewer's marks, and other potentially private content are deleted, use the Remove Hidden Information dialog box shown in Figure 12-6.

12

Figure 12-6 *You can select which types of hidden data to remove from your diagram*

The Remove Hidden Information dialog box offers three check boxes:

- **Remove these items from the document** Removes editing and validation markup and data that appears in the document's Properties section

- **Warn me if I try to reinsert this information** Helps to protect you if you inadvertently add personal details back to the document after removing them

- **Remove data from external sources stored in the document** Removes private information from data sources to which this diagram has been linked

> **SEE ALSO** For information about linking diagrams to external data, see Chapter 10, "Link to external data."

Not all of the items you can remove are visible in the document properties, but if you compare Figure 12-7 with either Figure 12-4 or Figure 12-5, you'll see a number of important differences.

> ⚠ **IMPORTANT** Information Rights Management (IRM) is another means for helping to protect your Visio diagrams. See the "What is Information Rights Management?" sidebar following this topic for information about IRM.

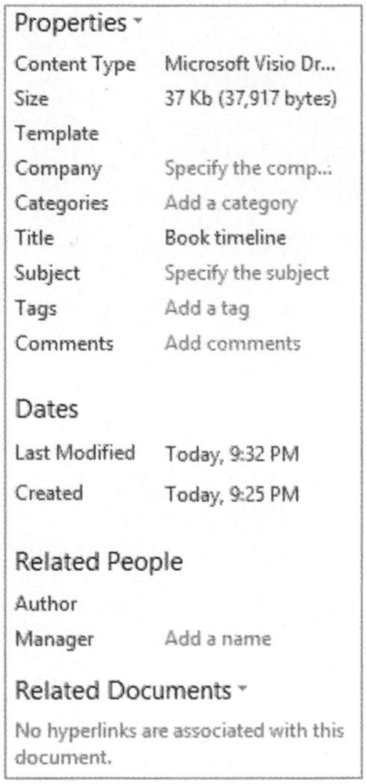

Properties ▾

Content Type	Microsoft Visio Dr...
Size	37 Kb (37,917 bytes)
Template	
Company	Specify the comp...
Categories	Add a category
Title	Book timeline
Subject	Specify the subject
Tags	Add a tag
Comments	Add comments

Dates

Last Modified	Today, 9:32 PM
Created	Today, 9:25 PM

Related People

Author	
Manager	Add a name

Related Documents ▾

No hyperlinks are associated with this document.

Figure 12-7 *Personal content has been removed from this diagram*

To view or edit document properties

1. Display the **Info** page of the Backstage view.

2. (*Optional*) Click the current value of the field you want to change, and then enter the required information.

Or

1. On the **Info** page of the Backstage view, click the **Properties** button, and then click the **Advanced Properties** button.

2. (*Optional*) Enter data into the appropriate fields.

3. Click **OK**.

To remove personal information

1. On the **Info** page of the Backstage view, click **Remove Personal Information**.

2. In the **Remove Hidden Information** dialog box, click the options you want, and then click **OK**.

12

What is Information Rights Management?

Visio 2016 provides the added security and control of Information Rights Management (IRM). You can help to protect the content in your Visio diagram by specifying who can view and who can edit your diagrams.

IMPORTANT Before you can use IRM in a Visio document, an administrator must have activated the rights management service within your organization's Office 365 or internal network.

In a Visio diagram, enabling IRM begins by clicking the Protect Document button on the Info page of the Backstage view to display the Restrict Access menu, as shown in Figure 12-8.

Figure 12-8 *You can choose an IRM protection template from the Restrict Access menu*

If you choose Restricted Access, you can configure the settings in the Permission dialog box, shown in Figure 12-9, to identify specific people who can read or change your diagram. The people you specify can be located both inside and outside your organization.

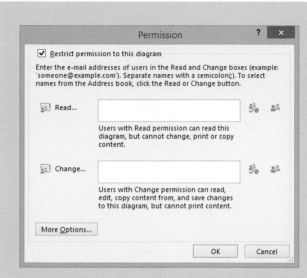

Figure 12-9 *You control who can read or change your diagram*

If you want to restrict access solely to people within your organization, you can select either of the Confidential options shown on the Restrict Access menu. Both Confidential entries shown in Figure 12-8 include the words *Visio Step by Step*, because that is the organization name for the author's Office 365 account. If you are connected to an organizational network when you display the Restricted Access menu, the name of your organization will be displayed.

When a Visio user opens a restricted document, the software displays an appropriate warning or error, depending on who the user is and what rights he or she has for the document. For example, the message in Figure 12-10 appears at the top of the drawing window when a user within my organization has been authorized to read, but not change, a document.

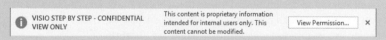

Figure 12-10 *A user has insufficient permission to edit this document*

Create graphics

A handy feature in Visio is the ability to create image files from some or all of the elements on a drawing page. The most frequently used image formats are located in the Graphic File Types section of the Export page in the Backstage view, as shown in Figure 12-11.

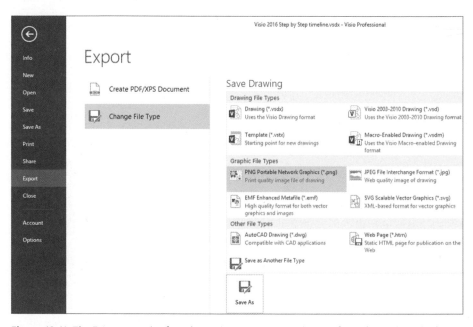

Figure 12-11 *The Export page is often the easiest way to create images from shapes in Visio diagrams*

The full range of graphical file types is available on the Save As menu, as noted by the boxed areas in Figure 12-12. The remaining file types shown in the figure are described in the following topic.

> **TIP** If you need a detailed description of any of these file formats, you can find plenty of information on the Internet. For example, a Wikipedia article describes most of the formats in the preceding list: *www.wikipedia.org/wiki/Image_file_formats*.

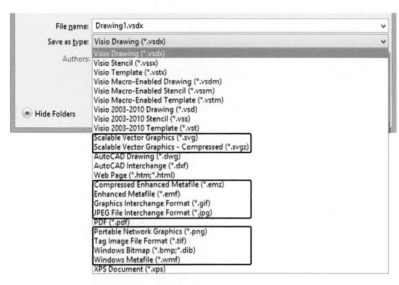

Figure 12-12 *All available file types are displayed in the Save As dialog box*

Most image types provide a dialog box you can use to configure the image format details. Figure 12-13 shows the PNG Output Options dialog box as an example.

Figure 12-13 *PNG image options are representative of the customizations you can make when you create image files*

> **TIP** If you need to manipulate a photo or other image and don't have image editing software, you can often use Visio to accomplish what you need. Either insert the image or paste it onto a Visio drawing page, and then use the buttons on the Picture Tools tab that appears when an image is selected. See Chapter 1, "Get started with Visio 2016" for more information about tool tabs.

In general, creating images in Visio is a shape-oriented, not a page-oriented, operation. To say that another way, Visio does not provide a built-in method to create an image of an entire page because it always creates images of shapes.

Figure 12-14 shows an entire Visio drawing page; it will serve as an example for the remainder of this section.

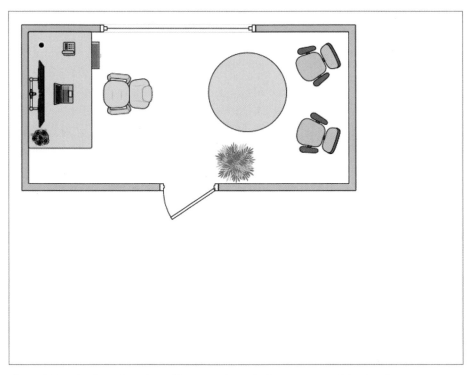

Figure 12-14 *The floor plan of an office occupying only the upper part of the drawing page*

If you select several shapes before exporting to an image file, the image will display just those shapes. To create Figure 12-15, only the desk and chair were selected.

Figure 12-15 *A close-up of a desk and chair*

However, if no shapes are selected when you export, Visio will create an image that is only as big as the rectangle surrounding the shapes on the page. White space between that rectangle and the page boundaries will not be included. For example, Figure 12-16 was created when no shapes were selected; compare this image with the one in Figure 12-14.

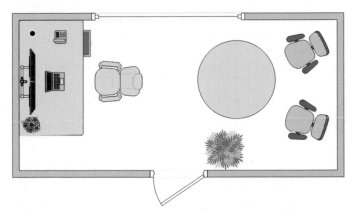

Figure 12-16 *The "full page" image includes shapes but not the surrounding white space*

12

 TIP If you want to create an image of an entire Visio drawing page, you must place one or more shapes at the page boundaries to force Visio to capture the entire page. The easiest techniques for accomplishing this are to: 1) draw a rectangle with no fill at the page margins, effectively creating a border around the page; or 2) place a pair of very small shapes in opposite corners of the page.

If you use the first technique, you can make the line nearly invisible by making it very thin and giving it a color that is almost the same as the page background. If you use the second method, you can make the small shapes nearly invisible by making them very, very tiny or by making their fill color nearly the same as the page background, or both. In either case, do not use a color that is the same as the page background. If your shapes and the background are the same color, Visio will not detect your shapes and will exclude them from the exported image.

To save selected shapes as an image

1. On the **Export** page of the Backstage view, click **Change File Type**.

2. In the **Graphic File Types** section, do either of the following:

   - Click the image type you want, and then click **Save As**.

   - Double-click the image type you want.

3. In the **Save As** dialog box, navigate to the location you want, and then click **Save**.

4. Accept or change the image-type-specific **Output Options**, and then click **OK**.

Or

1. On the **Save As** page of the Backstage view, click the storage location you want.

2. In the **Save As** dialog box, click the **Save as type** arrow, and then click the file type you want.

3. Enter the file name you want, and then click **Save**.

4. Accept or change the image-type-specific **Output Options**, and then click **OK**.

To save all shapes on the page as an image

1. Do either of the following:

   - Select all shapes on the page.

   - Click the page background to deselect all shapes.

2. Follow the instructions in the "To save selected shapes as an image" procedure to save selected shapes.

Save drawings in other file formats

In addition to creating multiple types of graphics files for shapes located on a single page, with Visio, you can save your entire drawing in more than a dozen formats shown in Table 12-1 and Table 12-2.

> **⚠ IMPORTANT** The standard file formats for Visio 2016 and Visio 2013 drawings, stencils, and templates cannot contain macros. In Table 12-1, notice that a separate, macro-enabled file format exists for each of those three file types for situations in which you need to include macros with the file.

Table 12-1 Visio file types

Save As format name	File extension	Description
Visio Drawing	.vsdx	Visio 2016 and Visio 2013 drawing (cannot contain macros)
Visio Stencil	.vssx	Visio 2016 and Visio 2013 stencil (cannot contain macros)
Visio Template	.vstx	Visio 2016 and Visio 2013 template (cannot contain macros)
Visio Macro-Enabled Drawing	.vsdm	Visio 2016 and Visio 2013 macro-enabled drawing
Visio Macro-Enabled Stencil	.vssm	Visio 2016 and Visio 2013 macro-enabled stencil
Visio Macro-Enabled Template	.vstm	Visio 2016 and Visio 2013 macro-enabled template
Visio 2003-2010 Drawing	.vsd	Visio drawing in file format used in Visio 2003 through Visio 2010
Visio 2003-2010 Stencil	.vss	Visio stencil in file format used in Visio 2003 through Visio 2010
Visio 2003-2010 Template	.vst	Visio template in file format used in Visio 2003 through Visio 2010

12

> **TIP** Visio 2016 can create files that are compatible with Visio versions back to Visio 2003 but cannot create files that are compatible with Visio 2002 or earlier.

Table 12-2 Non-Visio (and non-image) file types

Save As format name	File extension	Description
AutoCAD Drawing	.dwg	AutoCAD drawing format; file can be opened directly by AutoCAD and other CAD systems that use this file format
AutoCAD Interchange	.dxf	AutoCAD drawing exchange format; intended to provide greater interoperability among systems that do not use .dwg extensions
PDF	.pdf	Adobe Portable Document Format; accurate rendering of a Visio drawing, including most hyperlinks, that is intended to be read-only; requires free PDF viewer
XPS Document	.xps	XML Paper Specification; an alternative to PDF for creating high-quality, read-only renderings of a document; requires free XPS viewer
Web Page	.htm/.html	HTML rendering of a Visio drawing that is viewable with a web browser

All of the entries in Table 12-1 and the first two entries in Table 12-2 always save the entire Visio drawing in the new format. However, the last three entries in Table 12-2— PDF, XPS, and Web Page—give you the choice of saving a subset of your pages into the format you want. Each offers an options dialog box, similar to the one for PDF documents shown in Figure 12-17.

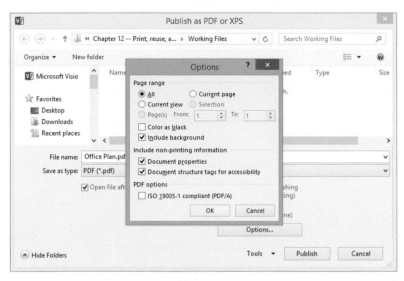

Figure 12-17 *You can select a page range along with other format-specific options in the Options dialog box*

To save a diagram as a PDF

1. On the **Export** page of the Backstage view, click **Create PDF/XPS**.

2. Navigate to the location you want, and then click **Publish**.

Or

1. On the **Save As** page of the Backstage view, click the storage location you want.

2. In the **Save As** dialog box, click the **Save as type** arrow, and then click **PDF (*.pdf)**.

3. Enter the file name you want, and then click **Save**.

To customize PDF output

1. Open the **Save As** dialog box, and then click the **Options** button.

2. Change the options that you want to be different, click **OK**, and then click **Publish**.

To save a diagram in another file format

1. On the **Export** page of the Backstage view, click **Change File Type**.

2. Do either of the following:

   - In either the **Drawing File Types** section or the **Other File Types** section, click the file type you want, and then click **Save As**.

   - In the **Graphic File Types** section, double-click the image type you want.

3. Navigate to the location you want, and then click **Save**.

4. Accept or change the image-type-specific **Output Options**, and then click **OK**.

Or

1. On the **Save As** page of the Backstage view, click the storage location you want.

2. In the **Save As** dialog box, click the **Save as type** arrow, and then click the file type you want.

3. Enter the file name you want, and then click **Save**.

Create templates

Technically, saving a diagram as a Visio template is no different than saving it in any of the other file formats described in the preceding topic. Despite the ease of creating them, templates are described separately in this topic because of their potential importance.

Why would you want to save a diagram as a template? Because despite the dozens of templates provided with Visio, Microsoft can't possibly envision every type of diagram you will want to create.

In addition, although you can open a diagram and reuse it as is, a key advantage of a template is that the template document is never modified by accident. This is especially valuable if you share your template with other people; just like the templates that are packaged with Visio, whenever a user selects your template, Visio creates a new diagram and leaves the template untouched.

You might create a custom template simply by enhancing one of the standard Visio templates with a background page that displays your organization's logo on every page. Or you might create a very elaborate template that includes your own stencils and shapes, multiple foreground and background pages, preset shapes on certain pages, and a legal notice on the bottom of every page. There are no limitations on the contents of a template; you can include anything that will make creating a new diagram easier.

To save a diagram as a template

1. Follow the steps in the "To save a Visio diagram in another file format" procedure at the end of the preceding topic, choosing **Template (*.vstx)** or **Visio Template (*.vstx)** as the file type.

Where do I store custom templates?

You can store custom templates in any location you want—for example, on your own computer if only you will use them, or on a server to share them with other people.

You can use a template by double-clicking its file name in File Explorer, but you can make custom templates more accessible by configuring Visio to include them on the New page in the Backstage view.

The following example uses a folder called *Trey Research Templates* that contains three custom templates. To inform Visio of the location for your template folder:

1. On the **Options** page of the Backstage view, click **Advanced**.

2. Scroll to the bottom of the **Advanced** settings, and then click the **File Locations** button.

3. In the **Templates** field of the **File Locations** dialog box, enter the path to the folder that contains the Trey Research Templates folder.

   IMPORTANT Note the wording in the preceding sentence: "enter the path to the folder that contains the Trey Research Templates folder." In other words, do not include the target folder in the template path—stop one folder above that folder. This ensures that your folder name appears in the Template Categories pane along with the Visio-supplied template categories. For example, in Figure 12-18, the Trey Research Templates folder is located within the Documents folder, so the words *Trey Research Templates* are not included in the path.

Figure 12-18 *In addition to templates, you can set custom locations for drawings, stencils, and add-ons*

12

4. After you enter the template path, click **OK** twice. When you restart Visio, the Template Categories section of the New page should look similar to Figure 12-19.

Figure 12-19 *Your custom templates can be available on the New page*

5. Double-click **Trey Research Templates** to display the templates in that folder, as shown in Figure 12-20.

Figure 12-20 *Custom templates for office layouts, org charts, and timelines*

Share diagrams by using the Visio Viewer

Microsoft Office 2016 includes the Visio Viewer as a default installation option. Consequently, if your system includes Office but not Visio, you can still view any Visio diagram.

The Visio Viewer runs as an add-on to Internet Explorer, which displays Visio diagrams in the browser, as shown in Figure 12-21.

 IMPORTANT The first time you use the Visio Viewer, you might be required to grant permission for Internet Explorer to load the Visio Viewer add-on.

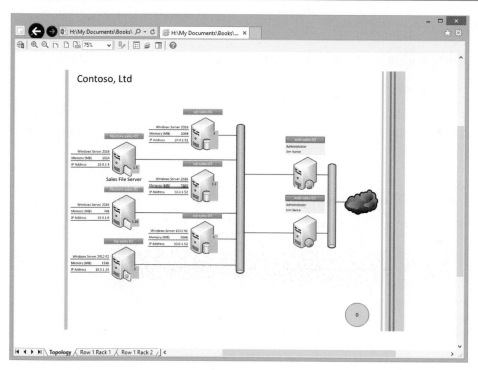

Figure 12-21 *A high-quality view of a Visio diagram on a device that does not have Visio*

12

The upper-left corner of the Internet Explorer window includes buttons for zooming, displaying shape data, viewing and controlling layers, and viewing comments. The lower-left edge offers page navigation buttons along with page name tabs in a multipage diagram.

 IMPORTANT On a device that includes both Office and Visio, Visio drawings always open in Visio.

Publish diagrams to the web

Visio 2016 retains a long-time feature that automatically builds a website from any diagram. You can use this capability to share diagrams with people who might not have Visio installed on their computers.

A Visio-generated website includes all foreground pages, provides a table of contents, and preserves both page-to-page and external hyperlinks. Although the website will be viewable with almost any web browser, the results are enhanced by using Internet Explorer because it provides the following additional features:

- A pan-and-zoom pane, which you can click and drag to zoom and navigate around any page

- A details window to present shape data

- Full-text search for all text in the drawing

Whether you want to share drawings with colleagues by using your intranet site, or publish drawings on the public World Wide Web, the Save As Web Page feature can make your diagrams more accessible.

View web-published diagrams

Figure 12-22 shows a network diagram that has been published to the web by using default options.

> ⚠ **IMPORTANT** Depending on where your Visio-generated webpages are stored, a warning might appear when you attempt to view the pages. To proceed, click Allow Blocked Content.

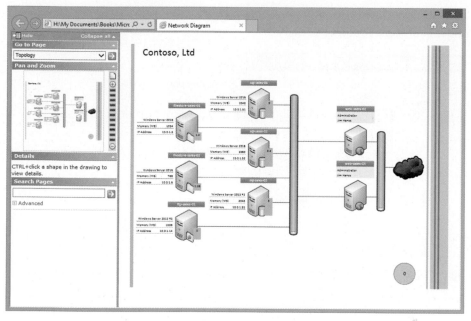

Figure 12-22 *A network diagram rendered as a webpage*

> ⚠ **IMPORTANT** The four left-panel navigation panes shown in Figure 12-22 are special
> features that require Internet Explorer and Microsoft Silverlight. If you have not
> previously installed Silverlight when you view a Visio-generated website, a button will appear
> in Internet Explorer that you can click to install it. Information about Silverlight is available at
> *www.microsoft.com/silverlight*.

You can use the navigation panes on the left side of the browser window to do the
following:

- **Go To Page** Select from the list of all pages in the current diagram, as shown in
  Figure 12-23.

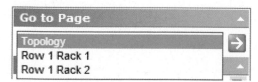

Figure 12-23 *The diagram in the web browser contains three pages*

12

■ **Pan And Zoom** Set the zoom level and pan position for the viewing pane, as shown in Figure 12-24.

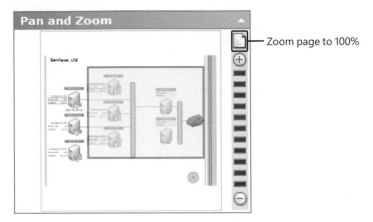

Figure 12-24 *You can set pan and zoom by dragging in the pane or by using the buttons on the right*

 TIP You can't control the shape of the box you draw in the Pan And Zoom pane. It will maintain the same aspect ratio as the viewing pane to the right.

■ **Details** View shape data, as shown in Figure 12-25.

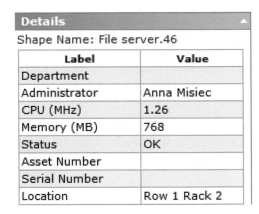

Figure 12-25 *Shape data details are available in the webpage version of a Visio diagram*

- **Search Pages** View results of full-text search, as shown in Figure 12-26.

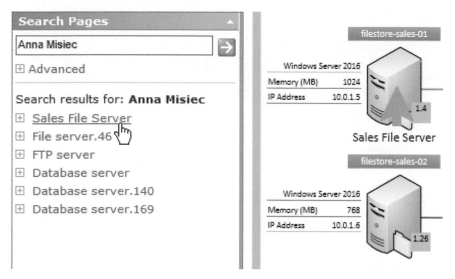

Figure 12-26 *Clicking a result highlights the target shape*

> ✓ **TIP** The full-text search feature creates a hyperlinked list of search results. Clicking any result presents the page containing the selected shape and highlights the target shape with an orange arrow for two or three seconds.

> ✓ **TIP** The default behavior for full-text search is to examine the shape name, shape text, and all shape data fields. You can alter that behavior by clicking Advanced below the search box.

When you point to a shape containing a hyperlink, a ScreenTip appears with up to three entries, as shown in Figure 12-27. The first entry is the shape text and will not be present if the shape does not contain text. The second entry provides instructions that result in the display of shape data in the Details pane, as shown in Figure 12-25. The third entry describes standard web behavior—click to follow a link.

12

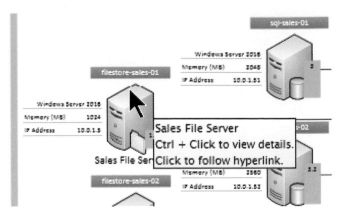

Figure 12-27 *The Sales File Server is hyperlinked to another page in the diagram*

If you view the Visio-generated website without Silverlight, or in a browser that does not support Silverlight, the main content—the webpages—will appear. However, the left panel is reduced to a hyperlinked list displaying each of the page names in the Visio diagram; you can click a page name to view that page, as shown in Figure 12-28.

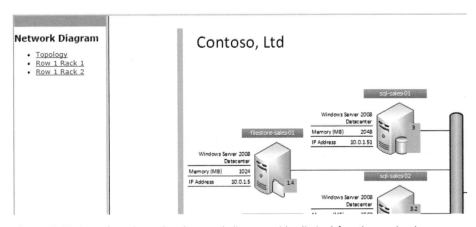

Figure 12-28 *Part of a web-rendered network diagram with a limited-function navigation pane*

To create a website from a diagram

1. On the **Export** page of the Backstage view, click **Change File Type**.

2. In the **Other File Types** section, click **Web Page (*.htm)**, and then click **Save As**.

3. In the **Save As** dialog box, navigate to the location you want, and then click **Save**.

Or

1. On the **Save As** page of the Backstage view, click the storage location you want.

2. In the **Save As** dialog box, click the **Save as type** arrow, click **Web Page (*.htm; *.html)**, and then click **Save**.

To view a different page

1. In the **Go to Page** pane, click the down-arrow, and then click the page name you want.

2. Do either of the following:

   - Press **Enter**.

   - Click the green **Go to selected page** button.

To change the zoom setting

1. Do any of the following in the **Pan and Zoom** pane:

   - Click the webpage thumbnail and draw a bounding box around the area of interest.

   - If there is a red-bordered rectangle on the webpage thumbnail, drag any edge of the rectangle.

   - Click the **Zoom in** (+) or **Zoom out** (-) button.

   - Click any of the **Zoom to** x% buttons.

   - Click the **Zoom page to 100%** button.

To pan the webpage

1. If there is not a red-bordered rectangle on the webpage thumbnail in the **Pan and Zoom** pane, drag to create one.

2. Drag the red-bordered rectangle to a new location.

To view shape data

1. Hold down the **Ctrl** key while clicking the shape whose data you want to view.

To search for text

1. In the **Search Pages** text box, enter the text you want to locate.

2. Click any of the search results to view the shape containing your search text.

12

To follow a hyperlink

1. Click the shape containing the hyperlink you want to follow.

Set publishing options

Web-published Visio drawings include full support for embedded hyperlinks along with rich navigation and search capabilities, as you discovered in the preceding section. However, you don't necessarily need all of those capabilities in every Visio-generated website, so it is convenient to be able to change the publishing options.

In addition, you might want to change the format in which Visio creates your website. By default, Visio 2016 creates webpages by using the Extensible Application Markup Language (XAML). XAML is responsible for the left-pane navigation features and requires Silverlight. If you prefer a webpage format that doesn't require Silverlight, you can select one of the five alternatives described later in this section.

The key to customizing Visio webpages is a pair of buttons in the lower portion of the Save As dialog box (shown in Figure 12-29):

- You can click the Change Title button to modify the text that will be displayed in the title bar of the web browser.

- The Publish button opens the Save As Web Page dialog box, which includes both General and Advanced tabs.

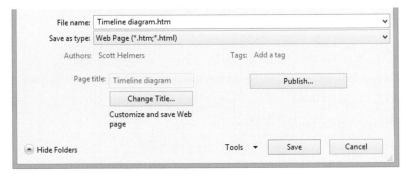

Figure 12-29 *You use the Change Title and Publish buttons to customize your Visio-generated website*

Use the settings on the General tab

The General tab of the Save As Web Page dialog box, shown in Figure 12-30, includes one note-worthy feature that is easy to miss: you can include report output along with the pages of your diagram. The list in the Publishing Options section includes both navigation panes and reports.

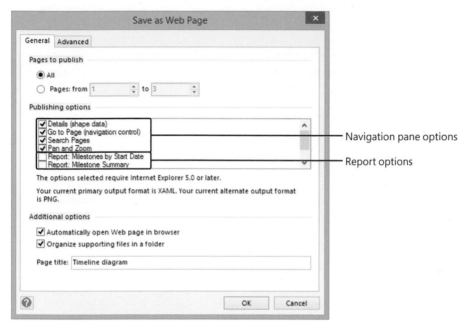

Figure 12-30 *When you create a website, you can change what content it will contain*

The General tab is divided into three sections:

- **Pages to publish** You can select a subset of the diagram's pages to include in the web-published output.

- **Publishing options** You can select which navigation pane options and which reports, if any, should be included in your website.

> ⚠ **IMPORTANT** The only way to view reports in your web-published drawing is via the Go To Page navigation pane. Consequently, if you include reports as part of your website, you must leave the Go To Page check box selected.

> ✓ **TIP** Visio remembers the settings for the navigation pane options you select; the same settings will appear the next time you save a drawing as a webpage. However, Visio *does not* remember the settings for the reports you choose; none of the report check boxes will be selected the next time you save a drawing as a webpage.

12

- **Additional options** This section contains three options:

  - Each time you create a website, Visio opens it in your browser. You can clear the Automatically Open Web Page In Browser check box to prevent this from occurring.

  - Visio normally creates a subfolder to store the majority of website files. You can clear the Organize Supporting Files In A Folder check box to instruct Visio to store all website files in a single folder.

    > **SEE ALSO** For information about the files created by the Save As Web Page function, see the "What's in a Visio-generated website and where is it stored?" sidebar later in this section.

  - You can enter a different title in the Page Title text box as an alternative to using the Change Title button shown in Figure 12-29.

Figure 12-31 provides one example of customizing webpage output. The webpage appears with only the Go To Page and Pan And Zoom navigation panes.

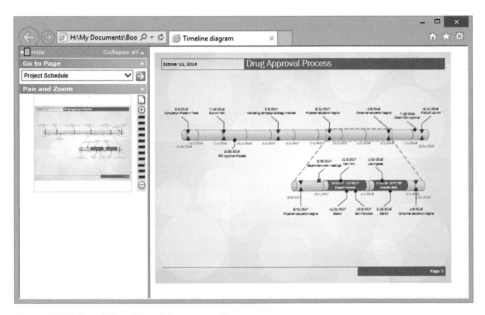

Figure 12-31 *A website with only two navigation panes*

Figure 12-32 shows that the customized website includes three Visio diagram pages plus the Milestones By Start Date report.

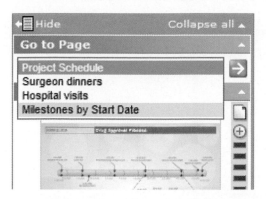

Figure 12-32 *A report name appears with diagram page names*

A portion of the Milestones By Start Date report is shown in Figure 12-33.

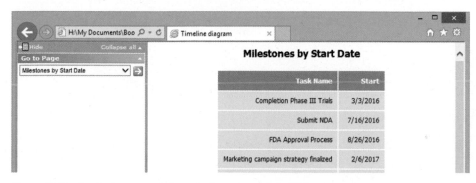

Figure 12-33 *A milestone report shows task names and start dates*

12

Use the settings on the Advanced tab

Figure 12-34 shows the Advanced tab of the Save As Web Page dialog box.

Figure 12-34 *XAML is the default, but you can select other output formats*

You can use the Output Formats list to select any of the following instead of XAML:

- VML is the webpage format used by Visio 2007 and earlier versions of Visio. The features of VML websites are very similar to websites created with XAML but require Internet Explorer.

- SVG is a specialized format that is supported by some but not all browsers. Like the three image formats described in the following bullet point, SVG websites display fixed-size pages with no Pan And Zoom pane.

- GIF, JPG, and PNG provide fewer capabilities than either VML or XAML. For example, the viewing window for these formats is a fixed size and does not include the Pan And Zoom pane in the left navigation pane. However, websites produced in these formats retain all hyperlinks and are likely to be compatible with a wider range of web browsers. (Note that you can have the best of both worlds—full navigation functions in Internet Explorer and support for older browsers; refer to the following paragraph.)

If you select XAML, VML, or SVG as the output format, Visio defaults to selecting the Provide Alternate Format For Older Browsers check box, as shown in Figure 12-35. You can use the list under this heading to select GIF, JPG, or PNG output as a backup to your primary choice.

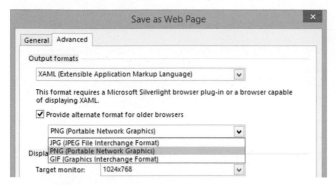

Figure 12-35 *PNG is one of three alternate output formats*

In the Display Options section, you can use the Target Monitor, Host In Web Page, and Style Sheet settings to further customize your webpages. The second and third settings, in particular, are intended to help you integrate a Visio-generated website with another existing website.

To change the title of a Visio-generated website

1. Open the **Save As** dialog box, and then click the **Change Title** button.

2. In the **Enter Text** dialog box, enter a title, click **OK**, and then click **Save**.

To customize the appearance of a Visio-generated website

1. Open the **Save As** dialog box, and then click the **Publish** button.

2. In the **Save as Web Page** dialog box, change the items you want to customize, and then click **OK**.

To customize the format of a Visio-generated website

1. Open the **Save As** dialog box, and then click the **Publish** button.

2. In the **Output formats** section of the **Save as Web Page** dialog box, click the name of the format you want.

3. (*Optional*) Click the name of an alternate format in the **Provide Alternate Format For Older Browsers** list.

4. (*Optional*) Change the **Display options**.

5. Click **OK**.

12

What's in a Visio-generated website and where is it stored?

When you use the Save As Web Page feature, Visio creates a home page for the website. It also creates a supporting files folder that contains graphics and webpages for each page in the drawing, in addition to JavaScript, XML, and other files that comprise the website.

By default, Visio places the home page in the same Windows folder that contains your Visio drawing, and gives it the same name as the drawing plus an .htm file extension. For English versions of Visio, the name of the supporting files folder is the same as the drawing name but appended with _files_.

For example, if you use an English-language version of Visio and create a website for a diagram called *Timeline diagram.vsdx*, the folder that houses the Visio diagram also contains the following:

- A file called *Timeline diagram.htm*
- A folder called *Timeline diagram_files*

If you want to copy or move your new website, it's important to copy or move both the .htm file and the supporting files folder to the new location. You can copy your website to a shared drive, to your organization's intranet, or to any web server to provide access to your Visio diagram.

IMPORTANT The default name for the companion subfolder varies based on the language version of Office that is installed on your computer. For a complete list of default names for various language versions, go to *support. office.com/en-us/article/Save-all-or-part-of-a-workbook-to-a-static-Web-page-5AD26DEE-8739-4D80-B9D9-CF0530AB1968*. Even though the article applies to Microsoft Excel, the list is also correct for the Visio 2016 website folder.

Skills review

In this chapter, you learned how to:

- Preview and print drawings
- Remove personal information
- Create graphics
- Save drawings in other file formats
- Create templates
- Share diagrams by using the Visio Viewer
- Publish diagrams to the web

12

Practice tasks

The practice files for these tasks are located in the Visio2016SBS\Ch12 folder. You can save the results of the tasks in the same folder.

Preview and print drawings

Open the PreviewDrawings diagram in Visio, and then perform the following tasks:

1. Display the **Print** page of the Backstage view to preview the diagram.

2. (*Optional*) Print the diagram.

3. Add a header and footer. Notice that the change is visible in the print preview.

4. Move shapes off the page breaks to improve the printed output.

Remove personal information

Open the PreviewDrawings diagram you used in the "Preview and print drawings" practice task, and then perform the following tasks:

1. View the document properties, and then change the name of the company.

2. Remove personal information from the diagram.

Create graphics

Open the CreateGraphics diagram in Visio, and then perform the following tasks:

1. Create a PNG image of the round table and two adjacent chairs.

2. Create a JPEG image of the plant and green desk chair.

3. Create any type of image of all shapes on the page.

4. Create any type of image of the entire printable area of the page. (See the tip following Figure 12-16 for assistance with this task.)

Save drawings in other file formats

Open the SaveInFormats diagram in Visio, and then perform the following tasks:

1. Create a PDF of all pages in the diagram.

2. Create a PDF that includes only pages **1** and **2**.

3. Save the diagram as a macro-enabled document.

4. Save the diagram as a Visio 2003-2010 diagram.

Create templates

Open the CreateTemplates diagram in Visio, and then perform the following tasks:

1. Save the diagram as a template.

2. Create a diagram from the new template.

Share diagrams by using the Visio Viewer

There are no practice tasks for this topic.

Publish diagrams to the web

Open the PublishToWeb diagram in Visio, and then perform the following tasks:

1. Create a website.

2. View the **Hospital Visits** page.

3. Return to the **Project Schedule** page.

4. Zoom in on the expanded timeline below the main timeline.

5. Pan up to the main timeline.

6. View the shape data for the main timeline.

7. Search for FDA, and then click **FDA Approval Process**.

8. Follow the hyperlink on the **FDA Approval Process** milestone located on the left end of the main timeline.

9. Republish the website with a new title, omit the **Pan and Zoom** pane, and include the **Milestone Summary** report.

10. Republish the website in **VML** format.

Add structure to your diagrams

In many types of Visio diagrams, it's useful to create visual or logical relationships among a set of shapes. The traditional technique for doing this in Visio has been to use background shapes and groups. However, Visio 2016 offers three special shape types—containers, lists, and callouts—that can be even more effective when you want to establish relationships and add structure to your diagrams.

Structured diagram shapes are so useful that Visio itself relies on them for a growing number of templates and special uses. For example, you will find lists and containers in swimlane diagrams, wireframes, and data graphic legends; and you will encounter callouts in the Business Process Model and Notation (BPMN) template (Visio Professional only).

This chapter guides you through procedures related to organizing shapes by using containers or lists, finding containers and lists in Visio, and annotating shapes by using callouts.

In this chapter

- Understand containers, lists, and callouts
- Compare groups and containers
- Organize shapes by using containers
- Organize shapes by using lists
- Find containers and lists in Visio
- Annotate shapes by using callouts

Practice files

For this chapter, use the practice files from the Visio2016SBS\Ch13 folder. For practice file download instructions, see the introduction.

Understand containers, lists, and callouts

Visio 2010 introduced three structured diagram shape types:

- **Containers** A container provides a visual boundary around a set of objects, but it also establishes a logical relationship between the container and the objects within it—shapes know when they are members of a container and containers know which shapes they contain.

  The key advantage of a container is that while you can move, copy, or delete it and its members as a unit, each contained shape maintains its independence. Unlike grouped shapes, selecting an object inside a container only requires one click, which makes it simple to access the shape data and other properties of a container member.

   TIP A container can contain shapes, other containers, and lists.

- **Lists** A list is a special type of container that maintains an ordered relationship among its members. Each object in a list knows its ordinal position, and new objects are not merely added to a list but are added to a specific position in a list.

   TIP A list can contain shapes and containers but cannot contain other lists.

- **Callouts** In previous versions of Visio, a callout was merely a shape that you glued to another shape to add a comment. A Visio 2016–style callout still provides a way to add annotation to a shape, but the callout knows the shape to which it is attached, and the shape can identify any attached callouts.

What is the value to you if shapes know where they live and containers and lists know what they contain? Think about a shape that automatically knows whether it's first, second, or third in a list and displays that data (explained in the section "Add shapes to lists" in the "Organize shapes by using lists" topic later in this chapter). Or think about the potential uses for a shape that displays data from its parent container—and the data changes automatically if you move the shape to a different container (covered in the "Explore swimlanes" section in the "Find containers and lists in Visio" topic later in this chapter).

Although it's true that containers, lists, and callouts are just Visio shapes, each includes unique properties and formulas that give it special capabilities.

Compare groups and containers

You can use either groups or containers to visually connect a set of shapes. However, the two have key behavioral differences that are likely to lead you in one direction or the other. The diagrams in this topic contain two sets of shapes that will serve to illustrate the similarities and differences. The green shapes on the left in the diagrams are part of a group; the gold shapes on the right are located inside a container.

In the image on the left in Figure 13-1, the arrows and square are grouped with a gold rectangle by using the traditional Visio technique:

1. Draw a rectangle (or other shape).

2. Send the new shape to the back of the Z-order.

3. Select the rectangle and the shapes you want in the group.

4. Group the selected shapes.

> ✓ **TIP** For information about creating and using groups, see Chapter 3, "Manage text, shapes, and pages." The same chapter also describes moving shapes backward and forward in the Z-order of a page.

Prior to the introduction of containers in Visio 2010, this was the only technique for creating a visual association among a set of shapes.

In contrast, the shapes on the right in Figure 13-1 were placed into a container. One difference is immediately apparent: containers are not just plain rectangles; they include both a main section and a heading.

13

 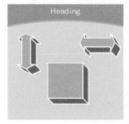

Figure 13-1 *Shapes are grouped or contained*

Three additional differences that are not easily captured in a screenshot become obvious when you work with groups and containers in Visio:

- If you click a shape that is located in a group, you select the group and not the shape. However, if you click a shape in a container, the first click selects the shape. In essence, a group stands between you and its shapes, but a container is invisible as you select shapes.

> **TIP** If you run Visio in developer mode, you can alter the selection characteristics of a group. For more information about developer mode, see Appendix A, "Look behind the curtain."

- To select a container and not a member of the container, you must click the heading or an edge of the container.

- As a result of the click behavior described in the preceding bullets, using a bounding box to select interior shapes in a container is easy—just click inside or outside the container, and then drag. However, to select shapes in a group by using a bounding box, you must start the bounding box outside of the group or you will inadvertently drag the group.

Groups and containers share several behaviors. For example, if you move either one, you move all shapes. If you delete either one, you delete everything. Similarly, you can copy and paste either as a unit.

One difference arises when you want to label the collection, however. When you click a group and start entering text, the text appears in the center of the group shape by default. Sometimes this placement is fine, but other times it's not. The usefulness of the text in a group also depends on the color and style defaults of the theme you're using.

In the group shown on the left in Figure 13-2, for example, the text is illegible because its default color is too similar to the color of the background shape. You can, of course, use the Text Block tool you worked with in Chapter 3, "Manage text, shapes, and pages," to move the text, or you can change its color, but that requires extra steps.

Clicking a container and entering text, on the other hand, automatically places the text in the heading, as shown on the right in Figure 13-2.

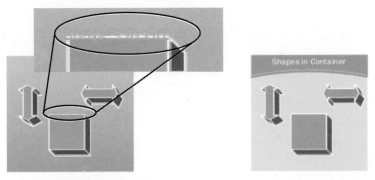

Figure 13-2 *Text in a group can be obscured by the default font color or by the shapes in the group*

If you drag a shape out of a group, is it still part of the group? What if you drag a shape out of a container?

The upper half of Figure 13-3 shows a double-headed arrow that has been dragged out of the group on the left and another that has been removed from the container on the right. In the lower half of the figure, the group and container have been moved to the right.

Notice the following:

- The green arrow moved with the group.
- The gold arrow remained in a fixed location.

From these observations, you can conclude the following:

- Dragging a shape from a group does not remove it from the group.
- Dragging a shape from a container removes it from the container.

13

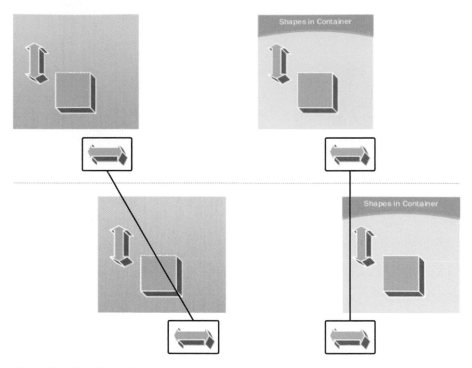

Figure 13-3 *The effects of dragging a shape out of a group and a container*

Attempting to add shapes exposes a similar difference. In the upper half of Figure 13-4, a circle has been placed on top of the group on the left and the container on the right. In the lower half of the figure, the group and the container have been moved to the right.

Here are the conclusions you can draw from this:

- Placing a shape on top of a group does not add it to the group.

> **✓ TIP** If you run Visio in developer mode, you can change the behavior of a group so it will accept dropped shapes. For more information about developer mode, see Appendix A, "Look behind the curtain."

- Placing a shape on top of a container adds it to the container.

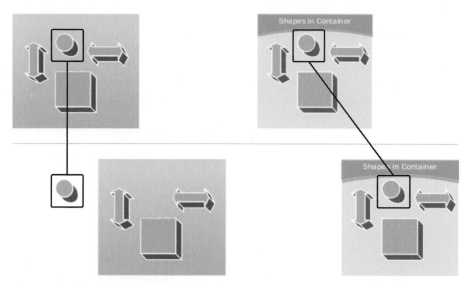

Figure 13-4 *The effects of placing a shape on top of a group and a container*

The primary lesson from Figure 13-3 and Figure 13-4 is that unlike groups, Visio containers behave like physical containers: if you put an object in, it becomes part of the container; if you remove an object, it is no longer associated with the container.

Figure 13-5 illustrates a final behavior difference: resizing groups and containers produces strikingly different results. In the figure, both the group and the container were stretched by dragging the bottom resize handle downward.

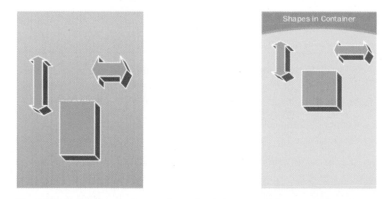

Figure 13-5 *Resizing a group resizes all subshapes; resizing a container does not affect member shapes*

13

> **TIP** If you run Visio in developer mode, you can change the behavior of a group so the interior shapes do not resize. For more information about developer mode, see Appendix A, "Look behind the curtain."

The following table summarizes the key differences between groups and containers.

Action	Groups	Containers
Resize	Contents are resized with the group	Contents are not changed
Select an interior shape	Requires two clicks (unless default group behavior has been changed)	Requires one click
Select interior shape(s) by using a bounding box	Cannot start a bounding box by clicking inside a group	Can start a bounding box by clicking anywhere
Drop a new shape inside	Dropped shapes are not added to the group (unless default group behavior has been changed)	Dropped shapes are added to the container
Drag a shape out	Shape is physically outside the group but remains part of the group	Shape is removed from the container
Enter text	Text is placed in the center of the group	Text is placed in the container's heading

> **TIP** Containers, lists, and callouts were introduced in Visio 2010 and were described by the Visio development team in a series of blog posts that are summarized at *blogs.msdn.com /b/visio/archive/2010/09/02/new-structured-diagrams-whitepaper-for-visio-2010.aspx*.
>
> Visio 2013 included additional containers and callouts and upgraded the style and appearance of both, as described in a blog post at *blogs.office.com/2012/11/05/containers-and-callouts-in-visio/*.
>
> For the technically inclined, the following article provides details about the inner workings of containers, lists, and callouts and is still relevant for Visio 2016 structured diagrams: *msdn.microsoft.com/en-us/library/ff959245.aspx*.

Organize shapes by using containers

Grouped shapes are still valuable for many purposes, including holding collections of subshapes that are unlikely to change. However, Visio containers offer numerous advantages, especially for dynamically grouping, moving, and managing a set of related shapes.

One regular ribbon tab and one tool tab are vital for working with containers. The Insert tab, shown in Figure 13-6, is home to the Container gallery, which you use to add containers to a page.

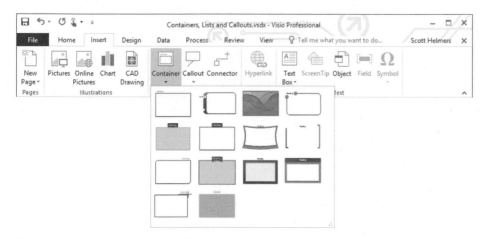

Figure 13-6 *The Container gallery offers 14 container styles*

You use various functions on the Format tool tab in the Container Tools tab group, shown in Figure 13-7, to manage containers in ways you will explore in the sections of this topic.

13

Figure 13-7 *The Format tool tab appears only when you select a container*

Use containers

You can create an empty container and add shapes to it later, or you can create a container around existing shapes. In either case, your containers can appear in a variety of styles. Figure 13-8 shows the same set of network shapes in five different containers to illustrate the range of choices.

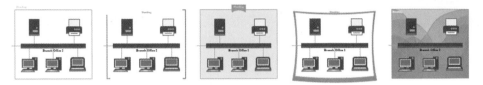

Figure 13-8 *Examples of diverse container styles from simple to highly stylized*

Containers provide visual feedback while you interact with them. As shown on the left in Figure 13-9, dragging a shape into a container causes the border of the container to "light up" in green. This type of feedback is a way to distinguish a container from a group or an ordinary shape.

The container border also lights up when you select any contained shape, as shown on the right in Figure 13-9. This behavior is evidence of the relationship between containers and members that was described in "Understand containers, lists, and callouts" earlier in this chapter.

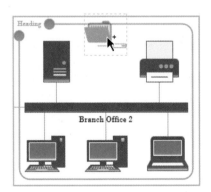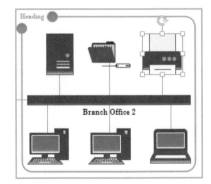

Figure 13-9 *Adding or selecting shapes highlights the surrounding container*

Because containers were designed to remain connected to their members, it's easy to copy or delete both as a unit by selecting the container. The only trick when selecting the container is to remember that the body of a container is invisible to mouse clicks. You must click the header or one of the edges to select it.

If you want to copy or delete just the members but not the container, that's also easy because there are several techniques for selecting all members of a container—then you can just copy or delete the shapes in the usual way.

To delete the container but leave its contents behind, you could drag the contents out and then delete the container. However, Visio provides a Disband Container command for this purpose.

> **TIP** You can lock a container to prevent shapes from being added or deleted. If you attempt to add a shape to a locked container, the border does not light up as you drag the shape onto the container and the new shape sits on top of the container. If you attempt to delete a contained shape, you receive an error message.

To place an empty container on the page

1. On the **Insert** tab, in the **Diagram Parts** group, click **Container**.

2. In the **Container** gallery, click the thumbnail of the container type you want.

To contain existing shapes

1. Select one or more existing shapes, and then do one of the following:

   - Display the **Container** gallery, and then click the thumbnail of the container type you want.

   - Right-click one of the selected shapes, and then click **Add to New Container**.

   - If the shapes are on top of, but are not members of, a container, right-click one of the selected shapes, and then click **Add to Underlying Container**.

To add shapes to a container

1. Drag one or more shapes into the container.

Or

1. Do either of the following:

   - Resize a container until it covers the shapes you want to add.

   - Drag a container until it's on top of the shapes you want to add.

2. Right-click one of the shapes, and then click **Add to Underlying Container**.

13

To select a container

1. Do either of the following:

   - Click the heading section of the container.

   - Click any edge of the container.

To select all contained shapes

1. Do either of the following:

   - Select the container, and then on the **Format** tool tab, in the **Membership** group, click the **Select Contents** button.

   - Right-click any edge of the container, point to **Container**, and then click **Select Contents**.

To remove shapes from a container

1. Drag the shape you want to remove until it is outside the container.

To delete a container but leave contained shapes

1. Do either of the following:

   - Select the container, and then on the **Format** tool tab, in the **Membership** group, click the **Disband Container** button.

   - Right-click any edge of the container, point to **Container**, and then click **Disband Container**.

To lock or unlock a container

1. Do either of the following:

   - Select the container, and then on the **Format** tool tab, in the **Membership** group, click the **Lock Container** button.

   - Right-click any edge of the container, point to **Container**, and then click **Lock Container**.

Format containers

When you drag a container onto the page, it includes a set of predefined style attributes. You can change some of the most visible container attributes by using the commands on the Format tool tab that is shown in Figure 13-7. You can alter other container characteristics by using buttons on the other Visio tabs.

Container attributes you can alter include the following:

- You can switch to another of the 14 container styles.

- You can choose alternate heading styles; Visio offers either two or four heading styles per container type. You can also hide the heading.

- You can select different themes, variants, and effects. Because containers respond to those changes, the appearance of the containers on your drawing page (and their thumbnails in the gallery) can be very different from one diagram to the next.

- You can change the fill, line, and shadow attributes of a container as you would any other Visio shape.

To choose a different container style

1. Do any of the following:

   - On the **Format** tool tab, in the **Container Styles** group, display the **Container Styles** gallery.

   - On the **Home** tab, in the **Editing** group, click the **Change Shape** button.

   - Right-click the heading or edge of the container, and then on the mini toolbar, click the **Change Shape** button.

2. Click the container style you want.

To choose a different heading style

1. On the **Format** tool tab, in the **Container Styles** group, click the **Heading Style** button.

2. In the **Heading Styles** gallery, click the thumbnail of the heading style you want.

To hide the heading

1. Display the **Heading Styles** gallery, and then in the **No Heading** section, click the **No Heading** thumbnail.

13

On the border

When you drag a shape into a container, a green outline appears on the border of the container. This is true even when you drag a shape most of the way, but not fully into the container. In Figure 13-10, the wireless access point is being dragged into a container and will be added to the container when it is released, even though it is not fully within the borders of the container. (Depending on the resize options described just after this sidebar, the container might expand to encompass the new shape.)

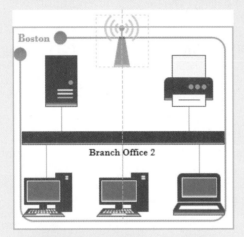

Figure 13-10 *The majority of the wireless access point is within the container*

The pair of images in Figure 13-11 shows a different container behavior that can be useful in some diagrams. In the image on the left, the wireless access point has not been dragged quite as far into the container as it was in Figure 13-10. The container signals the difference by displaying a green outline only on the top border and not all the way around.

When you release the wireless access point in this situation, it becomes a member of the container, but it remains attached to the edge. If you expand the size of this container upwards, the border shape will move along with the top of the container, as shown in the image on the right.

Another example of a shape on the border of a container is included in the "Build wireframes" section of the "Find containers and lists in Visio" topic later in this chapter.

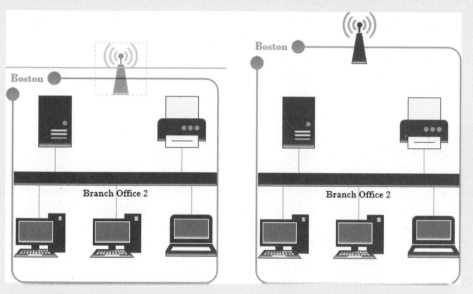

Figure 13-11 *A wireless access point is added to the border because it was dropped on the edge*

Control container size

Visio containers expand automatically when you add shapes near the edge of the container. You can change this default behavior by using the Automatic Resize button located in the Size group on the Format tool tab. Clicking the Automatic Resize button, which is shown in Figure 13-7, reveals three mutually exclusive options:

- **No Automatic Resize** The container does not expand when you drag shapes near the edge.

- **Expand as Needed** The container expands when you drop shapes near the edge. Note that the opposite is not true—the container does not shrink when you remove shapes.

- **Always Fit to Contents** The container expands and contracts automatically when you add or remove shapes.

13

You can also affect container size by using the other buttons in the Size group:

- **Margins** Sets the spacing between the edges of the container and the contained shapes

- **Fit to Contents** Sets the container size to the minimum required for the contained shapes plus the margin

 TIP You can also resize a container to fit its contents by opening the container's shortcut menu and then choosing from the options on the Container submenu.

Organize shapes by using lists

A *list* is a special type of container that maintains its members in ordered sequence. When you drag an object into a list, it takes a specific place before, between, or after existing members. Each list member knows its relative position in the list.

Visio doesn't provide a list gallery on the Insert tab in the same way that it offers a Container gallery. Consequently, creating a list either requires reusing an existing list shape or having enough technical knowledge to make changes to the ShapeSheet.

 SEE ALSO For information about modifying the ShapeSheet and creating custom list shapes, see Appendix A, "Look behind the curtain."

This topic explores adding shapes to a list and reordering shapes within a list. The list shape for this hypothetical scenario is called *My New PC*, to which will be added rectangular shapes that represent the software to load onto the PC. The starting point is shown in Figure 13-12, with the list in the center and the software shapes on either side.

Figure 13-12 *A list shape surrounded by candidate members*

The software shapes for this example were created with two special attributes:

- Each shape displays the name of a software product that is stored as shape data. The shape data value is displayed by using a Visio field.

> **SEE ALSO** For more information about Visio fields, see Chapter 8, "Work with shape data."

- Each shape displays its relative position in the list when it is in a list. When the shape is not in a list, it doesn't display any number. Display of the list position for each shape was accomplished by using two ShapeSheet formulas.

The goal for the example in this topic is to create a list that shows the installation sequence for a new PC. Although you are unlikely to use a Visio list for this specific purpose, this example might stimulate you to think of your own applications for position-aware shapes.

Add shapes to lists

Dragging a shape into a list triggers the same response shown for a container earlier in this chapter: the list is surrounded by a green rectangle, as shown on the left in Figure 13-13. Also like a container, the list displays the green border when any member shape is selected, as shown on the right.

Figure 13-13 *List borders illuminate when shapes are being added or are contained*

In the real world, it isn't possible to install Visio without installing Windows first, so Figure 13-14 shows the Windows 10 shape being dragged into the list. On the left, as the Windows rectangle first approaches the list, there are three visual responses:

- The list border turns green.

- A ScreenTip appears, displaying the words *Insert Shape*.

- A horizontal, orange insertion bar appears below the Visio 2016 shape.

13

The insertion bar is Visio's way of telling you that the new shape will be added to the list at that specific location.

The image in the center shows the Windows shape positioned partially above the Visio shape, with the result that the insertion bar is now located above the Visio rectangle.

The result of dragging the Windows rectangle above the Visio shape is shown on the right. Notice that the label *Windows 10* is now preceded by the number 1 and the digit in front of *Visio 2016* has changed from a 1 to a 2.

Figure 13-14 *New shapes are added to a list in specific positions*

You can insert new shapes between existing list shapes. In Figure 13-15, the Office 2016 shape is being added before Visio 2016 and after Windows 10.

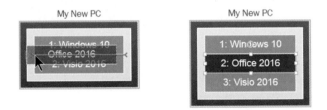

Figure 13-15 *You can insert a shape between existing list shapes*

> ✓ **TIP** Although the blue triangle that appears at the left end of the orange insertion bar in the image on the left in Figure 13-15 might appear when you drag a shape into a list, it is primarily useful when you are not dragging a shape.
>
> If you pause when pointing to the edge of a list between existing shapes, the Insert Shape triangle appears. Clicking the triangle causes Visio to insert a shape at that location in the list. If the shape designer specified a default list shape, then that shape is inserted. If there isn't a default list shape, the shape adjacent to the insertion bar is added to the list. "Find containers and lists in Visio" later in this chapter includes an example of shape insertion.

The preceding figures illustrate a key behavior difference between Visio lists and containers: container members can be located anywhere within a container, but list members are always in fixed positions.

Figure 13-16 illustrates another important difference: unlike shapes in a container, list members cannot reside on the border of the list. On the left, the Visio Add-In shape is positioned on the border of the list. Only a small percentage of the rectangle is actually touching the list, and yet releasing the shape at this point causes it to "fly" into the list.

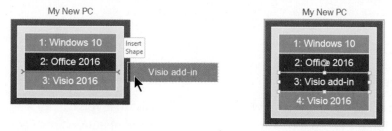

Figure 13-16 *Lists do not allow border shapes*

Not only can shapes be inserted into specific positions in a list, they can be rearranged within the list. On the left in Figure 13-17, the Visio 2016 shape is being relocated so it will appear above the Visio add-in shape. Notice that each shape is renumbered automatically based on its new list position.

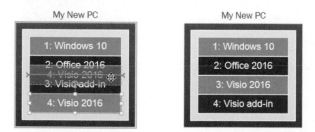

Figure 13-17 *List shapes can be dragged to new locations*

The example in this section uses a vertical list in which shapes are automatically placed from top to bottom. A Visio list can be either vertical or horizontal and can sequence shapes in either direction within the list. These attributes are controlled by parameters and don't require writing code, but you can't change them from the Visio ribbon; you must make changes in the ShapeSheet for the list.

13

To add shapes to a list

1. Do either of the following:

   - Drag one or more shapes into the list.

   - Use the **Insert Shape** arrow to position a shape where you want it.

> (Q) **SEE ALSO** For procedures related to selecting a list, selecting all members of a list, locking or unlocking a list, deleting a list, or disbanding a list, see the procedures in the "Use containers" section of the "Organize shapes by using containers" topic earlier in this chapter.

Format and size lists

You can adjust most of the same format and size options for a list that you can for a container, with one notable exception: you cannot change the size of a Visio list shape. Visio controls the size by expanding and contracting a list so it is the exact size of its member shapes plus the margin around the shapes.

The Format tool tab described earlier in this chapter provides the following list-related groups and the functions within them:

- **Size group** You can use the Margins button to adjust the spacing between the edges of the list and the contained shapes. Because Visio controls the size of a list shape, Fit To Container and Automatic Resize are dimmed.

- **Container Styles group** You cannot change the style of a Visio 2016 list. However, you can change the style of a list created in Visio 2010 by using the Container Styles gallery. This is true even if the Visio 2010 list is located in a Visio 2016 diagram. You can use the Heading Style gallery to choose alternate heading placement and style options.

- **Membership group** The Lock Container, Select Contents, and Disband Container buttons provide the same functions for lists that they do for containers.

Find containers and lists in Visio

Several Visio 2016 templates take advantage of the properties of containers and lists to enhance ease of use and to add valuable features. In this section, you will discover three examples.

Explore swimlanes

Cross-functional flowcharts, also known as swimlane diagrams, provide one of the most prominent examples of list and container usage in Visio.

 SEE ALSO For more information about swimlane diagrams, see Chapter 4, "Create business process diagrams."

The swimlane add-in was completely redesigned when lists and containers were introduced in Visio 2010. The net effect of the redesign is that a cross-functional flow-chart (CFF) is a list of containers: the framework that holds swimlanes is a list, and each swimlane is a container.

⚠ **IMPORTANT** Swimlane diagrams created in Visio 2016, Visio 2013, or Visio 2010 will open directly in Visio 2016 because they share the same underlying container and list structure. However, swimlane diagrams created in earlier versions of Visio must be converted to the new swimlane structure, and, once converted, they can no longer be edited with the older software. To warn about the impending conversion when you open an older diagram, Visio displays a dialog box that gives you an opportunity to save the older version of the diagram before converting it.

Evidence of containers and lists appears as soon as you drag a shape into a swimlane—a green border appears around the lane, as shown in Figure 13-18.

✓ **TIP** Notice that two Dynamic Grid feedback elements also appear inside the swimlane, informing you that the new shape is at the left margin of the lane and is centered vertically within the lane. For more information about the Dynamic Grid, see Chapter 2, "Create diagrams."

Because the overall swimlane structure is a list, it includes a heading. Similarly, each swimlane has a heading. You can change the text of either, which was done in the image shown in Figure 13-18, by selecting the swimlane structure or a swimlane and then entering text.

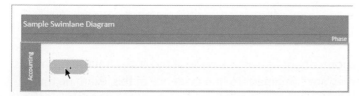

Figure 13-18 *The combination of container feedback and the Dynamic Grid simplify positioning of new shapes in a swimlane*

13

Further evidence that the swimlane structure is a list is shown in Figure 13-19. With the pointer at the left end of the lanes and positioned on the boundary between two lanes, the Insert Shape triangle appears.

> ✓ **TIP** If you compare the Insert Shape triangle in Figure 13-19 with the one shown in Figure 13-12, you'll notice that the one in Figure 13-19 includes the name of a specific shape. The name appears because the swimlane list was preconfigured to insert a specific shape.

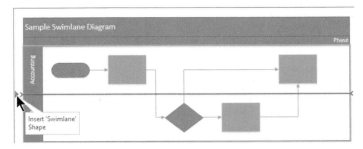

Figure 13-19 *Adding new lanes to a diagram is easy because of the list structure*

Clicking the Insert Shape triangle produces the result shown in Figure 13-20. Notice that Visio extends dynamic connectors, as required, to accommodate the new lane.

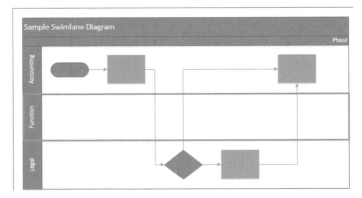

Figure 13-20 *Visio rearranges existing lanes when you add or remove lanes*

Because swimlanes reside in a list, you can rearrange the sequence of swimlanes by dragging the heading of a lane up or down.

Swimlane diagrams derive another benefit from being built by using containers: shapes in a container know where they are contained. To find evidence of this, examine the Function field in the shape data for any flowchart shape in a swimlane.

As an example, data for the process shape in the upper left of Figure 13-20 is shown in the image on the left in Figure 13-21, and the data for the decision diamond is shown on the right. In both cases, the value in the Function field is derived dynamically from the swimlane heading. If you change the value of the swimlane title, the Function field will be updated for all contained shapes. If you move a shape to a new lane, the Function field will reflect the heading of the new lane.

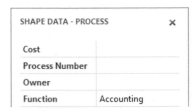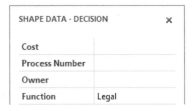

Figure 13-21 *The Function field automatically displays the name of the swimlane that contains each flowchart shape*

Build wireframes

 IMPORTANT The information in this topic applies only to the Professional edition of Visio 2016.

Visio 2016 includes a revamped set of user interface (UI) design shapes that were initially introduced in Visio 2010. For this topic, the key point of interest about the redesigned shapes is that many of them are either containers or lists.

Software designers use wireframe shapes to create mockups of dialog boxes and other visual elements that will be displayed by their applications. When you use Visio 2016 to create a mockup of a dialog box, you will find that the Dialog Form shape is a container. Consequently, as you add buttons and controls to your dialog box, those buttons and controls become container members. If you move, copy, or delete your dialog box, all of the contained shapes are automatically included. If you have ever created a UI mockup by using Visio 2007 or earlier, it won't take more than a moment or two of experimentation to realize how significant an improvement this is.

Some Visio 2016 UI shapes are lists, including, not surprisingly, the List Box control. When you drag one into a Dialog Form container, the list is prepopulated with three list members. You can add, delete, and resequence list members by dragging them, as described in "Add shapes to lists" earlier in this chapter.

13

> **TIP** As a shape designer, you can configure a list to automatically add one or more member shapes when the list is added to a page. Creating a shape with that feature is outside the scope of this book, but you can find information on this subject at *msdn.microsoft.com /en-us/library/ff959245.aspx*.

The following three figures highlight some of the containers and lists in the wireframe template.

Adding a button control to a Dialog Form container lights up the border of the dialog box shape, as shown in Figure 13-22.

Figure 13-22 *The Dialog Form shape is a container*

On the left in Figure 13-23, a panel is added to the dialog box container. Because the panel shape is, itself, a container, adding a tab to the top edge of the panel causes the top panel border to illuminate.

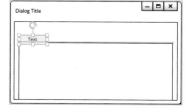

Figure 13-23 *Multiple containers comprise the wireframe shapes*

> **SEE ALSO** For information about border shapes, see the "On the border" sidebar earlier in this chapter.

> **TIP** Because the panel shape is a container but doesn't have a visible heading, you can select it only by clicking its edges.

The list box control exhibits standard list behavior when adding new list elements, as shown in Figure 13-24.

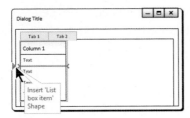

Figure 13-24 *A list inside a container inside a container.*

The wireframe shapes provide further evidence that nested containers and lists are practical solutions for creating Visio diagrams.

Insert data graphic legends

> ⚠️ **IMPORTANT** The information in this topic applies only to the Professional edition of Visio 2016.

In Chapter 9, "Visualize your data," you worked with data graphics and then added an automatically generated legend to your diagram. A data graphic legend is actually a structure consisting of an outer list, one or more containers as list members, and lists within those containers.

For example, the same legend is shown in both images in Figure 13-25. The structure is loosely visible on the left. However, after selecting the entire legend, the telltale green borders are apparent on the right. You can identify three containers—Legend, Owner, and Risk—and two vertical lists, one in each of the Owner and Risk containers.

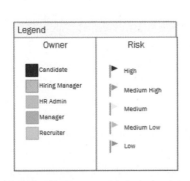
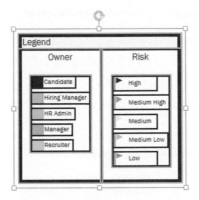

Figure 13-25 *Data graphic legends are created from lists and containers*

13

When you work with data graphic legends, you will discover that you can add, delete, rename, edit, and move legend components, just as you can with the headings and members of any unlocked containers and lists.

Annotate shapes by using callouts

Many generations of Visio have included more than three dozen callouts that you can use to add comments to any shape on the drawing page. Those callouts still exist in Visio 2016. Figure 13-26 shows some examples.

Figure 13-26 *Six classic callout examples*

 TIP To locate the classic callouts, in the Shapes window, click More Shapes, click Visio Extras, and then click Callouts.

However, using classic callouts is often a challenge because fundamentally they are just ordinary shapes. For example, all of the following are common annoyances of the classic callouts:

- Deleting the shape to which a callout is attached does not delete the callout, which can leave orphan callouts throughout your diagram.

- Moving the shape to which a callout is attached does not move the callout.

- Moving a callout disconnects the callout from the shape to which it's attached unless you know exactly which control handle to drag.

Visio 2016 structured callouts behave more logically, primarily because, like containers and their members, there is an active association between a callout and the shape to which it's attached.

Just as there is a Container gallery, there is also a Callout gallery, as shown in Figure 13-27.

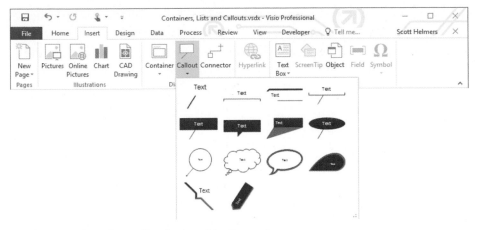

Figure 13-27 *The Callout gallery features 14 callout styles*

Figure 13-28 illustrates the following ways that structured callouts appear and behave more logically than groups:

- In the image on the left, selecting a callout highlights the shape to which it's attached by using a familiar green border. Note that the opposite is not true: selecting the attached shape does not highlight the callout.

> ✅ **TIP** The callout in this image is connected to the shape by a visible tail, which might make the green highlight seem redundant. Not all callout styles have visible tails, however. Consequently, this feature is particularly valuable for those styles.

- In the center image, moving a callout by dragging it appears to disconnect it. However, when you release the connector it is still attached, as shown on the right.

13

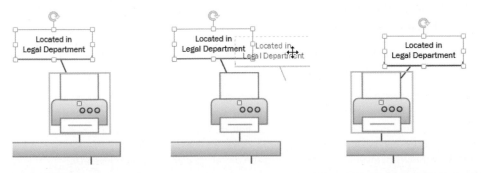

Figure 13-28 *Structured callouts are associated with the attached shape and remain attached even when you move them*

Unlike containers and lists, callouts do not have a tool tab that you can use to switch styles. However, you can take advantage of the Change Shapes feature in Visio to replace any callout style with a different one. Figure 13-29 uses Live Preview and the mini toolbar to show how the callout from Figure 13-28 can be changed to the Word Balloon style.

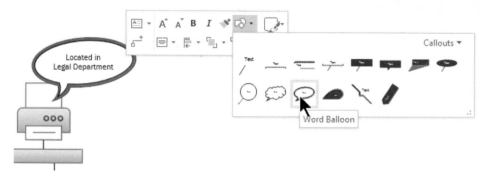

Figure 13-29 *Alternate callout styles are available via the Change Shapes feature*

The following list summarizes the behavior of new style callouts:

- If you delete a callout, it doesn't affect the shape to which it was attached. However, if you delete the shape, the callout is also deleted.

- If you copy a shape that has a callout attached, both the shape and the callout are copied.

- You can attach more than one callout to a shape.

- If you do not have any shapes selected when you insert a callout, Visio inserts the callout in the center of the drawing window.

- If you select more than one shape before inserting a callout, Visio attaches a callout to each selected shape.

- Callouts respond to themes and variants, so their appearance on the page remains consistent with the rest of your diagram.

> **SEE ALSO** For information about configuring callouts to read and display shape data from the shape to which they are attached, go to *blog.bvisual.net/2014/04/08 /adding-configure-callout-functionality-to-visio-callouts/.* For more information about callouts, visit the Visio development team blog at *blogs.office.com/b/visio/archive/2012 /11/05/containers-and-callouts-in-visio.aspx.*

To attach a callout to a selected shape

1. On the **Insert** tab, in the **Diagram Parts** group, click the **Callout** button, and then click the callout style you want.

To change a callout to a different style

1. Do one of the following:

   - On the **Home** tab, in the **Editing** group, click the **Change Shape** button, and then click the callout style you want.

   - Right-click the callout, and on the mini toolbar, click the **Change Shape** button, and then click the callout style you want.

To relocate a callout

1. Click anywhere on the callout or its tail, and then do one of the following:

   - Drag the callout to a new location.

   - Move the callout by using the arrow keys.

Or

1. Relocate the shape to which the callout is attached.

To detach a callout

1. Select the callout, and then drag the yellow control from the center of the attached shape to anywhere outside the attached shape.

To delete a callout

1. Do one of the following:

   - Click the callout, and then delete it.

   - Click the shape to which the callout is attached, and then delete the attached shape.

13

Skills review

In this chapter, you learned how to:

- Understand containers, lists, and callouts
- Compare groups and containers
- Organize shapes by using containers
- Organize shapes by using lists
- Find containers and lists in Visio
- Annotate shapes by using callouts

Practice tasks

The practice files for these tasks are located in the Visio2016SBS\Ch13 folder. You can save the results of the tasks in the same folder.

Understand containers, lists, and callouts

There are no practice tasks for this topic.

Compare groups and containers

There are no practice tasks for this topic.

Organize shapes by using containers

Open the OrganizeByContainers diagram in Visio, and then perform the following tasks:

1. Place an empty container on the page, and then label the container Datacenter.

2. Place the **Branch Office 1** shapes into a container, and then label the container Chicago.

3. Add several new shapes from the **Servers** stencil to the empty container.

4. Add several new shapes from the **Servers** stencil to the **Chicago** container.

5. Enlarge the **Chicago** container, select all shapes in the **Datacenter** container, and then move them to the **Chicago** container.

6. Drag two network shapes from the **Chicago** container to the **Datacenter** container, and then lock the **Chicago** container.

7. Disband the **Datacenter** container.

8. Place all of the **Branch Office 2** shapes into a new container.

9. Change the style of the **Branch Office 2** container, and then move the heading to a new location.

Organize shapes by using lists

Open the OrganizeByLists diagram in Visio, and then perform the following tasks:

1. Drag various software shapes into the **My New PC** list, being sure to add shapes at the top and bottom of the list and between existing list members.

2. Move a shape from the middle of the list to the top.

3. Make a copy of the **My New PC** list, and then lock the copied list.

4. Drag shapes from the **Rack Mounted Servers** stencil to the **Store Shelf** list. Notice that the list grows from left to right and not from top to bottom.

5. Move the **Store Shelf** list to another part of the page.

Find containers and lists in Visio

There are no practice tasks for this topic.

Annotate shapes by using callouts

Open the AnnotateShapes diagram in Visio, and then perform the following tasks:

1. Attach a callout to the park shape, and then assign a name to the park.

2. Attach a different style of callout to the airport shape.

3. Move the airport shape and observe the change in its callout.

4. Change the location of the callout attached to the park.

5. Detach the callout from the airport and attach it to the city instead.

6. Delete the city.

7. Delete the callout that is attached to the park.

Validate diagrams

Is your diagram correct? Are all of the shapes linked as they should be? Did you complete all of the requirements for a diagram of this type?

The Check Diagram feature in Visio Professional 2016 can help you answer these and many other questions. You will find predefined validation rules built into selected Visio templates, which is a good place to begin exploring this powerful tool. You can also create custom rules to check the validity of your own diagrams.

 IMPORTANT The information in this chapter applies only to the Professional edition of Visio 2016.

This chapter guides you through procedures related to validating flowchart, swimlane, and Business Process Model and Notation (BPMN) diagrams, and reusing existing validation rule sets. It also provides references to learn how to list the rules in a rule set and create new validation rules.

In this chapter

- Understand Visio rules
- Validate flowcharts and swimlane diagrams
- Validate BPMN diagrams
- Reuse existing validation rule sets
- List the rules in a rule set
- Create new validation rules

Practice files

For this chapter, use the practice files from the Visio2016SBS\Ch14 folder. For practice file download instructions, see the introduction.

Understand Visio rules

It's possible to create a validation rule to check virtually any aspect of a Visio diagram, from a single condition to a sophisticated set of interrelated conditions. Multiple rules are then grouped into a rule set for use by Visio.

For example, a rule developer might create a rule to answer any of the following questions:

- Are there any shapes on the page with one connection but not two?

- Are there any unconnected shapes on the page?

- Are there any shapes derived from the "widget" master that are located on the bottom half of the page?

- Are there more than three blue shapes on any one page or more than five red shapes in the entire diagram?

- Are there any containers with fewer than three or more than seven shapes?

- Are there any shapes of type X, containing a field named Y with a value of Z?

Although a few of these examples might be a bit fanciful, they are intended to demonstrate the flexibility of the validation capability in Visio.

Six Visio 2016 templates include predefined business rule sets:

- Basic Flowchart

- Cross-Functional Flowchart

- Six Sigma Diagram

- BPMN Diagram (Professional only)

- Microsoft SharePoint 2010 Workflow (Professional only)

- Microsoft SharePoint 2016 Workflow (Professional only)

It's also possible to create your own custom rule sets for validating any kind of Visio diagram. Although the specific techniques for editing or creating custom rule sets are beyond the scope of this book, links to appropriate resources are in the "Reuse existing validation rule sets" and "Create new validation rules" topics later in this chapter.

Validate flowcharts and swimlane diagrams

Despite their visual differences, flowcharts and swimlane diagrams use the same flow-chart shapes and share a common validation rule set, as you'll discover in the following sections.

The same rule set is used to validate Six Sigma Diagrams, although this chapter does not include a Six Sigma example.

Validate flowcharts

A good way to get started with the Check Diagram feature is to validate a familiar diagram. In this section, you will experiment with rules by applying them to a flow-chart you worked with in Chapter 4, "Create business process diagrams." There is one important difference in the version used in this section: it contains deliberate errors.

If validation issues exist when you check a diagram, they appear in the Issues window, as shown in Figure 14-1. Clicking a rule name in the Issues window typically highlights the corresponding shape in the drawing window. In Figure 14-1, the pointer is resting on Decision Shape Should Have More Than One Outgoing Connector. As a result, the Candidate Accepts? shape is selected.

> **✓ TIP** Clicking a rule does not always result in a selected shape; some rules, by their nature, don't apply to a specific shape. One example: when a rule reports that a shape is missing, there is nothing to select.

14

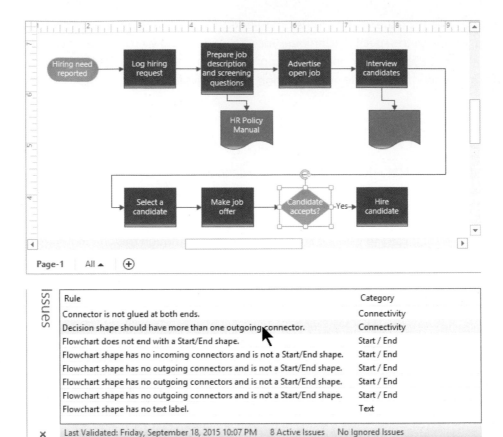

Figure 14-1 *Selecting almost any rule in the Issues window selects the offending shape*

> ✓ **TIP** You can click any column header to sort issues into a different sequence. You can also right-click anywhere inside the Issues window and then click Arrange By to select a different sequence.

The fact that Visio selects a shape when you click a rule in the Issues window is even more valuable when the violation applies to a very small shape or to an obscure violation. For example, you can't tell by looking at the top row of the flowchart in Figure 14-1, but one of the dynamic connectors is unglued at one end. However, the offending connector becomes obvious when you click Connector Is Not Glued At Both Ends., as shown in Figure 14-2.

> ✓ **TIP** If the gap is so small that you can't see an unglued connection, why does it matter? For many diagrams it won't, but it might in certain circumstances. For example, a workflow based on a flowchart could be halted by an unconnected link, or a custom report that creates a bill of materials from an engineering drawing might be incomplete if a connection is missing.

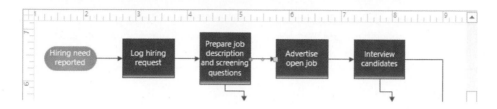

Rule	Category
Connector is not glued at both ends.	Connectivity
Decision shape should have more than one outgoing connector.	Connectivity
Flowchart does not end with a Start/End shape.	Start / End

Figure 14-2 *Some issues would be very difficult to locate without the Check Diagram feature*

The unconnected shape in Figure 14-2 is a good example of a violation that generates more than one issue. The selected issue and shape in Figure 14-3 are actually the result of the same underlying error. Gluing the connector to the Advertise Open Job shape will remove both errors from the Issues window the next time you validate the diagram.

> ✓ **TIP** You can click the Check Diagram button in the Diagram Validation group on the Process tab at any time to refresh the Issues window.

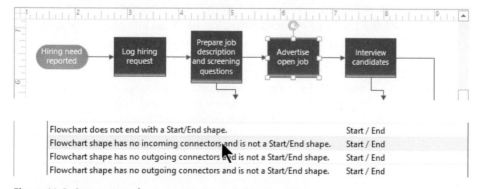

Flowchart does not end with a Start/End shape.	Start / End
Flowchart shape has no incoming connectors and is not a Start/End shape.	Start / End
Flowchart shape has no outgoing connectors and is not a Start/End shape.	Start / End
Flowchart shape has no outgoing connectors and is not a Start/End shape.	Start / End

Figure 14-3 *Some types of errors generate more than one issue*

14

Not all issues need to be corrected, so you can tell Visio to ignore any violation. The issue highlighted in Figure 14-4 is a good example. Although the message is correct—the document shape does not have any outgoing connectors—that's acceptable for this shape because a document isn't a process step. It's simply a representation of a process artifact and does not need an outgoing connector.

 TIP If your diagram has more than one page and there are issues on multiple pages, the Issues window will include a Page column.

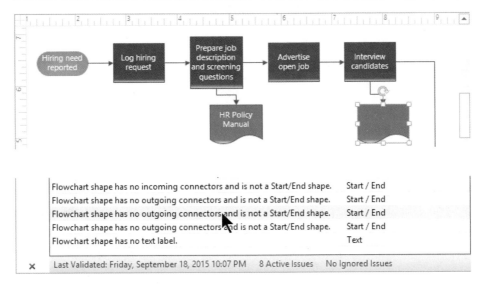

Figure 14-4 *Some issues can be ignored*

When you ignore an issue, Visio removes it from the Issues window but doesn't lose track of it. For example, ignoring the issue for the document shape in Figure 14-4 causes Visio to update the count of ignored issues in the status line at the bottom of the Issues window, as shown in Figure 14-5.

 TIP Right-clicking in the Issues window provides options besides Ignore This Issue and Ignore Rule. You can also reverse your choice to ignore issues and rules, make ignored issues visible in the Issues window, and change the sort sequence of displayed issues.

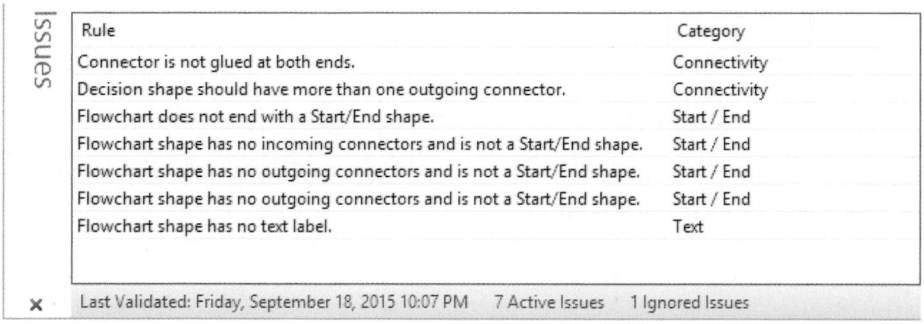

Rule	Category
Connector is not glued at both ends.	Connectivity
Decision shape should have more than one outgoing connector.	Connectivity
Flowchart does not end with a Start/End shape.	Start / End
Flowchart shape has no incoming connectors and is not a Start/End shape.	Start / End
Flowchart shape has no outgoing connectors and is not a Start/End shape.	Start / End
Flowchart shape has no outgoing connectors and is not a Start/End shape.	Start / End
Flowchart shape has no text label.	Text

✕ Last Validated: Friday, September 18, 2015 10:07 PM   7 Active Issues   1 Ignored Issues

Figure 14-5 *Visio tracks ignored issues and displays a count on the status bar below the Issues window*

⚠ **IMPORTANT** Although you can safely ignore the issue described in Figure 14-4, other violations of the same rule should not be ignored, which is why Visio provides two options for ignoring an issue: Ignore This Issue and Ignore Rule. The distinction between the two is critical—the former ignores a single issue, whereas the latter ignores all issues created by a rule. You should use Ignore Rule very carefully, or you might inadvertently hide important issues.

To validate a flowchart

1. On the **Process** tab, in the **Diagram Validation** group, click the **Check Diagram** button.

To highlight a shape that violates a rule

1. Click the rule name in the **Issues** window.

To ignore an issue

1. Do either of the following:
   - Right-click the name of the rule, and then click **Ignore This Issue**.
   - On the **Process** tab, in the **Diagram Validation** group, click the **Ignore This Issue** button.

To ignore all issues that result from a rule

1. Do either of the following:
   - Right-click the name of the rule, and then click **Ignore Rule**.
   - In the **Diagram Validation** group, click the **Ignore This Issue** arrow (not its button), and then click **Ignore Rule**.

To show or hide ignored issues

1. Do either of the following:

   - Right-click in the **Issues** window, and then click **Show Ignored Issues**.

   - In the **Diagram Validation** group, click the **Ignore This Issue** arrow, and then click **Show Ignored Issues**.

To stop ignoring an issue or a rule

1. With ignored issues visible, right-click the name of an ignored issue, and then do either of the following:

   - Click **Stop Ignoring This Issue**.

   - Click **Stop Ignoring Rule**.

Or

1. With ignored issues visible, click the name of an ignored issue.

2. In the **Diagram Validation** group, click the **Ignore This Issue** arrow, and then do one of the following:

   - Click **Stop Ignoring This Issue**

   - Click **Stop Ignoring Rule**

To close the Issues window

1. Do either of the following:

   - Click the **Close** button (**X**) in the corner of the **Issues** window.

   - In the **Diagram Validation** group, clear the **Issues Window** check box.

Validate swimlane diagrams

Swimlane diagrams are validated by using the same rule set that you worked with in the preceding section. However, the flowchart rule set includes a few rules that apply only to swimlanes. Figure 14-6 shows an example of this type of rule.

After you resolve all active issues and no ignored issues remain, Visio displays the message shown in Figure 14-7.

If there are no active issues but the diagram still contains ignored issues, the Issues window displays the message shown in Figure 14-8.

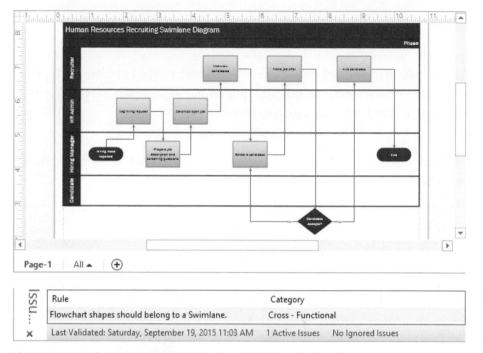

Rule	Category
Flowchart shapes should belong to a Swimlane.	Cross - Functional
Last Validated: Saturday, September 19, 2015 11:03 AM	1 Active Issues No Ignored Issues

Figure 14-6 *The flowchart rule set includes special rules for swimlane diagrams*

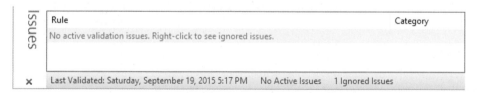

Figure 14-7 *A message confirming that no active nor ignored issues remain*

Rule	Category
No active validation issues. Right-click to see ignored issues.	
Last Validated: Saturday, September 19, 2015 5:17 PM No Active Issues 1 Ignored Issues	

Figure 14-8 *A message noting that the diagram contains ignored issues but no active issues*

To validate a swimlane diagram

1. On the **Process** tab, in the **Diagram Validation** group, click the **Check Diagram** button.

14

Validate BPMN diagrams

You worked with BPMN diagrams in Chapter 4, "Create business process diagrams." The BPMN validation rule set includes a few rules that are similar to those used with flowcharts and swimlane diagrams, but the complex nature of BPMN means that its rule set also contains many unique rules. By way of comparison, the flowchart rule set includes 11 rules, but BPMN includes 76 rules.

Figure 14-9 shows an example in which the wrong connector type between the Start and Check Seat Inventory shapes causes three issues.

> **TIP** Because of the potential complexity of BPMN diagrams, the text of many BPMN rule descriptions is longer than the width of the Issues window. However, if you position the pointer over any item in the Issues window, Visio displays the full text in a ScreenTip, as shown in Figure 14-9.

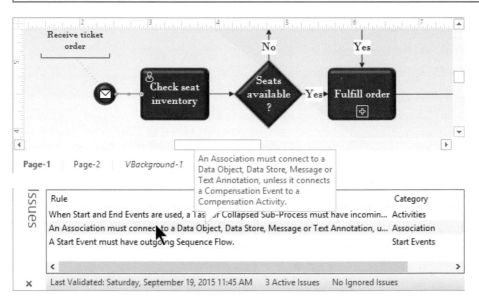

Figure 14-9 *BPMN diagrams include many rules that are more sophisticated*

To validate a BPMN diagram

1. On the **Process** tab, in the **Diagram Validation** group, click the **Check Diagram** button.

Reuse existing validation rule sets

You can import a rule set into any diagram. For example, if you have a flowchart that was created prior to Visio 2010, which was when validation rules were introduced, you can add rules to the diagram.

Figure 14-10 shows the dialog box that appears if you attempt to validate a diagram that does not contain any rules. Note that the dialog box provides specific instructions for adding rules.

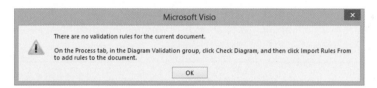

Figure 14-10 *Older diagrams might not contain rule sets*

Clicking Rules To Check, shown in Figure 14-11, confirms that the diagram contains no rules.

Figure 14-11 *There are no validation rules in the current document*

To import a rule set

1. On the **Process** tab, in the **Diagram Validation** group, click the **Check Diagram** arrow, and then click **Import Rules From**.

2. Click the name of the rule set you want to import.

> ✓ **TIP** The flowchart rule set is available to import into any diagram. In addition, if you have other diagrams open that contain rule sets, you will find them listed and can import their rules.

14

List the rules in a rule set

The Visio 2016 user interface does not provide a way to list the rules in a rule set. However, an experienced Microsoft Visual Basic for Applications (VBA) programmer can write a short program to list all of the rules in a set. Even better, Visio MVP David Parker has already done the work for you by including code samples for this and other diagram validation purposes in an article he wrote for MSDN. Although he wrote the article about the 2010 release of Visio, it applies equally to Visio 2016.

 **SEE ALSO** For detailed information about rules, see David Parker's article, "Introduction to Validation Rules in Visio Premium 2010" at *msdn.microsoft.com/en-us/library /ff847470.aspx*.

Although not used in the practice tasks, you will find listings of all of the rules in each of the five Visio 2016 rule sets in the Visio2016SBS\Ch14 practice files folder. Look for the five .html files whose names start with the word *RuleSets*. The listings were produced by using David Parker's Rules Tools, which are described in the next topic.

Create new validation rules

Having seen the value that rules add to business process diagrams, you might be imagining ways that you would like to validate other diagram types. Perhaps you want to do one of the following:

- Verify connectivity in a network diagram.

- Ensure that the number of links on each network device doesn't exceed the maximum allowable for that brand and model of equipment.

- Confirm that each piece of furniture in an office floor plan was selected from an approved list and meets budget guidelines.

- Verify that all parts of an electrical schematic meet minimum and maximum power thresholds.

- Ensure that a building plan conforms to local building codes.

The good news is that you can both edit existing rules and create new rules. The bad news is that Visio does not provide an easy means to accomplish either task.

One resource for learning about custom rule development is a brief article written by the Visio development team. Although it was written for Visio 2010, the article still applies to Visio 2016 and can be found at *blogs.msdn.com/b/visio/archive/2009/09/10 /creating-custom-validation-rules-for-visio-2010.aspx.*

The most complete resource for learning more about editing and designing validation rules is a book written by David Parker. His book, *Microsoft Visio 2013 Business Process Diagramming and Validation* (Packt Publishing, 2013), provides extensive, technical coverage of validation, in addition to details about many parts of Visio that touch, or are touched by, diagram validation. The validation features of Visio 2016 are largely unchanged from Visio 2013, so David's book is still relevant.

David also filled a significant gap left by Microsoft: he wrote a Visio add-in called *Rules Tools* that provides a user interface for exploring and working with validation rules. If you install David's Rules Tools and run Visio in developer mode, you'll find an additional group of buttons on the right end of the Process tab, as shown in Figure 14-12.

 SEE ALSO For information about running Visio in developer mode, see Appendix A, "Look behind the curtain."

Figure 14-12 *The Rules Tools group on the Process tab provides rule management functions*

14

 SEE ALSO For information about David Parker's book and about Rules Tools, go to *www.visiorules.com.*

After you create a custom rule set, you can import it into any diagram. It's also useful to know that one diagram can contain multiple rule sets, as shown in Figure 14-13.

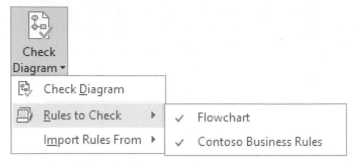

Figure 14-13 *The current diagram contains two rule sets*

Skills review

In this chapter, you learned how to:

- Understand Visio rules

- Validate flowcharts and swimlane diagrams

- Validate BPMN diagrams

- Reuse existing validation rule sets

- List the rules in a rule set

- Create new validation rules

Practice tasks

The practice files for these tasks are located in the Visio2016SBS\Ch14 folder. You can save the results of the tasks in the same folder.

Understand Visio rules

There are no practice tasks for this topic.

Validate flowcharts and swimlane diagrams

Open the ValidateFlowcharts and ValidateSwimlanes diagrams in Visio, and then perform the following tasks:

1. Validate the flowchart diagram.

2. Resolve or ignore the **Flowchart shape has no text label** issue.

3. Ignore the **Flowchart shape has no outgoing connectors and is not a Start/End shape** issue for the two document shapes. Do not ignore the rule.

4. Resolve the **Flowchart shape has no outgoing connectors and is not a Start/End shape** issue for the **Hire candidate** shape.

5. Resolve the **Connector is not glued at both ends** issue.

6. Rerun the validation, and then resolve any remaining issues.

7. Rerun the validation.

8. Show the issues that you previously ignored.

9. Validate the swimlane diagram.

10. Resolve all open issues, and then rerun the validation.

Validate BPMN diagrams

Open the ValidateBPMN diagram in Visio, and then perform the following tasks:

1. Validate the diagram.

2. Resolve any open issues.

Reuse existing validation rule sets

Open the ReuseRules diagram in Visio, and then perform the following tasks:

1. Import the **Flowchart Rule Set**.

2. Validate the flowchart.

3. Resolve any open issues.

List the rules in a rule set

There are no practice tasks for this topic.

Create new validation rules

There are no practice tasks for this topic.

Collaborate and publish diagrams

Chapter 12, "Print, reuse, and share diagrams," described techniques for sharing Visio diagrams in a variety of formats, including as collections of webpages. All of the techniques described in that chapter are valuable, but sometimes you need more, such as dynamic updates to web-published diagrams, threaded comments among team members, or even live, simultaneous coauthoring of a diagram in progress.

The combination of Visio and the Visio Services component of Microsoft SharePoint 2016 provides all of these capabilities. Even better, two of those three features can be used by people who do not have Visio, further extending the power and reach of the diagrams you create.

 IMPORTANT The information in this chapter applies only to the Professional edition of Visio 2016.

This chapter guides you through procedures related to storing, viewing, and refreshing Visio diagrams in SharePoint, and collaborating by commenting on and coauthoring Visio diagrams.

In this chapter

- Understand Visio Services in SharePoint
- Store diagrams in SharePoint
- View diagrams by using a web browser
- Refresh diagrams saved in SharePoint
- Collaborate on diagrams
- Comment on diagrams
- Coauthor diagrams

Practice files

No practice files are necessary to complete the practice tasks in this chapter.

Understand Visio Services in SharePoint

Visio Services is a Microsoft SharePoint Server 2016 feature you can use to share diagrams with people who don't have Visio. There are four key advantages to sharing diagrams via Visio Services instead of publishing static webpages as described in Chapter 12, "Print, reuse, and share diagrams":

- The Visio Web Access browser view is dynamic and reflects nearly all diagram changes. The web view can be updated either automatically by a program or timer, or manually by the user.

  Data-connected Visio diagrams that use data graphics provide particularly impressive results when published to SharePoint, because whenever the source data changes, the data graphics on the webpage change.

- Visio Services supports interactive commenting on diagrams by multiple people, regardless of whether they are using the Visio client or a web browser.

- You can incorporate Visio diagrams into SharePoint apps in the following ways:

  - You can embed a Visio web drawing in a SharePoint Web Part.

  - You can create dynamic connections between Web Parts that contain Visio web drawings, and between the drawings and other types of Web Parts.

  - You can use the Visio Services Mash-up API to program dynamic changes in the browser as the user navigates around a drawing or takes other actions on a SharePoint page.

 TIP Creating SharePoint Web Parts and apps is outside the scope of this book.

- The Visio client and Visio Services use the same .vsdx file format. Consequently, either you can save directly to SharePoint from the Visio client or you can copy a Visio diagram file to SharePoint after creating or editing it locally.

 SEE ALSO For information about the Visio .vsdx file format, see Appendix A, "Look behind the curtain."

In addition to the preceding advantages, the user experience in the web browser is enhanced in the following ways in Visio web drawings when compared to Visio websites:

- Pan and zoom are provided by click-and-drag techniques and by rolling the mouse wheel, respectively. (Other techniques are also available.)

- Shape data is easier to view via a floating properties window.

- The properties window that displays shape data also lists the hyperlinks, if any, that are attached to the selected shape.

- Microsoft Silverlight is not required.

 TIP One key feature is missing from Visio web drawings: full-text search. It is an important part of Visio-created webpages but is not available in diagrams saved to Visio Services.

As you plan the best way to use data-linked diagrams in conjunction with Visio Services, keep in mind one important limitation, which is that connections in a diagram published to SharePoint are refreshable only if you link your diagram to one of the following data sources:

- Microsoft Excel workbooks that are stored on the SharePoint site

- SharePoint lists

- Microsoft SQL Server tables and views

- Databases accessed via OLE DB or ODBC drivers

 TIP Linking to SQL Server and OLE DB/ODBC databases is not supported for SharePoint Online in Microsoft Office 365.

Visio has always been good for building data-driven, visual representations of processes, networks, organizations, or other entities. When you add the capability to create dynamically updateable webpages via SharePoint, Visio becomes a key contender for building business intelligence solutions in almost any work domain.

15

 TIP For detailed reasons to use Visio as part of a business intelligence solution, including numerous examples, refer to Chapter 9, "Visio and Visio Services," in *Business Intelligence in Microsoft SharePoint 2013* by Norm Warren, Mariano Neto, Stacia Misner, Ivan Sanders, and Scott Helmers (Microsoft Press, 2013).

Store diagrams in SharePoint

> ✓ **TIP** The diagram used in this topic was created by using the Business Process Model and Notation (BPMN) 2.0 template that is packaged with Visio Professional 2016. For more information about BPMN, refer to Chapter 4, "Create business process diagrams."

As noted in the preceding topic, Visio 2016 files can be saved directly to a SharePoint server. Visio 2016 makes this easy to do by including SharePoint servers on the Save As page of the Backstage view, as shown in Figure 15-1. You can save directly to a recently used folder or browse to locate a different folder on any previously configured SharePoint server.

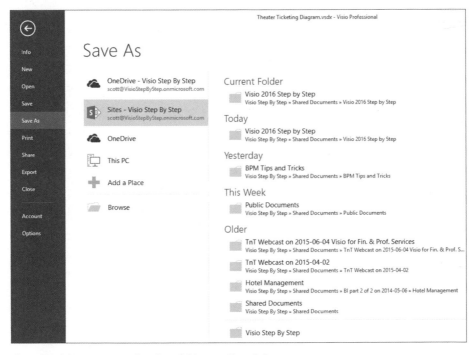

Figure 15-1 *You can save directly to folders on SharePoint servers*

You can also save to a SharePoint site that isn't listed by using either of two techniques:

- You can make an ad hoc selection by clicking the Browse button and then locating the server you want.

- You can add a server to the Save As menu by clicking the Add A Place button.

 TIP Often the easiest way to select the folder you want on the correct SharePoint site is to navigate to it first in your web browser. After locating the correct folder, copy and paste its URL into the address bar at the top of the Save As dialog box.

 TIP Visio Services operates the same way on both in-house SharePoint servers and Office 365 SharePoint servers.

Regardless of which technique you use to select a server, the Save As dialog box, shown in Figure 15-2, opens so you can complete the action.

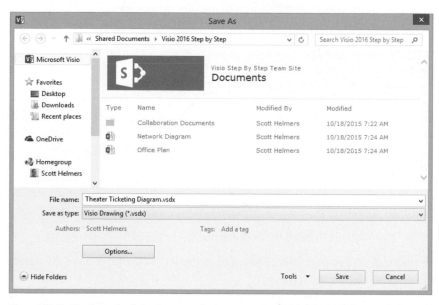

Figure 15-2 *The Save As dialog box can display contents of either local folders or folders on SharePoint*

The Save As dialog box includes an Options button in the lower section that you can use to refine how your document is saved. Clicking the Options button displays the Publish Settings dialog box shown in Figure 15-3.

15

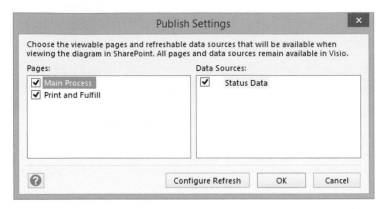

Figure 15-3 *You can control which pages or data refresh options are available in the web browser view of a Visio document*

In the Pages area on the left, you can select a subset of the diagram's pages if there are some you don't want to include in your web-published drawing.

If your diagram is linked to one or more data sources, you can use the Data Sources area on the right to allow or disallow refreshing from specific sources.

 SEE ALSO For information about linking diagrams to data, see Chapter 10, "Link to external data."

⚠ **IMPORTANT** Note the comment at the top of the Publish Settings dialog box: clearing the check box for pages or data sources in this dialog box eliminates them from the browser view of the drawing. However, the unselected pages and sources are still available to anyone who opens the diagram in Visio.

To save a diagram to SharePoint

1. In the Backstage view, click **Save** or **Save As**.

2. Click the name of an existing SharePoint site in the left side of the **Save As** page, and then do either of the following:

   - Click a folder on the right side.

   - Click the **Browse** button.

   Or

   Click **Browse.**

3. In the **Save As** dialog box, navigate to the SharePoint site and folder where you want to save the file, and then enter a file name.

4. (*Optional*) Click **Options**, and then in the **Publish Settings** dialog box, select a subset of pages and data sources to make available in the web-rendered view of the diagram, and click **OK**.

5. Click **Save**.

View diagrams by using a web browser

With your document saved in Visio Services on SharePoint, you can click the file name in any web browser to open the Visio Web Access view shown in Figure 15-4. Notice that this view can include the Shape Info pane.

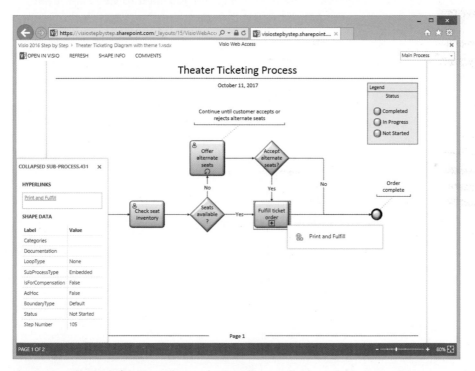

Figure 15-4 *The high-fidelity rendering of a Visio diagram that is available via a web browser can include additional shape details*

If your diagram is linked to a data source, the message shown in Figure 15-5 might appear in your browser. You can click the Allow Refresh button to proceed.

15

Figure 15-5 *Visio Web Access notifies you if a diagram is linked to a data source*

The Visio Web Access pane provides buttons and controls in both upper corners and in the lower-right corner so you can manipulate the viewed image and open other viewing panes or the Visio application.

To view a diagram stored in SharePoint

1. Open the SharePoint site in a web browser.

2. Navigate to the folder that contains the diagram you want to view, and then click the file name.

To zoom in and out

1. Do any of the following by using the controls in the lower-right corner of the browser window:

   - Click the **Zoom Out** (-) or **Zoom In** (+) button to decrease or increase the zoom level.

   - Use the zoom slider.

   - Click the displayed percentage and enter a new percentage.

   - Click the **Zoom To Fit Page To View** button to view the entire Visio page in the browser window.

   Or

   Roll the mouse wheel.

To pan the diagram

1. Click and drag anywhere within the viewing pane.

To view a different page

1. In the upper-right corner, click the arrow next to the current page name, and then click the name of the page you want to view.

To view shape data

1. If the Shape Info pane is not visible, in the upper-left corner, click **Shape Info**.

2. Click the shape whose data you want to view.

To close the Shape Info pane

1. Do either of the following:

   - Click **Shape Info**.

   - Click the **Close** button (**X**) in the upper-right corner of the **Shape Info pane**.

To show or hide the comments pane

1. In the upper-left corner, click **Comments**.

To open the diagram in Visio

1. In the upper-left corner, click **Open in Visio**.

Refresh diagrams saved in SharePoint

Now that you can save diagrams in SharePoint, the next step is to make changes to the diagram or its linked data source to discover how that affects the web view.

For example, you can apply data graphics to the diagram shown in Figure 15-4, save the changes, and refresh the Visio Web Access pane to produce the view shown in Figure 15-6.

15

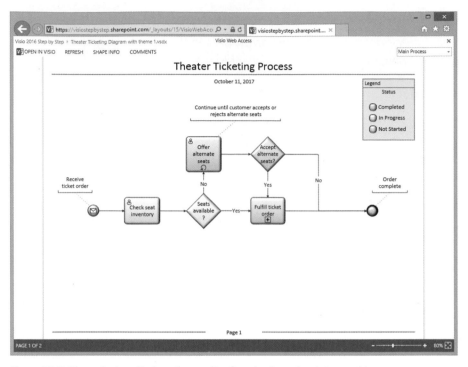

Figure 15-6 *The web view displays the results of a color-by-value data graphic*

When you save changes to a diagram that is stored in SharePoint, Visio displays two messages in the status bar at the bottom of the Visio window while the save is in progress. The message in the upper half of Figure 15-7 appears first, followed by the message in the lower half.

Figure 15-7 *Visio keeps you informed about the save status of your diagram*

The Theater Ticketing Process diagram is linked to an Excel workbook that is also stored in SharePoint and has the data values shown in Figure 15-8. You can compare the data values in this figure to the shape colors and legend in Figure 15-6.

> **IMPORTANT** In order for Visio Services to have access to data in an Excel workbook, the workbook must be stored in SharePoint prior to linking to it from your Visio drawing.

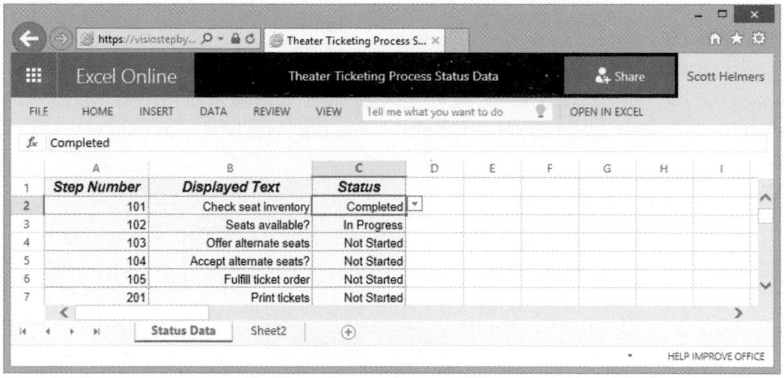

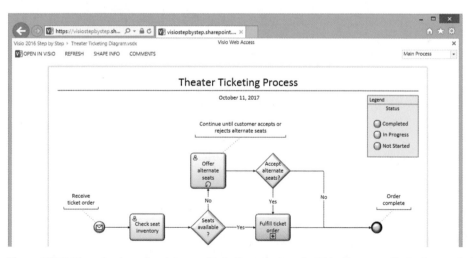

Figure 15-8 *Excel data displayed by Excel Online*

Changing the values for the Status field to those shown in Figure 15-9, and then refreshing the browser view of the Visio diagram results in the view shown in Figure 15-10.

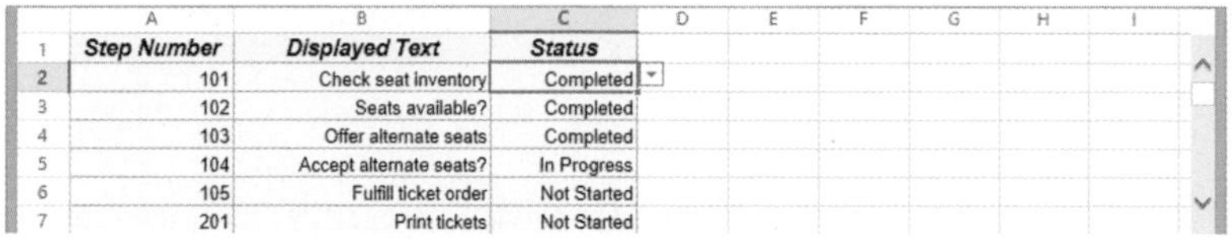

	A	B	C	D	E	F	G	H	I
1	**Step Number**	**Displayed Text**	**Status**						
2	101	Check seat inventory	Completed						
3	102	Seats available?	Completed						
4	103	Offer alternate seats	Completed						
5	104	Accept alternate seats?	In Progress						
6	105	Fulfill ticket order	Not Started						
7	201	Print tickets	Not Started						

Figure 15-9 *Updated process status data*

Figure 15-10 *The color-by-value data graphic in the web view of a Visio diagram reflects changes in the linked data*

15

473

> **TIP** The refresh interval for data and diagrams stored in SharePoint is managed by SharePoint administrators. If you use in-house servers, diagram refresh might happen immediately or after a short interval. If you use SharePoint Online in Office 365, refresh might be immediate, but even if you never click the refresh button, the diagram will update in a maximum of five minutes.

Diagram refresh is not limited to updating data graphics. For example, the second page of the ticketing diagram consists of the fulfillment process shown in Figure 15-11.

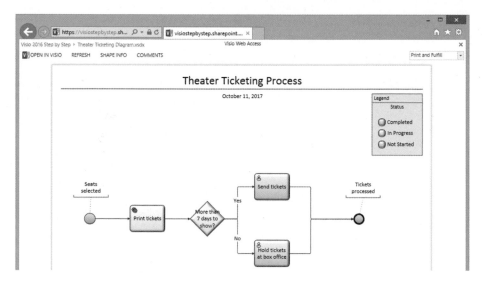

Figure 15-11 *The Print And Fulfill page of the Theater Ticketing Process*

You might decide to change the look of the page and update the process to accommodate eTickets. To do so, you open the diagram in Visio and perform the following actions:

- Add an eTickets? decision shape with two outcome paths.

- Shift existing shapes to the right to accommodate the new shape.

- Apply a new border style.

- Change the text on the existing decision diamond.

- Save the changes.

After you refresh the diagram, the browser view is updated automatically and might look like Figure 15-12.

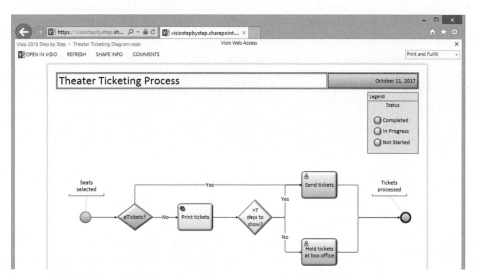

Figure 15-12 *A shape has been added to the Print And Fulfill page*

The example in this topic uses a diagram linked to an Excel workbook, but remember that your Visio diagram can be linked to a variety of data sources and even to multiple data sources at once.

Picture a more elaborate scenario in which:

- A web-rendered diagram is linked to several data sources.
- Some data sources are updated by people, but some are updated by IT systems.
- Various data graphics are attached to the shapes and change color, size, shape, or text labels as the underlying data changes.

You can create powerful dashboards and visual renderings of day-to-day operations in any organization by using Visio and SharePoint. Best of all, you already know everything that is required to make it work: you can create a diagram, link it to data, add data graphics, save it in SharePoint, and automatically or manually refresh it when the data changes.

> **SEE ALSO** For information about creating and using data graphics, see Chapter 9, "Visualize your data." For information about creating and linking to data, see Chapter 10, "Link to external data."

As a final note, you can create even more sophisticated views in SharePoint by using Web Part pages. In this scenario, each Web Part can contain different items. For example, one or more Web Parts might contain Visio diagrams, while other Web Parts display supporting data that might reside in Excel, a SharePoint list, or another data source. It's also possible to link Web Parts to each other so that an action in one Web Part updates the view in one or more of the other Web Parts on the page.

Although building Web Part pages is outside the scope of this book, resources are available online, including these two:

- "Visio Services in SharePoint 2013" at *msdn.microsoft.com/en-us/library/office /jj164027.aspx*

- "Connect a Visio Web drawing to another Web part" at *support.office.com /en-us/article/Connect-a-Visio-Web-drawing-to-another-Web-part-D04356A5-0E1E-46E3-9EF6-814D8CB554BF*

> ⚠️ **IMPORTANT** Both of the articles cited apply to Visio 2013 and SharePoint 2013. At the time of this writing, comparable resources for the 2016 versions are not yet available, but they might be by the time you are reading this.

To refresh the diagram view

1. Do either of the following:

   - In the upper-left corner of the **Visio Web Access** pane, click **Refresh**.

   - Wait until the update interval for your diagram expires.

Collaborate on diagrams

The collaboration capabilities in Visio 2016 take two principal forms: commenting and coauthoring. Both capabilities recognize the growing importance of collaboration among geographically dispersed workers and are implemented by using Visio Services, either via SharePoint within an enterprise or SharePoint Online through an Office 365 subscription. Coauthoring capabilities are also supported when a diagram is stored in OneDrive.

The "Comment on diagrams" topic that follows explores a scenario in which two people read and write comments in a Visio drawing, even though one of them does not use Visio.

The "Coauthor diagrams" topic later in this chapter examines the simultaneous editing capabilities of Visio.

Both topics use the diagram shown in Figure 15-13, which was created from the Brainstorming Diagram template that is located in the Business template category.

 TIP The content of the diagram used in the remainder of this chapter is a convenient summary of the collaboration capabilities of Visio 2016.

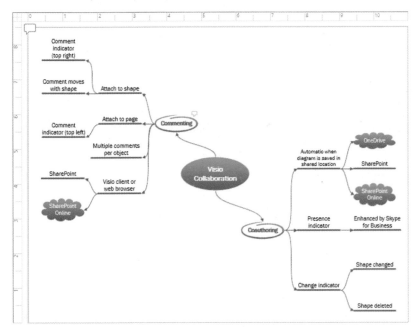

Figure 15-13 *A brainstorming diagram summarizing the commenting and coauthoring features of Visio 2016*

Comment on diagrams

Commenting in Visio 2016 is flexible and includes the following features:

- You can read and write comments from either the Visio client or a web browser; the latter requires storing the Visio diagram on a SharePoint server or in SharePoint Online in Office 365.

- You can attach comments to shapes and to the drawing page.

- A comment indicator appears in the upper right of a shape or the upper left of a page that contains a comment.

15

- When you move or copy and paste a shape containing a comment, the comment travels with the shape.

- You can view all comments at once by opening the Comments pane.

 SEE ALSO For additional information about comments, see Chapter 3, "Manage text, shapes, and pages."

Figure 15-13 is a full-page view of a brainstorming diagram that contains two comment balloons, one in the upper-left corner that is attached to the page, and one near the center that is attached to the brainstorming shape labeled *Commenting*.

In the scenario for this topic, two people are collaborating on the diagram. Scott Helmers is using Visio 2016 on his computer, and Rebecca Laszlo is using Internet Explorer on her computer.

When Scott clicks a comment indicator, Visio opens the comment on the drawing page, as shown in Figure 15-14.

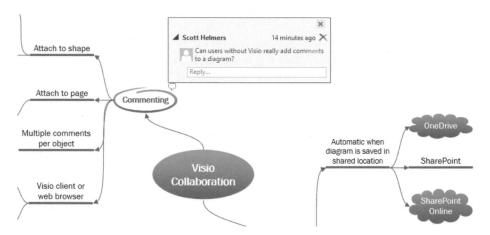

Figure 15-14 *Clicking a comment balloon in Visio displays the text of the comment*

Figure 15-15 was captured on Rebecca's computer. When she uses Internet Explorer to open the Visio diagram, it appears in the Visio Web Access pane. Then, when she clicks the Comments button in the upper left, she sees Scott's comments.

> ✓ **TIP** The default view in the Visio Web Access pane hides comment indicators unless the Comments pane is open. However, the default presentation for comments in Visio is the opposite: comment balloons are visible regardless of the state of the Comments pane.

In Figure 15-15, Rebecca clicked the comment balloon attached to the upper-left corner of the page. Consequently, both the comment balloon and the frame around the corresponding comment in the Comments pane are blue.

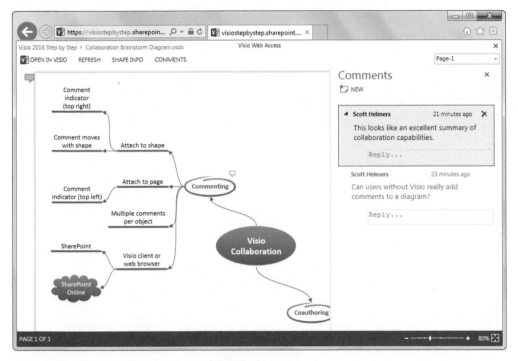

Figure 15-15 *Comments displayed in the web view of a Visio diagram*

Rebecca responds to Scott's comments by entering text in the Reply box beneath each comment.

> ✓ **TIP** When you enter a comment via a web browser, an explicit save is not required. When you click anywhere outside the Reply box, Visio immediately saves the changes to the diagram.

15

Meanwhile, back in Visio on Scott's PC, he notices that the text *Updates Available* has appeared in the lower-right section of the status bar, as shown in Figure 15-16.

Figure 15-16 *A notification appears on the Visio status bar when diagram updates are available from the SharePoint server*

Scott clicks the words *Updates Available*, and Visio applies the changes to his view of the diagram. When Scott opens the Comments pane, both of Rebecca's replies are visible, as shown in Figure 15-17.

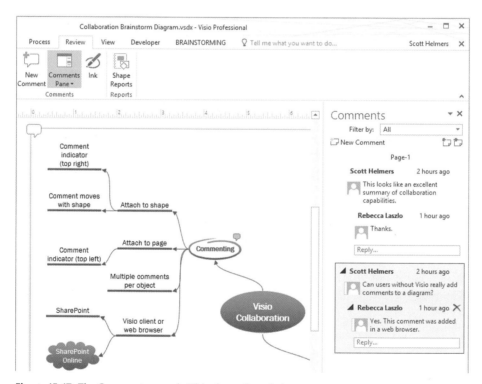

Figure 15-17 *The Comments pane in Visio shows threaded comments*

At the conclusion of this commenting scenario, the diagram contains only four comments. In a diagram that includes a large number of comments, you can navigate through the comments by using the Previous and Next buttons at the top of the Comments pane (shown on the left in Figure 15-18). You can also select subsets of comments based on location, timing, author, and whether the comments in the diagram are expanded or collapsed, by using the Filter By list (shown on the right in Figure 15-18).

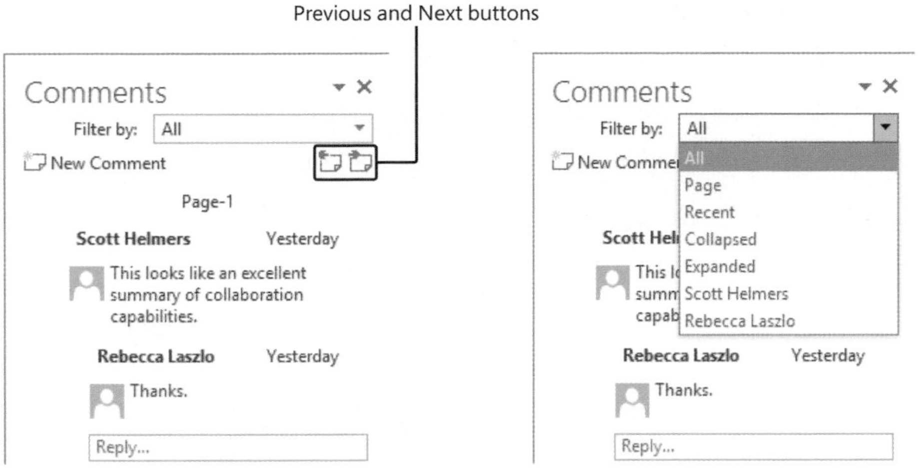

Previous and Next buttons

Figure 15-18 *Comment pane viewing controls*

The Visio commenting feature makes it easy to connect in other ways with another person who has entered comments. If you point to the commenter's name or photo-graph, either in the Comments pane or in a comment displayed on the drawing page, a mini contact card displays the contact's photo and up to four ways to connect. The mini contact card is similar to the one shown in Figure 15-24 in the topic that follows this one.

The connection options include telephone, video, email, and live chat if both parties are online at the same time. Clicking the arrow in the lower-right corner of the Screen-Tip opens a contact card for this person.

The specific communication options that appear on the ScreenTip, and which details appear on the full-sized contact card, depend on the user's software, connectivity, and privacy settings. Generally, if both users run Skype for Business and are within the same organization, all four options should be available.

To show or hide the Comments pane in the Visio client

1. On the **Review** tab, in the **Comments** group, click the **Comments** button.

To show or hide the Comments pane in a web browser

1. In the upper left of the **Visio Web Access** pane, click **Comments**.

To add a comment in the Visio client

1. Right-click a shape or a blank place on the page, and then click **Add Comment**.

Or

15

1. Click a shape or a blank place on the page.
2. Do either of the following:
   - On the **Review** tab, in the **Comments** group, click the **New Comment** button.
   - Open the **Comments** pane, and then click **New Comment**.

To add a comment in a web browser

1. Open the **Comments** pane.
2. Click a shape or a blank place on the page, and then in the **Comments** pane, click **New**.

To filter the comments in the Comments pane in the Visio client

1. In the **Comments** pane, click the **Filter by** arrow, and then click the filter type that you want.

To show or hide comment indicators in the Visio client

1. On the **Review** tab, in the **Comments** group, click the **Comments** arrow, and then click **Reveal Tags**.

To apply diagram updates in the Visio client

1. On the status bar, click **Updates Available**.

To apply diagram updates in a web browser

1. In the upper left of the **Visio Web Access** pane, click **Refresh**.

To view a comment in the Visio client or web browser

1. Click the comment indicator.

To edit a comment in the Visio client or web browser

1. Click the text of the comment, enter changes, and then click outside the text of the comment.

To reply to a comment in the Visio client or web browser

1. Click the **Reply** box beneath the comment to which you want to respond.

To delete a comment or a reply in the Visio client or web browser

1. Click the **Close** button (**X**) in the corner of the comment or reply.

Coauthor diagrams

Coauthoring in Visio 2016 means that multiple people can edit the same diagram simultaneously when the diagram is stored on OneDrive, SharePoint, or SharePoint Online. Nothing else is required other than opening the drawing—coauthoring is automatic.

In the Visio 2016 implementation, shapes and pages are not locked during a coauthoring session. The assumption is that there are so many possible things to change in a Visio diagram that it's unlikely two people will be changing exactly the same thing at the same time. On the rare occasion that does occur, the last change wins.

To prevent possible conflicts and to help everyone working on a diagram understand what is happening, Visio provides several markers in the upper-right corner of a shape during coauthoring sessions. The markers indicate when another user is editing some aspect of a shape (the left image in Figure 15-19), when changes to a shape have been synchronized among authors (center), and when another author has deleted a shape (right).

 TIP Clicking the change indicators shown on the left and right in Figure 15-19 tells you which author is making that change.

Figure 15-19 *Coauthoring indicators appear on the upper right of a Visio shape*

⚠ **IMPORTANT** Normally, if one coauthor deletes a shape and then saves changes, the shape will disappear from other authors' diagrams when they apply updates. There is an important exception: the shape is retained and marked as shown on the right in Figure 15-19 if one of the coauthors made what Visio determines to be significant changes to the shape. If that author then saves the diagram, Visio reinstates the shape for all authors and adds a different indicator icon.

It is possible for more than one marker icon to appear at the same time. In addition, under certain circumstances, Visio might add a comment like the one shown in Figure 15-20.

15

Figure 15-20 *Visio warns you of potential overlap conditions*

The status line at the bottom of the Visio window also shows important coauthoring information, such as the following:

- Toward the left end of the status bar, an icon indicates that other users are editing the diagram and displays how many are doing so. Pointing to or clicking the icon can provide additional details.

    - Each time a new coauthor opens the diagram, he or she is announced in a text balloon, as shown in Figure 15-21.

Figure 15-21 *New coauthors are announced when they open a diagram*

    - At any time after the announcement box has disappeared, pointing to the icon prompts you to click for details, as shown in Figure 15-22.

Figure 15-22 *ScreenTip text describes how to view a list of coauthors*

    - Clicking the icon produces a list of coauthors with green presence indicators, as shown in Figure 15-23.

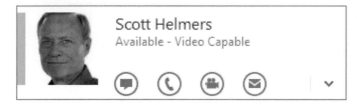

Figure 15-23 *Photos, if available, are displayed with the names of coauthors*

Pointing to one of the coauthor's names produces the short form contact card shown in Figure 15-24; the card indicates how the person can be contacted via a series of icons. The number of illuminated icons depends on the connectivity available for the authors and whether both are using Skype for Business.

Figure 15-24 *A mini contact card for Scott Helmers*

Clicking the arrow in the lower-right corner yields a full contact card that displays as much information about the coauthor as that person has chosen to make available.

- Toward the right end of the status bar, you will sometimes find several transient messages that were shown earlier in this chapter in Figure 15-7 and Figure 15-16.

> ⚠ **IMPORTANT** Unlike commenting, coauthoring is not possible via a web browser. All authors must use the Visio client, via either a desktop software license or a Visio Pro for Office 365 subscription.

The commenting scenario from the preceding topic continues here; the opening state of the diagram is shown in Figure 15-13 earlier in this chapter. After exchanging comments, Scott and Rebecca decide to work together on editing part of the diagram.

Rebecca starts Visio and opens the diagram from the SharePoint site. Her first action is to add text to the shape that describes the role of SharePoint in coauthoring. She wants to clarify that coauthoring applies to corporate (on-premises) SharePoint installations and to SharePoint Online. Consequently, she makes the change shown in Figure 15-25.

15

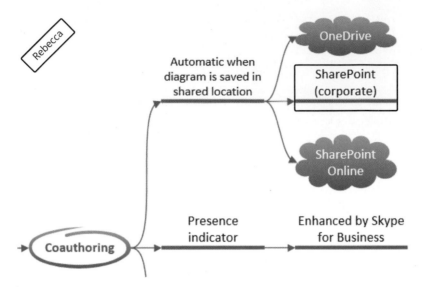

Figure 15-25 *Rebecca edited text on one shape*

In his copy of Visio, Scott receives the text changes along with a notification marker that is attached to the altered shape, as shown in Figure 15-26.

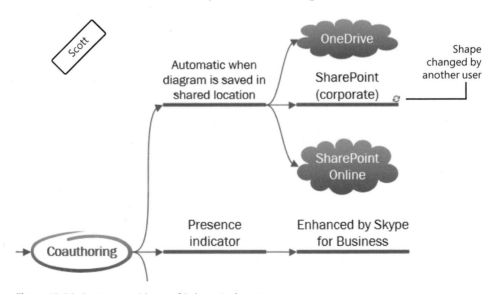

Figure 15-26 *Scott sees evidence of Rebecca's changes.*

Meanwhile, Rebecca decides to delete the OneDrive shape. When she does so, Visio also removes the arrow leading to it. Both changes are shown in Figure 15-27.

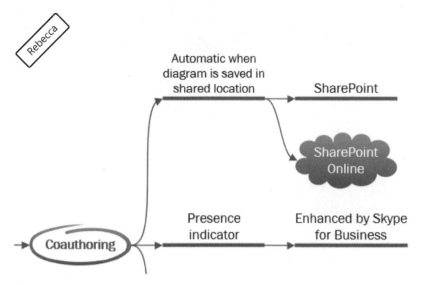

Figure 15-27 *Rebecca deleted the OneDrive shape*

Not knowing yet that Rebecca is deleting a shape, Scott decides he likes the change she made to the SharePoint shape, and chooses to make the following edits:

- He takes advantage of a brainstorming template feature to change the shape type by right-clicking the shape and selecting the Cloud symbol.

- He changes the text on the OneDrive shape to *OneDrive for Business*.

- He increases the height of both the OneDrive for Business and the SharePoint (Corporate) cloud shapes.

When Rebecca saves her changes that include removing a shape, Scott is notified by the shape-deleted symbols that appear on the OneDrive For Business shape and the arrow pointing to it, as shown in Figure 15-28.

Scott immediately saves his changes, which preserves the shape Rebecca deleted. In addition, the next time Rebecca applies updates to her diagram, the OneDrive for Business shape will reappear.

15

> ⚠ **IMPORTANT** If Scott had not previously made changes to the same shape Rebecca deleted, the shape would have been deleted from his diagram also.

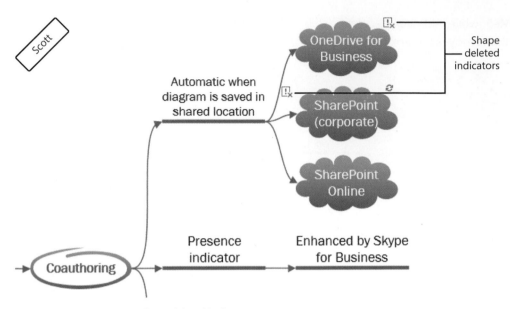

Figure 15-28 *Scott notices shape deleted indicators*

Finally, when both Scott and Rebecca have saved changes, the diagram appears in final form, as shown in Figure 15-29.

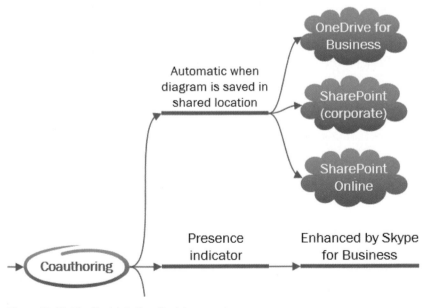

Figure 15-29 *The final, jointly edited document*

To begin coauthoring

1. Open a diagram located in either OneDrive for Business or SharePoint.

To determine who else is editing the same diagram

1. Click the **Authors editing this document** indicator on the Visio status bar to reveal a list of all coauthors.

To find contact information for a coauthor

1. Click the name of the coauthor after opening the list of coauthors.

To apply updates made by a coauthor

1. Click the **Updates Required** button on the right side of the Visio status bar.

Skills review

In this chapter, you learned how to:

- Understand Visio Services in SharePoint

- Store diagrams in SharePoint

- View diagrams by using a web browser

- Refresh diagrams saved in SharePoint

- Collaborate on diagrams

- Comment on diagrams

- Coauthor diagrams

15

Practice tasks

No practice files are necessary to complete the practice tasks in this chapter.

> ⚠️ **IMPORTANT** The tasks for all topics in this chapter require access to Visio Services on a SharePoint 2016 server. Visio Services are available with a SharePoint Server 2016 Enterprise Client Access License (ECAL) or by using SharePoint Online in Office 365.

Understand Visio Services in SharePoint

There are no practice tasks for this topic.

Store diagrams in SharePoint

Start Visio, and then perform the following tasks:

1. Do either of the following:

   - Create a diagram by using any of the Visio 2016 templates.

   - Open an existing Visio 2016 diagram.

2. Save the diagram to SharePoint.

Or

1. Copy a Visio diagram to a folder on a SharePoint site.

View diagrams by using a web browser

Start a web browser, and then perform the following tasks:

1. Click the name of a Visio diagram located in a SharePoint site.

2. Zoom in and out on the diagram.

3. Pan the viewing area of the diagram.

4. If the diagram has multiple pages, view a different page.

5. Open the **Shape Info** pane and view data for one or more shapes.

6. Close the **Shape Info** pane.

7. Open the **Comments** pane.

8. Open the diagram in Visio.

Refresh diagrams saved in SharePoint

Start a web browser, and then perform the following tasks:

1. View a Visio diagram that is stored on SharePoint and is linked to data.

2. Make changes to data values in the data source.

3. Make changes to the shapes on one or more pages in the diagram.

4. Refresh the browser view.

Collaborate on diagrams

There are no practice tasks for this topic.

Comment on diagrams

Start Visio, and then perform the following tasks:

1. Do either of the following:

   • Open an existing Visio 2016 diagram that is stored in SharePoint.

   • Either create a diagram by using any of the Visio 2016 templates or open an existing Visio 2016 diagram, and then save the diagram to SharePoint.

2. Have a colleague view the same diagram in a web browser, and then open the **Comments** pane.

3. Enter several comments by using Visio.

4. Enter several comments by using the web browser.

5. Reply to the other person's comments.

6. Delete a comment.

Coauthor diagrams

Start Visio, and then perform the following tasks:

1. Do either of the following:

   - Open an existing Visio 2016 diagram that is stored in SharePoint.

   - Either create a diagram by using any of the Visio 2016 templates or open an existing Visio 2016 diagram, and then save the diagram to SharePoint.

2. Have a colleague open the same diagram in Visio.

3. Determine the name of the colleague who is coauthoring with you.

4. Locate contact information for your colleague.

5. Make changes to the diagram and have your colleague do the same, and then save changes.

6. Apply updates made by your colleague.

Appendix A

Look behind the curtain

Visio 2016 serves two distinct communities that sometimes overlap. On one hand, there are people who create diagrams by using just the tools in the standard user interface. The diagrams they create might be simple or sophisticated, but this group of people completes their diagrams without needing to look "behind the curtain." The second group of people loves to push Visio beyond its off-the-shelf capabilities by exploring and modifying the ShapeSheet or by writing code to drive the behavior of Visio.

The purpose of this appendix is not to turn members of the first group into coders and ShapeSheet developers. However, you can accomplish so much more with Visio if you have just a little bit of extra knowledge. Consequently, the goal for this appendix is to equip you with a few extra tips, techniques, and tools so you can customize Visio and create even more interesting, attractive, and functional diagrams.

Customize the Visio user interface

Visio 2016 employs the familiar and easily customizable ribbon and Quick Access Toolbar user interface.

Customize the ribbon

You can alter the built-in tabs on the ribbon by adding or removing buttons (although not all buttons can be removed). You can also design your own tabs to hold your most frequently used buttons.

You begin by opening the Visio Options dialog box, which you can do in either of two ways:

- Right-click an unused area of the ribbon, and then click Customize The Ribbon.

- Click the File tab to display the Backstage view, click Options, and then click Customize Ribbon.

The left side of the Visio Options dialog box presents all possible Visio commands and functions, organized into eight groups in the list named Choose Commands From. One of the groups is All Commands, and as the name suggests, it provides a full list of all possible Visio commands, including those that are not configured to appear on the ribbon.

If you point to any command in this section, a ScreenTip indicates its location on the ribbon. For example, the pointer in Figure A-1 is resting on Automatic Resize, a command that is on the Format tab in the Container Tools tab group. If you point to a command that is not on the ribbon, the ScreenTip begins with the words *Commands Not In The Ribbon.*

The right side of the Visio Options dialog box controls the sequence and names of tabs, groups, and buttons. Each tab and group can be expanded or collapsed by clicking the plus or minus sign in front of the name. In addition, tabs can be included or excluded from the ribbon by selecting or clearing the appropriate check box.

To create your own tab, click the New Tab button located in the lower-right side of the dialog box, and then add and arrange buttons from those available on the left. You can create groups by clicking the New Group button, and then rename tabs or groups by clicking the Rename button. Finally, you can change the position of your new tab relative to the other tabs on the ribbon by using the Move Up and Move Down arrows located on the right side of the Main Tabs area.

 TIP You can restore the Quick Access Toolbar and the ribbon to a clean starting state by clicking the Reset button that is located in the lower-right corner of the Visio Options dialog box.

Figure A-1 shows the settings for a tab named My Tab to which several buttons have been added in a group named My Favorite Buttons.

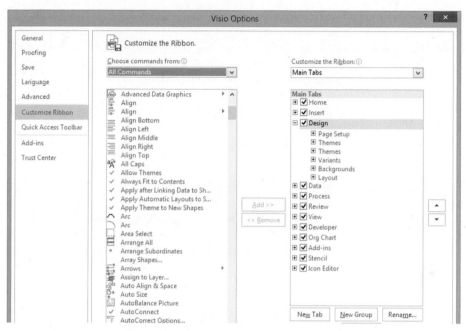

Figure A-1 *Creating a custom tab on the Visio ribbon*

Because it is located below the Developer entry on the right in Figure A-1, the new tab is positioned to the right of the Developer tab, as shown in Figure A-2.

Figure A-2 *A tab with user-selected buttons*

A

If you create a combination of tabs and buttons that you like and want to use them on another computer or share them with colleagues, use the Import and Export buttons in the lower-right corner of the dialog box in Figure A-1.

SEE ALSO For more information about customizing ribbon tabs, go to *office.microsoft. com/en-ca/visio-help/customize-the-ribbon-HA010355697.aspx.*

Customize the Quick Access Toolbar

The Quick Access Toolbar resides in the upper-left corner of the Visio window and provides easy access to commonly used functions. Visio provides a default set of buttons, but you can add buttons. One technique is to right-click any button on the ribbon, such as the New Comment button shown in Figure A-3, and then click Add To Quick Access Toolbar. The result of adding the New Comment button is visible in Figure A-4.

Figure A-3 *Customizing the Quick Access Toolbar*

The pointer in Figure A-4 is resting on the arrow at the right end of the Quick Access Toolbar that provides a list of common functions you can add to or remove from the toolbar with a click. If you want to add buttons that are not on the shortcut menu, click More Commands to display the Quick Access Toolbar page of the Visio Options dialog box. You can use the Quick Access Toolbar page to add, remove, or rearrange toolbar buttons, just as described for the ribbon in the preceding section. (You can also display the toolbar configuration page by clicking Options in the Backstage view, and then, in the Visio Options dialog box, clicking Quick Access Toolbar.)

Figure A-5 shows one convenient combination of file and window management functions that you can add to the Quick Access Toolbar. It includes, from left to right, Open, Open Recent File, Save, Save As, Publish As PDF Or XPS, Undo, Redo, Switch Windows, and Touch/Mouse Mode.

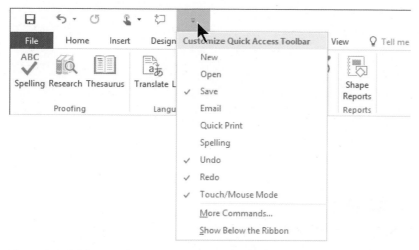

Figure A-4 *Select any options on this menu to add them to the Quick Access Toolbar*

Figure A-5 *A highly customized Quick Access Toolbar*

Although the Quick Access Toolbar usually shows file and window management functions, don't restrict your thinking to those categories. Do you use a certain fill color regularly? Do you frequently open and close the Shape Data window? Do you frequently use the Check Diagram button? You can add those and almost any other button to the Quick Access Toolbar.

Create custom shapes and stencils

Several chapters in this book describe techniques for creating and altering Visio shapes. When you create shapes you would like to reuse, you can drag them into any open stencil.

You can also create a custom stencil: in the Shapes window, click More Shapes, and then click either New Stencil (US Units) or New Stencil (Metric). A new stencil header appears in the Shapes window and displays a red asterisk on the right end to indicate that the stencil is open, as shown in Figure A-6.

A

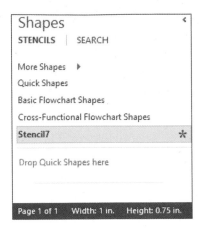

Figure A-6 *A user-created stencil is open in the Shapes window*

Like all Visio 2016 stencils, the new stencil is divided into two parts by a horizontal gray line. In Figure A-6, the line is visible below the words *Drop Quick Shapes here*. If you position a master so it is one of the first four above the gray line, it will appear on the Quick Shapes menu. If you position it below the line, it will be in the stencil but will not be one of the Quick Shapes.

When you drag a shape into an open stencil, Visio assigns a preview image and a name in the form of Master.*n*, where *n* is an integer. In addition, the red asterisk changes to a diskette icon, indicating that the stencil contains at least one unsaved change.

At this point, you can drag your new master onto the drawing page to create a shape. If you want to make the master more useful in the future, you can give it a more meaningful name by using one of the following techniques:

- Right-click the new master, and then click Rename Master.
- Double-click the current master name (do not double-click the icon).
- Select the master, and then press F2.

Regardless of which technique you use, enter a name, and then press Enter.

> ⚠️ **IMPORTANT** If you want to create new masters from several shapes, you must drag the shapes into the stencil one at a time. If you drag multiple shapes into the stencil at the same time, Visio will group the shapes and create a single master.

To save your stencil, right-click the stencil header, and then click Save. By default, the Save As dialog box opens to a special folder named My Stencils that is located in your Windows Documents folder. When you enter a name and click Save, your new stencil name appears on the stencil header.

The new stencil is available for use in any Visio diagram. To open it, point to More Shapes, and then point to My Shapes. A menu containing a list of any stencils you've saved in the My Shapes folder appears. As shown in Figure A-7, three stencils and a folder named Custom Network Shapes contain additional stencils. As is true for the stencils that come with Visio, you can click a stencil name to open it in the Shapes window.

Figure A-7 *Custom stencils are easily accessed when stored in the My Shapes folder*

🔍 **SEE ALSO** To learn more about the interactions among stencils, masters, and shapes, refer to "Visio Stencils, Masters and Shapes: How are they related?" written by Scott A. Helmers and published by Experts Exchange at *rdsrc.us/VXpJrB*.

Run in developer mode

When you decide to step beyond the ranks of ordinary Visio users, one of the first things you should do is run Visio in developer mode. Don't let the name frighten you—there are no programming or hardcore technical requirements for running Visio in this mode.

The primary advantage of developer mode is easy access to several useful features. In developer mode, you can perform the following functions:

- Create and run macros to automate Visio functions.
- Manage add-in programs.
- Add custom controls to Visio shapes.
- Design new shapes and alter the look and behavior of existing shapes.
- Create new stencils.

A

- View "behind the scenes" parts of Visio documents, most notably, the ShapeSheet.

 SEE ALSO For more information about the ShapeSheet, see "View and modify the ShapeSheet" later in this appendix.

- Open and close the Drawing Explorer pane. You can use the Drawing Explorer to navigate to and examine many diagram components, including pages, shapes, masters, themes, and data graphics.

The Developer tab is always available in Visio but is inactive by default. To activate developer mode, click Options in the Backstage view. Then on the left side of the Visio Options dialog box, click Customize Ribbon. On the right side of the dialog box, select the Developer check box, as shown in Figure A-8.

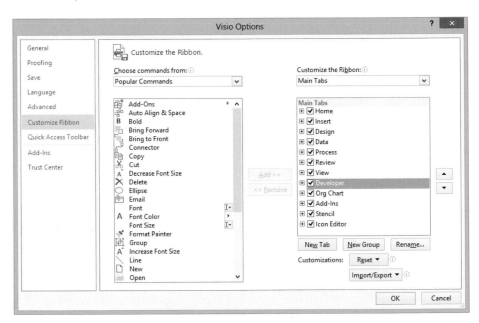

Figure A-8 *Activating the Developer tab in the Visio Options dialog box*

After you activate developer mode, the most obvious difference is the appearance of the Developer tab on the ribbon, as shown in Figure A-9.

Figure A-9 *The Developer tab on the ribbon*

Developer mode also adds the Show ShapeSheet entry to the shortcut menu for every Visio object, as shown in Figure A-10.

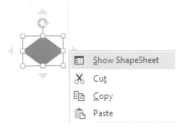

Figure A-10 *In developer mode, the shortcut menu for a shape includes a link to open the ShapeSheet*

> **TIP** There is no downside to running Visio in developer mode, even if you don't regularly use the features it provides.

> **SEE ALSO** For more information about running in developer mode, go to *www.visguy.com /2015/06/19/how-to-show-the-developer-ribbon-tab-and-why*.

Control shape properties and behavior

The Shape Design group on the Developer tab includes three buttons you can use to view and set selected shape properties:

- **Shape Name** This button displays a dialog box in which you can view key shape attributes such as the name of the shape and the name of the master from which it was derived.

- **Behavior** You can use the dialog box that opens when you click this button to adjust properties of both shapes and groups. Examples of the settings include Resize Behavior, Group Behavior, Double-Click behavior, and shape routing and placement.

- **Protection** You can use the dialog box that opens when you click this button to lock almost 20 shape attributes, including Width, Height, X Position, Y Position, and Text. You can also prevent a shape from being deleted or formatted.

A

View and modify the ShapeSheet

 IMPORTANT You must be running Visio in developer mode to access the ShapeSheet.

The following three elements combine to give Visio its power and versatility:

- **Visio engine** This is the preprogrammed heart of Visio.
- **Add-in programs** These typically extend Visio by providing features that the Visio engine does not. They are created by Microsoft, other software companies, or individuals.
- **ShapeSheet** This is a spreadsheet-like data store that exists behind every object in Visio. Every two-dimensional shape, every line, every container, every page, and even the document itself, has a ShapeSheet. The values and formulas in the ShapeSheet, in conjunction with the Visio engine and add-in code, control every aspect of the appearance and behavior of Visio objects.

 TIP For the technically inclined, you might prefer to think of the ShapeSheet as a window into parts of the Visio object model.

To view the ShapeSheet for any shape on the drawing page, select the shape, and then on the Developer tab, in the Shape Design group, click the Show ShapeSheet button. To view the ShapeSheet for the page or the document, click the Show ShapeSheet arrow (not the button) and choose a menu entry.

There is a quick alternative method for opening the ShapeSheet for each of the three primary types of Visio objects:

- **Shape** Right-click the shape, and then click Show ShapeSheet.
- **Page** Right-click the page background, and then click Show ShapeSheet.
- **Document** Right-click the page background, hold down the Shift key, and then click Show ShapeSheet.

The cells in the ShapeSheet are organized into sections and each section has a specific format. In Figure A-11, some sections are open and visible, such as Shape Transform, and some are closed, such as Protection. You can open or close any section by clicking the blue section header.

The Shape Data section, not shown in this figure, is the home for the attributes and values for all shape data fields. Visio developers often store data there in addition to the User-Defined Cells section, the header of which is visible in Figure A-11.

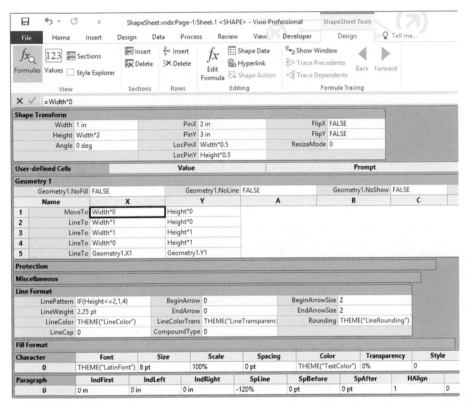

Figure A-11 *The Design tool tab provides ShapeSheet-specific functions whenever the ShapeSheet is open*

You can use ShapeSheet cells for two purposes: to observe the current attributes of a Visio object or to change the object's appearance or behavior. You do the latter by entering either a constant or a formula into a ShapeSheet cell. Examples of both appear in Figure A-11, which shows part of a ShapeSheet for a rectangular shape.

The Width cell in the Shape Transform section for the rectangle has a value of one inch, so the shape on the page is exactly one inch wide. If you drag either the left or right resize handle on the shape, the value in the Width cell will change to reflect the new width. Conversely, if you enter a different value into the Width cell, the shape on the page will react accordingly.

In contrast to that cell is the formula *Width*2* in the Height cell. This formula ensures that the height of the rectangle will always be two times its width. If you change the width of the shape by dragging a resize handle or by entering a new number into the Width cell, the height of the shape will adjust automatically.

A

Just as manually changing the width of the rectangle overwrites the value in the Width cell, the same is true for the formula in the Height cell. If you drag the resize handles to change the height of the shape, Width*2 will be overwritten by the new height value.

It's important to recognize that the ramifications of overwriting a formula can be more significant than overwriting a value—by overwriting a formula, you are changing the behavior of the shape. In our example, the height of the rectangle will no longer change in response to changes in the width.

> **TIP** One way to prevent a formula from being overwritten is by using a ShapeSheet function named GUARD(). Information about ShapeSheet functions is in the Software Developer's Kit that is cited in the list at the end of this topic.

Width*2 is obviously a simple formula. Many Visio shapes employ much more complex formulas. In addition, there are dozens of ShapeSheet functions that can be part of a formula and can take actions such as reading data from other cells in this ShapeSheet, reading data from the ShapeSheets of other objects in the document, performing sophisticated calculations, setting a value based on an "if" condition, triggering actions in the drawing, and responding to events.

The formula in the LineColor cell in the Line Format section shown in Figure A-11 provides an example. The THEME() function retrieves the default line color used in the current theme and applies it to the line on this shape. If a user applies a different theme to the diagram, the line color for this shape automatically changes to the line color in the new theme.

> **SEE ALSO** For information about Visio themes, see Chapter 6, "Add style, color, and themes."

As a second example, look at the formula for LinePattern in the Line Format section. The IF() function in that cell is interpreted this way: if the height of the shape is less than or equal to 2 inches, set the line around the shape to pattern number 1; if the height is greater than 2 inches, set the line pattern to 4. The results of this formula are apparent in the two shapes shown in Figure A-12, and are as follows:

- For the rectangle on the left, the width is 1 inch, which means the height is 2 inches; as a result, the line pattern is set to 1 (a solid line).

- For the rectangle on the right, the width is 1.25 inches, so the height now exceeds 2 inches, and the line pattern has changed.

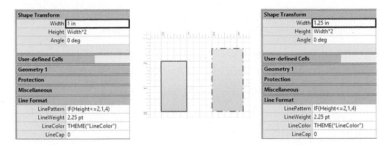

Figure A-12 *Shape appearance changed as a result of a ShapeSheet formula*

> ✓ **TIP** If you would like to experiment with a rectangle configured like the one just described, open the ViewShapeSheet diagram located in the Visio2016SBS\AppA practice file folder.

The preceding example is a simple one, but it should help you to understand the central role played by the ShapeSheet. It should also help you realize that one section in an appendix to a book like this can barely scratch the surface of the uses and functions of the ShapeSheet. Use the following references to continue your exploration of the Visio ShapeSheet:

- UK-based Visio Most Valuable Professional (MVP) John Goldsmith started his Visio blog in 2007 with a concise, nicely organized tutorial on the ShapeSheet, which can be found at *visualsignals.typepad.co.uk/vislog/2007/10/just-for-starte.html*. Be sure to check out other posts on John's blog for additional ShapeSheet-related examples.

- Two other Visio MVPs blog regularly about a broad array of topics and frequently describe clever manipulations of the ShapeSheet:

  - Chris Roth, also known as The Visio Guy, at *www.visguy.com*

  - David Parker at *blog.bvisual.net*

- The aforementioned David Parker wrote a book on diagram validation that is cited in Chapter 14, "Validate diagrams." Chapter 3 of David's book is available at *msdn.microsoft.com/en-us/library/gg144579.aspx*; the first third of the chapter is an excellent ShapeSheet overview.

- The ultimate reference for the ShapeSheet is contained in the Visio Software Development Kit (SDK). As of this writing, the 2016 SDK is not available, but the 2013 version is still valid. You can view it at *msdn.microsoft.com/en-us/library /ff768297.aspx* or download it from *www.microsoft.com/en-us/download /details.aspx?id=36825*.

A

Record and run macros

As with most of the programs in the Microsoft Office suite, you can record and run macros in Visio. A macro is a stored set of instructions. Macros are a great way to perform repetitive actions: you record a set of actions once and can replay it as many times as you'd like. To start recording a macro, click the Macro button that is located to the right of the Language section of the Visio status bar. The button is shown on the left in Figure A-13.

In the Record Macro dialog box that opens, click OK to begin recording. Note that the appearance of the button changes to a square stop button, as shown on the right in Figure A-13. When you complete the steps you want to capture, click the same button again.

> **IMPORTANT** The macro recorder does not record mouse movements or specific keystrokes. Instead, it records the instructions that produce the result of your actions.

Figure A-13 *The appearance of the macro button changes when a macro is running*

To run a macro that you've recorded, on the View tab, in the Macros group, click the Macro button. Select the appropriate macro in the Macros dialog box, and then click Run.

Although you are not required to be in developer mode to record and run macros, you can do both things very easily by using buttons in the Code group on the Developer tab.

> ⊘ **SEE ALSO** For information about the Developer tab, see "Run in developer mode" earlier in this appendix.

Macro security in Visio

The default security setting for macro code is Disable All Macros With Notification. This means that Visio opens any diagram containing macros in protected mode and displays a security warning bar above the drawing page, as shown in Figure A-14.

Figure A-14 *Visio displays a warning when you open a diagram that contains a macro*

If you ignore the warning, you will be able to edit the drawing but not run macros. If you click Enable Content, the drawing will close and reopen with macros enabled.

To change macro security settings, click Options in the Backstage view. In the left pane of the Visio Options dialog box, click Trust Center, and then click the Trust Center Settings button on the far right. When the Trust Center dialog box opens, as shown in Figure A-15, click Macro Settings if it's not already selected.

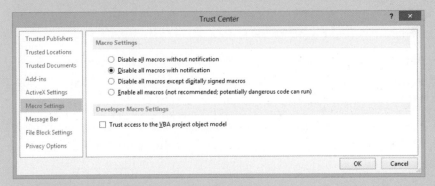

Figure A-15 *The Macro Settings page of the Trust Center*

In the Macro Settings section of the dialog box, click whichever setting meets your needs, and then click OK.

TIP If you are running Visio in developer mode, you can view the Macro settings with a single click: on the Developer tab, in the Code group, click Macro Security.

Program Visio by using Visual Basic for Applications

Microsoft Visual Basic for Applications (VBA) is the built-in programming language that accompanies most Microsoft Office applications. With VBA, you can extend or change the way that an Office application functions. In Visio, for example, you can automate tasks, add new features, or integrate Visio with other members of the Office suite.

Using VBA to integrate one Office application with another can yield very interesting results. For example, you might write Visio VBA code that creates a Microsoft Excel workbook and writes data to it, or you might write code to save all drawing pages as images and create a Microsoft PowerPoint presentation from them. These are just two examples among many other possibilities.

> **TIP** To read an article and view sample code for creating a PowerPoint presentation from a Visio diagram, refer to "How to Create PowerPoint Slides from a Visio Drawing" by Scott Helmers, published by Experts Exchange at *rdsrc.us/rRxZnU.*

To write a VBA program, you need to open the Visual Basic Editor (VBE) by pressing Alt+F11. Alternatively, on the Developer tab, in the Code group, click Visual Basic. This book will not teach you how to write VBA programs, but many books and online tutorials are available, including the following:

- "Getting Started with VBA in Office 2010" at *msdn.microsoft.com/en-us/library /ee814735.aspx* is still useful, despite the fact that Visio was omitted from the "Applies to" list of products on the page.

- The Visio page in the Office Dev Center at *msdn.microsoft.com/en-us/library /fp161226.aspx* includes links to a number of helpful pages, including the following:

  - "Visio VBA reference" at *msdn.microsoft.com/en-us/library/office /ee861526.aspx*

  - "Welcome to the Visio ShapeSheet reference" at *msdn.microsoft.com /EN-US/library/office/ff768297.aspx*

- If you've programmed Visio prior to Visio 2013, "New in Visio for developers" at *msdn.microsoft.com/en-us/library/ff767103.aspx* should be helpful for understanding what has changed since Visio 2010.

- The Visio SDK at *www.microsoft.com/en-us/download/details.aspx?id=36825* contains dozens of code samples that are excellent starting points for writing programs.

If you've never created a macro or written a VBA program, you might be wondering about the difference between the two because they sound similar. The answer is that a Visio macro is nothing more than a VBA program created for you by Visio. To discover this for yourself, record a macro by using the instructions in the preceding topic, and then open the Visual Basic Editor window. The module named *NewMacros* contains the macro code.

Because VBA and macros are closely related, recording macros is one of the best ways to learn how to write VBA programs. Let Visio generate the code for a task that you want to perform, examine the code, and then incorporate it into your VBA program. Although this is an excellent strategy, you should be aware that automatically generated macro code tends to be very verbose and is specific to the situation in which it was recorded. Over time, you will learn which parts of the macro code you need, which parts you don't need, and which parts you need to modify.

Create containers and lists

In Chapter 13, "Add structure to your diagrams," you learned about containers, lists, and callouts. You learned how to insert preformatted containers from the Container gallery, and how to add callouts from the Callout gallery. You also learned that there isn't a corresponding list gallery, which means that you can't create a list by using the Visio user interface.

So how do you create a list? The answer is surprisingly simple: you add one entry to the ShapeSheet for any shape and it becomes a structured diagram component.

 SEE ALSO If you're not familiar with modifying the ShapeSheet, see "View and modify the ShapeSheet" earlier in this appendix.

A

> **IMPORTANT** You must be running in developer mode to access the ShapeSheet. See "Run in developer mode" earlier in this appendix.

To create a list, follow these steps:

1. On the **Home** tab, in the **Tools** group, click the **Rectangle Tool** and draw a rectangle.

2. Right-click the rectangle, and then select **Show ShapeSheet**.

3. Right-click anywhere in the **ShapeSheet** window, and then click **Insert Section**.

4. In the **Insert Section** dialog box, select **User-defined cells**, and then click **OK**. The result should look like the cells shown in Figure A-16.

User-defined Cells	Value	Prompt
User.Row_1	0	""

Figure A-16 *A new row in the User-Defined Cells section of the ShapeSheet*

5. Click **User.Row_1**, enter **msvStructureType**, and then press **Enter**.

6. Click the **Value** cell, enter **"List"** (include the quotation marks), and then press **Enter**. The result will look like the image in Figure A-17.

User-defined Cells	Value	Prompt
User.msvStructureType	"List"	""

Figure A-17 *The only required entry in the ShapeSheet to turn a shape into a list*

You've just created a list! It isn't fancy and doesn't have any of the niceties like margins, a header, color, or style, but it is a list.

To test your new list, close the ShapeSheet window, and then drag several shapes into the list. As you add each shape, you'll find that your rectangle behaves exactly like the lists you worked with in Chapter 13, "Add structure to your diagrams."

Creating a container is as easy as creating a list: simply enter *Container* in the Value cell for msvStructureType. Creating a callout requires a few extra steps but can also be done fairly easily.

> ✓ **TIP** If you would like to enhance the appearance and behavior of your list, container, or callout, you will need to add additional rows to the User-Defined Cells section of the ShapeSheet. For an excellent summary of the user-defined rows and values required for structured diagram components, go to *blogs.msdn.com/b/visio/archive/2010/01/12/custom-containers-lists-and-callouts-in-visio-2010.aspx*. For additional technical details, including sample code for working with structured diagram components in VBA, go to *msdn.microsoft.com/en-us/library/ff959245.aspx*.

Insert fields: advanced topics

In Chapter 8, "Work with shape data," you learned how to display the value of a shape data field on a shape. Although that action is very helpful, you can do so much more than that with the Field dialog box.

To open the Field dialog box, select a shape, and then on the Insert tab, in the Text group, click the Field button. The first thing to notice about the Field dialog box, which is shown in Figure A-18, is that the Category section includes seven entries below Shape Data. Each of these categories contains multiple data fields. The Date/Time category, for example, shows four types of dates.

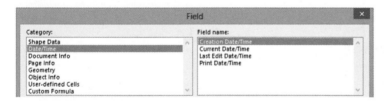

Figure A-18 *You can insert dates into a field*

Other categories display data about the document (shown in Figure A-19), the page, or detailed attributes of the selected shape.

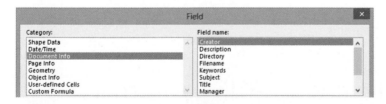

Figure A-19 *You can insert document properties into a field*

Finally, you can insert just about anything you'd like by selecting the Custom Formula category, shown selected in Figure A-20. A custom formula can include math and text functions, references to any of the data elements in the other seven field categories, and almost any ShapeSheet cell or function.

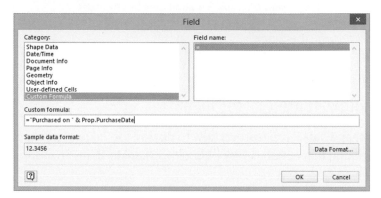

Figure A-20 *You can insert a custom formula into a field*

As one example, the custom formula shown in Figure A-20 consists of two parts: a text label, *Purchased on*, concatenated with a value stored in the PurchaseDate shape data field. The result, inserted on a conference table shape from the Office Layout template, is shown in Figure A-21.

Figure A-21 *A shape displaying a combination of text and shape data*

The Field dialog box offers a rich set of options for making the data in your document visible to users of your diagrams.

Understand the Visio 2016 file formats

All versions of Visio before the 2013 release used a proprietary file format. With the 2013 release, Visio joined most other members of the Office product family in using the XML-based Open Packaging Convention file format. The change won't be particularly noticeable to most Visio users, with the exception of encountering new file extensions; however, the new file format offers multiple advantages, such as the following:

- Most diagram files are significantly smaller than they were in the previous file format.

- Diagrams can be saved to, and then opened and read by, Visio Services on Microsoft SharePoint. Neither a file conversion nor a special file format is required.

- Diagrams can be opened directly in SharePoint Designer for editing and preparation for SharePoint Workflow. An intermediate file format is not required.

- Software developers can read and manipulate the XML files outside of Visio.

The Visio files for drawings, templates, and stencils each have two variations in the new file format, one that prohibits macros and one that allows macros:

- Macro-free drawings, templates, and stencils use .vsdx, .vstx, and .vssx, respectively.

- Macro-enabled drawings, templates, and stencils use .vsdm, .vstm, and .vssm, respectively.

The following notes relate to opening files from previous versions of Visio:

- Visio 2016 can open all files created in Visio 2010 through Visio 2003 and can save files in most 2010-2003 formats. See Chapter 12, "Print, reuse, and share diagrams," for details about saving Visio diagrams in other formats.

- Visio 2016 can open .vsd and .vdx files from Visio 2002 but cannot save in either of those formats.

- When you open a file from an earlier version of Visio, the words *Compatibility Mode* appear after the file name in the Windows title bar. The compatibility marker indicates that some newer features, including themes, variants, styles, and coauthoring, have been disabled.

- Opening a file created in an older version of Visio and then saving it into the Visio 2016 file format is not sufficient to enable Visio 2016 features. To upgrade a file you have opened in compatibility mode, you must click the Convert button on the Info page in the Backstage view.

The following resources are available for developers interested in learning how to work with the new XML file formats:

- "Welcome to the Visio file format reference" at *msdn.microsoft.com/en-us /library/office/jj684209.aspx* includes links to multiple articles.

- Former Visio MVP, Al Edlund, created a set of utilities for investigating and manipulating Visio files, which can be found at *pkgvisio.codeplex.com/documentation*.

Keyboard shortcuts for Visio

The keyboard shortcuts described in this appendix refer to the US keyboard layout.

 TIP Shortcuts styled as italic are among the author's favorites.

Zoom, pan, and navigate

Moving around within a Visio diagram can be significantly more efficient when you use keyboard or keyboard-plus-mouse shortcuts.

Zoom

The need to zoom in and out occurs so frequently that multiple techniques are available.

To do this	Press
Zoom in	Alt+F6 or Ctrl+Shift+left mouse button or *Ctrl+roll mouse wheel forward*
Zoom out	Alt+Shift+F6 or Ctrl+Shift+right mouse button or *Ctrl+roll mouse wheel backward*
Fit to window	*Ctrl+Shift+W*

Pan

To do this	Press
Pan up and down	*Roll mouse wheel backward and forward*
Pan left and right	*Shift+roll mouse wheel backward and forward*
Pan in any direction	Ctrl+Shift+drag right mouse button

Move around in the drawing window

To do this	Press
Move to the next page	*Ctrl+Page Down*
Move to the previous page	*Ctrl+Page Up*
Display the All Pages list	Alt+F3
Move from shape to shape on the drawing page (A dotted rectangle indicates the shape that has the focus.) **TIP** You cannot move to shapes that are protected against selection or are on a locked layer.	Tab
Move from shape to shape on the drawing page in reverse order	Shift+Tab
Select a shape that has focus **TIP** To select multiple shapes, press the Tab key to bring focus to the first shape you want to select, and then press Enter. Hold down the Shift key while you press the Tab key to bring focus to another shape. When the focus rectangle is over the shape you want, press Enter to add that shape to the selection. Repeat for each shape you want to select.	Enter
Clear selection of or focus on a shape.	Esc

Move around in full-screen view

Use these keyboard shortcuts to move between pages when you are in full-screen view.

To do this	Press
Enter full-screen view	F5
Exit full-screen view	Esc
Open the next page in the drawing	Page Down or Right Arrow or left mouse click
Return to the previous page in the drawing	Page Up or Left Arrow

Move around a webpage

Use these keyboard shortcuts to move around within a Visio-generated webpage or a drawing viewed in a Visio Web Access page.

To do this	Press
Cycle the focus among shapes, drawing controls, task panes, and other diagram elements	Tab
Activate the hyperlink for the shape or hyperlink on the drawing that has focus	Enter

Navigate the Ribbon

1. Press **Alt**.

   As shown in Figure B-1, the KeyTips are displayed over each feature that is available in the current view.

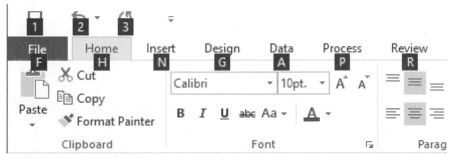

Figure B-1 *KeyTips are displayed as numbers or letters*

2. Press the letter shown in the KeyTip over the feature that you want to use.

3. Depending on which letter you press, you might be shown additional KeyTips. For example, if the Home tab is active and you press N, the Insert tab is displayed, along with the KeyTips for the groups and features on that tab.

4. Continue pressing letters until you press the letter of the command or control that you want to use. In some cases, you must first press the letter of the group that contains the command. For example, if the Home tab is active, pressing Alt+H, F, S will take you to the Size list box in the Font group.

 TIP To cancel the action that you are taking and hide the KeyTips, press Alt.

Visio shapes and windows

Use these shortcuts to organize and arrange shapes and windows in a Visio diagram.

Edit shape text

To do this	Press
Enter edit mode	F2
Exit edit mode	F2 or Esc
Open the Text dialog box	F11

Use the Snap & Glue features

To do this	Press
Open the Snap & Glue dialog box	Alt+F9

Move, group, rotate, and flip shapes

To do this	Press
Nudge a selected shape	*Arrow keys*
Nudge a selected shape 1 pixel at a time **TIP** Scroll Lock must be turned off.	*Shift+Arrow keys*
Group the selected shapes	*Ctrl+G* or Ctrl+Shift+G
Ungroup shapes in the selected group	*Ctrl+Shift+U*
Bring the selected shape to the front	Ctrl+Shift+F
Send the selected shape to the back	Ctrl+Shift+B
Rotate the selected shape to the left	Ctrl+L
Rotate the selected shape to the right	Ctrl+R
Flip the selected shape horizontally	Ctrl+H
Flip the selected shape vertically	Ctrl+J
Open the Align Shapes dialog box for the selected shape	F8

Arrange drawing windows

To do this	Press
Display the open drawing windows tiled vertically	Shift+F7
Display the open drawing windows tiled horizontally	*Ctrl+Shift+F7*
Display the open drawing windows so that you can view the title of every window	Alt+F7 or Ctrl+Alt+F7

B

Visio-specific toolbars

These keyboard shortcuts save considerable mouse movement and time when you are creating and editing Visio shapes.

Select tools

To do this	Press
Switch the Format Painter tool on or off	Ctrl+Shift+P
Select the Pointer Tool	*Ctrl+1*
Select the Text tool	Ctrl+2
Select the Connector tool	Ctrl+3
Select the Connection Point tool	Ctrl+Shift+1
Select the Crop tool	Ctrl+Shift+2
Select the Text Block tool	Ctrl+Shift+4

Select the drawing tools

To do this	Press
Select the Rectangle tool	Ctrl+8
Select the Ellipse tool	Ctrl+9
Select the Line tool	Ctrl+6
Select the Arc tool	Ctrl+7
Select the Freeform tool	Ctrl+5
Select the Pencil tool	Ctrl+4

Visio masters and stencils

These shortcuts are useful when you are creating masters and saving them in a stencil.

 SEE ALSO For information about creating masters and stencils, see Appendix A, "Look behind the curtain."

Work with masters in a stencil

To do this	Press
Move between masters in a stencil	Arrow keys
Move to the first master in a row of a stencil	Home
Move to the last master in a row of a stencil	End
Move to the first master in a column of a stencil	Page Up
Move to the last master in a column of a stencil	Page Down
Copy the selected masters to the Clipboard	Ctrl+C
Paste the contents of the Clipboard to a stencil **TIP** The stencil must be open for editing.	Ctrl+V
Select all the masters in a stencil **TIP** To select multiple masters (instead of all), press the arrow keys to bring focus to the first master you want. Hold down Shift while you press the arrow keys to bring focus to another master. When the focus rectangle is over the master that you want, press Enter to add that master to the selection. Repeat for each master that you want to select.	Ctrl+A
Select or cancel selection of a master that has focus	Shift+Enter
Cancel the selection of masters in a stencil	Esc
Insert the selected masters into the drawing	Ctrl+Enter

B

Work with stencils in edit mode

To do this	Press
Delete the selected master	Delete
Cut the selected master from the custom stencil and put it on the Clipboard	Ctrl+X
Rename the selected master	F2

Text

Your hands are already on the keyboard when you're working with text, so it only makes sense to use keyboard shortcuts in that situation.

Edit text

To do this	Press
Select all the text in a text block	Ctrl+A
Move to the beginning of the entry	Home
Move to the end of the entry	End
Select from the cursor to the beginning of the entry	Shift+Home
Select from the cursor to the end of the entry	Shift+End
Move to the next or previous character, respectively, in a line of text	Right Arrow or Left Arrow
Move to the next or previous word, respectively, in a line of text	Ctrl+Right Arrow or Ctrl+Left Arrow
Move to the next or previous line of text, respectively	Down Arrow or Up Arrow
Move to the next or previous paragraph, respectively	Ctrl+Down Arrow or Ctrl+Up Arrow
Select or cancel selection of the next or previous character, respectively	Shift+Right Arrow or Shift+Left Arrow
Select or cancel selection of the next or previous word, respectively	Ctrl+Shift+Right Arrow or Ctrl+Shift+Left Arrow

To do this	Press
Select the next or previous line, respectively	Shift+Down Arrow or Shift+Up Arrow
Select the next or previous paragraph, respectively	Ctrl+Shift+Down Arrow or Ctrl+Shift+Up Arrow
Delete the previous word	Ctrl+Backspace
Replace the selected text with the field height. If no text is selected, replace all text with the field height for the selected shape	Ctrl+Shift+H

Format text

To do this	Press
Turn bold on or off	Ctrl+B
Turn italic on or off	Ctrl+I
Turn underline on or off	Ctrl+U
Turn double underline on or off	Ctrl+Shift+D
Turn all caps on or off	Ctrl+Shift+A
Turn small caps on or off	Ctrl+Shift+K
Turn subscript on or off	Ctrl+=
Turn superscript on or off	Ctrl+Shift+=
Increase the font size of the selected text	Ctrl+Shift+>
Decrease the font size of the selected text	Ctrl+Shift+<

Align text

To do this	Press
Align text left	Ctrl+Shift+L
Center text horizontally	Ctrl+Shift+C
Align text right	Ctrl+Shift+R

B

To do this	Press
Justify text horizontally	Ctrl+Shift+J
Top-align text vertically	Ctrl+Shift+T
Center text vertically	Ctrl+Shift+M
Bottom-align text vertically	Ctrl+Shift+V

The Help window

The Help window provides access to all Office Help content. The Help window displays topics and other Help content.

To do this	Press
Open the Help window	F1
Close the Help window	Alt+F4
Switch between the Help window and the active app	Alt+Tab
Go back to Visio Help Home	Alt+Home
Select the next item in the Help window	Tab
Select the previous item in the Help window	Shift+Tab
Perform the action for the selected item	Enter
Select the next hidden text or hyperlink, including Show All or Hide All at the top of a topic	Tab
Select the previous hidden text or hyperlink	Shift+Tab
Perform the action for the selected Show All, Hide All, hidden text, or hyperlink	Enter
Move back to the previous Help topic (Back button)	Alt+Left Arrow
Move forward to the next Help topic (Forward button)	Alt+Right Arrow
Scroll small amounts up or down, respectively, within the currently displayed Help topic	Up Arrow or Down Arrow
Scroll larger amounts up or down, respectively, within the currently displayed Help topic	Page Up or Page Down

Glossary

1-D shape A Visio shape that has two endpoints and behaves like a line, sometimes in spite of its physical appearance. *1-D* is an abbreviation for *one-dimensional*.

2-D shape A Visio shape that has a border and an interior and behaves like a polygon. *2-D* is an abbreviation for *two-dimensional*.

absolute link A type of hyperlink that contains all of the information required to locate the linked object—such as D:\MyFolder\MyDocument.docx or *http://www.taskmap.com/Downloads.html*. See also *relative link*.

action tag Visio shapes can be designed to display a special icon when you point to the shape. Clicking an action tag displays a menu that contains one or more items. Prior to Visio 2010, action tags were called *smart tags*.

active page The drawing page that has the focus within the drawing window.

active window Of the windows inside the Visio window, this is the one that has the focus; most often the active window is the *drawing window*.

Activity (BPMN) One of a set of rectangle shapes that represents a step in a BPMN diagram. See also *Business Process Model and Notation (BPMN)*.

Activity (General) A task or step in a work process.

add-in Software written by Microsoft, other companies, or individuals that adds features and capabilities to Visio.

add-in tab A tab on the Visio ribbon that is present only when a Visio add-in is running—for example, the Org Chart tab for the Organization Chart add-in. See also *ShapeSheet*; *Visio engine*.

anchor shape The primary shape when multiple shapes are selected. If you select multiple shapes at one time by using a bounding box, the anchor shape is the one farthest to the back (see *Z-order*). If you select multiple shapes one at a time, the anchor shape is the first one you select. The anchor shape affects the results of alignment, spacing, and numbering operations.

Area Select A Visio tool used to select multiple shapes within a rectangular area. See also *bounding box*; *Lasso Select*.

Auto Size A Visio option that automatically expands or contracts the drawing page as you move shapes across page boundaries. Introduced in Visio 2010.

AutoAdd Occurs when you drop a shape onto an existing dynamic connector that is glued to two shapes. Visio disconnects the dynamic connector from the second shape, glues it to the shape you dropped, and automatically adds a new dynamic connector, which it then glues to the new shape and to the second shape. See also *AutoDelete*.

AutoConnect A Visio feature that glues a dynamic connector from one shape to another with a single click; AutoConnect arrows are small blue triangles that appear when you point to a shape.

AutoDelete Occurs when you delete a shape that is connected to two other shapes with dynamic connectors. Visio removes the deleted shape, deletes the dynamic connector glued to the second shape, and then glues the remaining dynamic connector to the second shape. See also *AutoAdd*.

background An area of the drawing page that does not contain any shapes.

background page A Visio page that can be attached both to *foreground pages* and to other background pages. Shapes on a background page appear on other pages to which the background page is attached; however, the shapes can be selected or altered only when the background page is the active page.

Backstage view A full-page UI view that exposes file-level functionality in Office applications. This is a companion feature to the Office ribbon and helps users discover and use the features that fall outside of the authoring features on the ribbon.

bounding box A temporary rectangular shape created by clicking the background of a page and dragging to select one or more shapes. By default, Visio selects all shapes that are fully contained within the area of the bounding box. See also A*rea Select*; *Lasso Select*.

BPMN See *Business Process Model and Notation (BPMN)*.

business process A collection of tasks and activities that leads to a desired result; also known as a *work process*, or just a *process*. See also *process map*.

Business Process Model and Notation (BPMN) A standard for graphically representing business processes. Visio 2016 conforms to the 2.0 version of the standard. See also *Activity (BPMN)*; *Connecting Object*; *Events*; *Gateway*.

callout A shape you use to annotate other shapes in a drawing. Visio 2016 callouts exhibit more intelligent behavior because they maintain a logical association with the shapes to which they are connected.

canvas See *drawing canvas*.

Change Shape A feature introduced in Visio 2013 that you can use to substitute a different shape for a shape already on the drawing page; shape data and most other shape attributes are preserved after the swap.

Check Diagram A Visio Professional feature that validates a diagram against a predefined set of rules. See also *rule*; *rule set*.

color by value A type of data graphic that applies color to shapes based on data values within the shapes. See also *data graphic*.

collaboration As it applies to Visio 2016, two new features: the capability for multiple authors to edit a diagram simultaneously, and the facility for multiple people to enter comments in a diagram by using either Visio or a web browser.

comma-separated value (CSV) A data file consisting of fields and records, stored as text, in which the fields are separated from each other by commas.

comment A Visio annotation object that can be attached to a shape or to the drawing page. See also *ScreenTip*.

Connecting Object One of a set of arrow shapes that links other shapes in a BPMN diagram. See also *Business Process Model and Notation (BPMN)*.

connection point A location on a Visio shape to which other shapes can be glued; represented by a small dark square that appears when you point to a shape.

connector Any one-dimensional (1-D) shape that can be glued between two shapes in a drawing to connect the shapes.

Connector tool A Visio tool that you use to add dynamic connectors to a drawing by dragging from one shape to another or from one connection point to another.

container A structured diagram shape that can contain other shapes. Containers know which shapes are members; member shapes know the identity of their container. Introduced in Visio 2010.

control handle A yellow square or diamond that you use to alter the appearance or function of a shape. Most shapes do not have control handles; when they do exist, they appear when you select a shape. See also *resize handle*; *rotation handle*; *selection handle*.

cross-functional flowchart A type of flowchart in which each process step is placed into a horizontal or vertical lane based on which person, department, or function is responsible for that step. Commonly referred to as a *swimlane diagram*.

CSV See *comma-separated value*.

Custom Import A Visio feature you can use to connect a diagram to an external data source. The Custom Import wizard guides you through identifying and configuring the connection to the data source. See also *data linking*; *Quick Import*.

custom property A data value that is stored inside a Visio shape. Starting with Visio 2007, custom properties are known as *shape data*.

data graphic A Visio feature that you use to annotate a shape by using icons and text callouts based on data in the shape. A data graphic contains one or more *graphic items*.

data graphic legend A key to the data graphics used on a Visio drawing page.

data linking The act of building a dynamic connection between a Visio diagram and an external data source; the data in the diagram can be refreshed manually or automatically whenever the linked data changes. See also *Custom Import*; *Quick Import*.

developer mode A special Visio operating mode that provides additional features and tools beyond the normal user interface. When you turn on developer mode, Visio activates a Developer tab on the ribbon.

diagram See *drawing*.

drawing A Visio document that contains a drawing window and can contain other open windows. Also referred to as a *diagram*. Visio drawings use the .vsd, .vsdx, or .vsdm file extension.

drawing canvas The space in the drawing window that is outside the Visio drawing page. If Auto Size is turned on when you place a shape on the drawing canvas, Visio automatically expands the page size to include the shape. If Auto Size is turned off, you can store shapes on the canvas; they are saved with the drawing but do not print. See also *drawing page*.

Drawing Explorer A window that shows a hierarchical view of a document and updates it to reflect the current drawing hierarchy as items (such as shapes or pages) are added or deleted.

drawing page The printable drawing surface within the drawing window. In some templates, the drawing page displays a grid to aid in positioning and aligning shapes. See also *drawing canvas; drawing window*.

drawing scale A ratio that expresses the size of an object in a drawing compared to its counterpart in the real world. In a metric drawing, 1:10 means that 1 cm on the page represents 10 cm in the real world. In a US units drawing, 1":1' means that 1 inch in the drawing represents 1 foot in the real world.

drawing tools A set of six tools—Rectangle, Ellipse, Line, Freeform, Arc, and Pencil—that enables the creation or alteration of shapes.

drawing window The Visio window that contains the drawing page. See also *drawing page*.

Duplicate Page A feature in Visio 2013 and later that you can use to copy both a page and its contents.

dynamic connector A special type of line that adds and removes bends as the shapes to which it is glued are moved or resized. Each end of a dynamic connector can be glued to another shape.

dynamic glue The result of attaching a dynamic connector to the body of a shape. When you move dynamically glued shapes, the point of attachment of the connector can change. See also *glue*; *static glue*.

Dynamic Grid A Visio feature that provides visual alignment and positioning feedback when you move shapes near other shapes or near the page margins. Visio 2016 also provides dynamic feedback as you resize shapes.

effect A coordinated set of fonts, fill patterns, gradients, shadows, and line styles. See also *theme*.

embellishment An extension of the theme concept that helps set the overall tone of a diagram by altering the geometry of selected shapes. Each theme has a default embellishment level, but you can choose a different level.

Events One of a set of circle shapes that mark start, intermediate, and end events in a BPMN diagram. See also *Business Process Model and Notation (BPMN)*.

Extensible Application Markup Language See *XAML*.

Extensible Markup Language See *XML*.

fixed list A type of shape data list from which users must select an entry. See also *variable list*.

flowchart A diagram that illustrates the activities, decisions, and events that occur in a work process or the logic of a program.

foreground page A Visio drawing page. A foreground page can have a *background page* attached to it.

functional band A vertical or horizontal rectangle in a cross-functional flowchart that contains process steps. Also known as a *swimlane*.

Gateway One of a set of diamond shapes that identify divergence and convergence in a BPMN diagram. Gateways often represent decisions. See also *Business Process Model and Notation (BPMN)*.

GIF See *Graphics Interchange Format*.

glue A property of a Visio shape that lets it remain attached to another shape. See also *dynamic glue*; *static glue*.

graphic item One graphic element within a data graphic. A graphic item represents one data field in a specific way. See also *data graphic*.

Graphics Interchange Format (.gif) A digital image file format developed by CompuServe that is used for transmitting raster images on the Internet. An image in this format can contain up to 256 colors, including a transparent color. The size of the file depends on the number of colors actually used.

gravity In Visio, a mathematical function that creates the appearance of gravity. For example, if the text angle in a shape is set by using the gravity function, the text remains upright when you rotate the shape.

grid The background pattern of intersecting, perpendicular lines on a drawing page. By default, shapes on a Visio drawing page snap to the gridlines as you move the shapes across the page.

group In a drawing program, to transform a number of objects into a group. A group also relates to a labeled collection of commands and controls that are grouped together on a ribbon tab.

guide A Visio shape you create by dragging either the horizontal or vertical ruler onto the drawing page; used to align other shapes.

handle See *selection handle*.

htm/html A file extension for webpages; short for *Hypertext Markup Language*.

Hue-Saturation-Lightness (HSL) A color model in which *hue* is the color itself as placed on a color wheel, where 0° is red, 60° is yellow, 120° is green, 180° is cyan, 240° is blue, and 300° is magenta; *saturation* is the percentage of the specified hue in the color; and *lightness* is the percentage of white in the color. See also *Red-Green-Blue (RGB)*.

hyperlink base The starting point for determining the path to a hyperlink target; Visio documents include a hyperlink base field, which is blank by default.

Hypertext Markup Language (HTML) A text markup language used to create documents for the web. HTML defines the structure and layout of a web document by using a variety of tags and attributes.

Information Rights Management (IRM) A policy tool that gives authors control over how recipients use the documents and emails they send.

insertion bar An orange horizontal or vertical line that appears when you drag a shape near the edge of a shape that is already in a Visio list. The insertion bar indicates where the shape you are dragging will be inserted. See also *list*.

JavaScript An object-oriented scripting language used by Visio to implement some navigation functions for websites created by using Save As Web Page.

JPG/JPEG A digital image file format designed by the Joint Photographic Experts Group for compressing either full-color or grayscale still images. It works well on photographs, naturalistic artwork, and similar material. Images saved in this format have .jpg or .jpeg file extensions.

Lasso Select A Visio tool used to select multiple shapes within a freeform area drawn by the user. See also A*rea Select*; *bounding box*.

layer A means for organizing sets of shapes in a drawing; layers have properties that affect all shapes in the layer at once. For example, with one or two clicks, you can show or hide all shapes on a layer, prevent shapes on a certain layer from printing, and recolor all shapes on a layer.

Line tool One of six drawing tools; used to create straight lines or combinations of multiple straight lines.

list A structured diagram shape that can contain other shapes. A list maintains its member shapes in ordered sequence; member shapes know their ordinal position within the list. Introduced in Visio 2010. See also *insertion bar*.

Live Preview An Office feature that shows the results of many operations before you implement the change. Used in Visio for many font, size, color, alignment, theme, and data graphic operations.

local area network (LAN) A network of computers, printers, and other devices located within a relatively limited area (for example, a building). A LAN enables any connected device to interact with any other on the network.

macro A stored set of instructions. In Visio, you can record a macro and play it back to repeat a set of actions.

master An object in a Visio stencil. Dragging a master from a stencil onto the drawing page creates a shape. See also *shape*; *stencil*.

metric A system of measurement used in Visio drawings and templates in most countries/regions outside North America. See also *US Units*.

mini toolbar A floating toolbar accessed by right-clicking either a shape or the drawing page. It contains the drawing tools and Connector tool, alignment and send to front/back buttons, font and text enhancement buttons, the Format Painter, and access to shape styles.

Object Linking and Embedding Database (OLE DB) A component database architecture that provides efficient network and Internet access to many types of data sources, including relational data, mail files, flat files, and spreadsheets. OLE DB comprises a specialized set of COM interfaces that expose data from a variety of data stores, both relational and nonrelational.

Open Database Connectivity (ODBC) In the Microsoft WOSA (Windows Open System Architecture) structure, an interface providing a common language for Windows applications to gain access to a database on a network.

org charts See *organization chart*.

organization chart A diagram that represents the structure of an organization.

page controls A collection of buttons and tabs at the bottom of the Visio drawing window that you can use to navigate from one page to another within the drawing.

page name tab A tab at the bottom of the Visio drawing window that displays the name of a page. Right-clicking the tab provides access to page management functions.

pan To change which part of a drawing is visible by moving the page horizontally, vertically, or both.

pin The center of rotation for a shape. See also *pin position*.

pin position The location of the pin for a shape. See also *pin*.

PNG See *Portable Network Graphic*.

Pointer Tool A Visio tool you can use to select shapes on the drawing page.

Portable Network Graphic (.png) A digital image file format that uses lossless compression (compression that doesn't lose data) and was created as a patent-free alternative to the .gif file format.

print tile The portion of the drawing page that is the size of a piece of printer paper; tiles are marked by dashed lines in print preview mode and on the drawing page if the Page Breaks check box is selected in the Show group on the View tab.

process See *business process*.

process map A diagram that shows the tasks and activities that comprise a business process. See also *business process*.

Quick Access Toolbar A customizable collection of buttons for frequently used functions that appears in the title bar of the Visio window and is always visible.

Quick Import A Visio feature you can use to connect a diagram to data in a Microsoft Excel workbook. After you select the workbook, Quick Import links to the workbook, links data rows to shapes on the drawing page, and applies one or more data graphics. See also *Custom Import*; *data linking*.

Quick Shape One of up to four masters that appear on a mini toolbar when you point to the AutoConnect arrow for a shape on the drawing page. Click on a Quick Shape to add it to the drawing page.

Quick Styles A set of predefined colors and styles that can be applied to one or more shapes. Each theme has its own set of Quick Styles, ensuring that you can apply styles while maintaining the overall look of the theme.

rack unit A unit of measure for the space occupied by equipment mounted in a network or data center equipment rack. Each rack unit, or *U*, equals 1.75 inches (44.45 mm); equipment height is described as a multiple of rack units, for example, 3U or 5U.

Red-Green-Blue (RGB) A color model that describes color information in terms of the red (R), green (G), and blue (B) intensities that make up the color. See also *Hue-Saturation-Lightness (HSL)*.

relative link A type of hyperlink that contains only part of the information required to locate the linked object. The remainder of the required information is derived from the location of the document containing the hyperlink or from the document's hyperlink base—for example: MyFolder2\MyDocument.docx or *Downloads.html*. See also *absolute link*.

replace shape See *Change Shape*.

report A Visio feature that you can use to generate a summary of the data on one or more pages in a drawing. A report can be exported in .html, Excel, or XML format or can be dropped on the drawing page as a Visio shape.

resize handle One of up to eight small squares that appear on the edge of a shape when you select the shape; two handles adjust the width; two adjust the height; the four corner handles adjust both dimensions proportionally. See also *control handle*; *rotation handle*; *selection handle*.

ribbon An area in a window in which commands and other controls are displayed in functionally related groups. A ribbon can be divided into multiple views, known as *tabs*, and every tab can contain multiple groups of controls. Typically, a ribbon appears at the top of a window.

rotation handle A circle that appears when you select a shape by using the Pointer Tool or the Text tool; dragging the handle rotates the shape or text. See also *control handle*; *resize handle*; *selection handle*.

rule A condition to be validated in a Visio drawing by using the Check Diagram feature. For example, a Visio validation rule might specify that all 1-D shapes must be connected on both ends. See also *Check Diagram*; *rule set*.

rule set A collection of Visio validation rules—for example, the flowchart rule set or the BPMN rule set. See also *Check Diagram*; *rule*.

ruler An on-screen scale marked off in inches or other units of measure and used to show line widths, tab settings, paragraph indents, and so on.

scaled drawing A diagram in which both the drawing page and objects on the page have been expanded or reduced proportionally from their size in the real world. Scale is expressed as a ratio—for example, a scale of 1:5 means that an object that occupies 1 unit of space in the diagram occupies 5 units of space in the real world.

ScreenTip A text annotation that can be added to a shape. The ScreenTip appears when you point to the shape on the drawing page. See also *comment*.

selection handle Small circles, diamonds, or squares that appear when you select a shape; used to resize or adjust the appearance of a shape. See also *control handle*; *resize handle*; *rotation handle*.

selection rectangle A rectangle with sizing handles that surrounds a selected object or objects.

shape An object on a Visio drawing page. You create shapes in three ways: 1) using tools from the Tools group on the Home tab to draw them; 2) dragging masters from stencils; or 3) pasting objects from the Clipboard. Alternatively, a program can create shapes for you. See also *master*; *stencil*.

shape data A data value stored inside a Visio shape; known as a *custom property* prior to Visio 2007. See *custom property*.

Shape Data window A window that displays shape data names and values for a selected shape. See *shape data*.

shape name The internal name of a Visio shape.

shape text Text that is part of a shape and is usually visible on or near the shape.

Shapes window A Visio window that contains one or more stencils.

ShapeSheet A spreadsheet-like data store that exists behind every object in Visio: every 1-D or 2-D shape, every container, every page, even the document itself. The values and formulas in the ShapeSheet, in conjunction with the Visio engine and add-in code, control every aspect of the appearance and behavior of Visio objects. See also *add-in; smart shape; Visio engine*.

sheet An internal Visio term for a shape.

smart shape A Visio shape whose appearance, behavior, or other attributes changes in response to events or to alterations within or outside the shape. Most smart features are implemented by placing formulas into the ShapeSheet of the smart shape. See also *ShapeSheet*.

static glue The result of attaching a dynamic connector or a line to a connection point on a shape. When you move statically glued shapes, the point of attachment for the connector remains fixed. See also *dynamic glue; glue*.

status bar An area at the bottom of the Visio window that displays information about the drawing page and selected shapes; also contains buttons and controls to adjust the page and selected shapes.

stencil A Visio document that contains a collection of masters. Stencils use a .vss, .vssx, or .vssm file extension. See also *master; shape*.

subnet A section of a network.

subprocess A subset of a process. In Visio, a subprocess shape on one page represents a collection of process steps that are typically located on another page; the subprocess shape is usually hyperlinked to the other page.

SVG Short for *Scalable Vector Graphics*; an XML-based format for describing and rendering vector graphics.

swimlane A vertical or horizontal rectangle in a swimlane diagram that contains process steps.

swimlane diagram A type of flowchart in which each process step is placed into a horizontal or vertical lane based on which person, department, or function is responsible for that step. Sometimes known as a *cross-functional flowchart*.

tab On the Visio ribbon, a set of buttons that provide related functions.

task pane A fixed pane that appears on one side of an app window and contains options related to the completion of a specific task.

task A step or activity in a *process map*.

template A Visio document that includes one or more drawing pages with preset dimensions and measurement units. A template can also include one or more stencils; it can include background pages and designs; its pages can contain shapes or text. A template can also include special software that operates only in that template. Templates use a .vst, .vstx, or .vstm file extension.

text block The part of a shape that contains text.

Text tool A Visio tool you can use to manipulate shape text when you use the tool to select a shape. You can also use it to create a text-only shape by dragging across the background of the drawing page.

theme A coordinated set of colors and effects designed to enhance the presentation of a Visio diagram. See also *effect*.

tile See *print tile*.

tool tab A tab on the Visio ribbon that appears only when you select an object for which it is relevant. Tool tabs are organized into tool tab groups.

tool tab group A collection of one or more tool tabs that appears only when you select an object for which it is relevant; for example, the Container Tools tab group appears when you select a container or a list.

U See *rack unit*.

URL Short for *Uniform Resource Locator*. URLs are used to identify the location of a document or other electronic object.

US Units A system of measurement used in Visio drawings and templates in the United States and parts of Canada and Mexico. See also *metric*.

user-defined cells Data names and values that can be stored in the User section of the ShapeSheet for a Visio shape, page, or document.

validation A Visio Professional feature that you can use to verify that a drawing meets certain predefined requirements. See also *rule*; *rule set*.

variable list A type of shape data list from which users can select an entry or can enter a new value. See also *fixed list*.

variant One of four variations on a theme that includes alternate colors and shape designs so you can add your own flair to a drawing while retaining the overall look of the theme.

VBA See *Visual Basic for Applications*.

VBE See *Visual Basic Editor*.

.vdw File extension for a Visio 2010 web drawing; not used in Visio 2013 and later. See also *Visio web drawing*.

Visio engine The core software that provides Visio features and functions. See also *add-in*; *ShapeSheet*.

Visio Services A service provided by SharePoint Server, which you can use to publish dynamically updateable Visio drawings so they can be viewed by people without Visio.

Visio web drawing A Visio 2010 file format that you can use to publish Visio drawings to SharePoint sites by using Visio Services. Visio web drawings can be viewed by anyone with Internet Explorer. Web drawings can be dynamically updated when the data in the Visio drawing changes. Uses a .vdw file extension. No longer used in Visio 2013 and later.

Visio Workflow Interchange A Visio 2010 file format that you can use to exchange Visio SharePoint Workflow drawings with SharePoint Designer. Uses a .vwi file extension. No longer used in Visio 2016.

Visual Basic Editor (VBE) An environment in which you write new and edit existing Visual Basic for Applications code and procedures. The Visual Basic Editor contains a complete debugging toolset for finding syntax, run-time, and logic problems in your code.

Visual Basic for Applications (VBA) A programming language built into many Microsoft Office products.

VML Short for *Vector Markup Language*. A markup language used to define and render webpages created by using Save As Web Page. VML was the primary Save As Web Page output format in versions of Visio before Visio 2010; it is still available in Visio 2010 and later versions as an alternate output format.

.vsdx The file extension introduced with Visio 2013. Uses Open Packaging Conventions to store Visio diagrams in a standards-based XML format.

.vwi See *Visio Workflow Interchange*.

work process See *business process*.

workflow A set of process steps, some or all of which have been automated. For the automated parts of a workflow, documents and files are stored and moved electronically, according to a set of pre-defined rules, so that they are available to participants as required.

workspace A collection of Visio windows and window settings. At minimum, the workspace consists of the drawing window and the zoom settings for the pages in the drawing; frequently, it also includes a Shapes window containing one or more stencils.

X-coordinate Defines the horizontal position of a shape on the drawing page.

XAML Short for *Extensible Application Markup Language*. A markup language based on XML that was created by Microsoft. Used by many Microsoft products. Visio creates XAML documents when you use the Save As Web Page function.

XML Short for *Extensible Markup Language*. A markup language for describing and exchanging structured data in a format that is independent of operating systems and applications. XML is a World Wide Web Consortium (W3C) specification and is a subset of Standard Generalized Markup Language (SGML).

Y-coordinate Defines the vertical position of a shape on the drawing page.

zoom To magnify (zoom in) or shrink (zoom out) the display of a drawing.

Z-order Defines the relative front-to-back position of a shape on the drawing page. The first shape you add to a page is at the back and each subsequent shape is in front of all previous shapes. You can change the Z-order by using the Send Forward/Send Backward or Send To Front/Send To Back buttons.

Index

Symbols

A

B

T